KU-363-232

Everyday Life in Ancient Mesopotamia

Everyday Life in Ancient Mesopotamia

by

Jean Bottéro

with contributions from

André Finet, Bertrand Lafont *and* Georges Roux

and translated by

Antonia Nevill

Edinburgh University Press

English edition first published 2001
by Edinburgh University Press Ltd
22 George Square, Edinburgh

Transferred to Digital Print 2009

Originally published in France as
Initiation à l'Orient ancien
by Editions du Seuil
27 rue Jacob, 75261 Paris, France

Published with the kind assistance of
the French Ministry of Culture

Typeset in 10 on 12 pt Sabon
by Hewer Text Ltd, Edinburgh, and
printed and bound in Great Britain by
CPI Antony Rowe, Chippenham and Eastbourne

A CIP Record for this book is available from the British Library

ISBN 0 7486 1387 0 (hardback)
ISBN 0 7486 1388 9 (paperback)

Contents

Part III Myth and Legend

Publisher's Acknowledgement

The publisher wishes to thank Antonia Nevill for providing, as always, a translation that captures the pace and *élan* of the original text; the French Ministry of Culture for generous assistance towards the cost of preparing the translation; and Dr Trevor Watkins of the Department of Archaeology at the University of Edinburgh for checking the English text for technical accuracy and for providing a guide to further reading in English.

A Note on Pronunciation

To read words and proper names in Sumerian, Akkadian or Hebrew, remember that:

- final *e* is never silent: so Abarage is pronounced Abaragay
- *u* is pronounced *oo*: so Abad-duri is Abad-doori
- all consonants are articulated
- all consonants are hard: Gilgamesh is Guilgamesh
- *h* is usually pronounced as *kh*, not unlike but harsher than *ch* in Scottish loch: Asalluhi is Asallukhi.

Foreword

Approaching a cultural system as complex and far removed from our own day as ancient Mesopotamia – the crowning glory of the ancient Near East – is somewhat difficult. Everyone agrees about that.

Rediscovered a good century and a half ago – since when people have tirelessly continued to decipher and dissect the gradually exhumed and copious archives – this ancient civilisation is decidedly too sumptuous, exuberant, inexhaustible and different from our own for a simple introduction. It makes our heads swim. There are so many things we have to know just to get our bearings in such a labyrinth: the impossible writing and the strange forgotten languages it portrays; its difficult geography; the historical sequence of reigns and dynasties, whose designations do not make them easy to commit to memory; its complex institutions with their slow and meandering progress; its opulent and entangled economy; its trade at home and abroad; its expeditions and wars; its technical, artistic and intellectual advances; and above all its luxuriant and unexpected religion, with dozens of divinities, sparkling myths and barbaric rites. Here we have a prodigious museum: taking the first few steps inside it may be quite an ordeal.

Those (rare) professionals capable of introducing and guiding the beginner make hardly any effort to make the task any easier. They do not often descend from the heights of their rostrum to meet their readers, speak to them clearly and try to capture these old ancestors and bring them close to us. However distant they may be, the Mesopotamians were none the less men and women like ourselves, and there must therefore be some way of communicating with them.

It would be wrong to try to launch ourselves into the accounts that learned scholars have written to entice us into their Holy of Holies. Let us leave such writings to those who are already fairly conversant with the arcane mysteries and who have been introduced and acclimatised to this old and labyrinthine citadel – yet even they may lack an overall plan, a panoramic view, a map to guide them and put their ideas in order. Meanwhile the novices, still outside the closed door and impatient to get in, may lose their enthusiasm, and be put off because they can find nothing else to get their teeth into – at least not of a serious nature.

Well then, why not tackle things differently? Instead of confining the visitors to an official tourist bus that sticks to the main road and has to travel to all the famous sites and monuments listed in the glum homily of the authorised guide, why not let them wander on foot into the odd little byways, along the paths where they can play truant? During these unpretentious roamings, there would be time to pick up a liking for the country as well as a few indispensable words of its language to enable them to get around more comfortably. Of course, to start with, they would not get a schematic and overall view; they would not immediately acquire a complete and ordered picture, but at least they would be able to breathe the ancient air and little by little discover the old ways of looking at and valuing things, the real and restless life of the ancients observed and experienced as if at first hand – despite the dozens of centuries separating us from them. Why not indeed? For when all is said and done, the fundamental and final goal of every historical investigation is surely to rediscover for ourselves and others the true life of our ancestors. That at any rate is the idea which has prompted this book and guided its contents and presentation.

Over more than a decade *L'Histoire* – by far the best if not the only French journal seriously and intelligently dedicated to the discovery and exploration of the past – has published a series of articles devoted to the ancient Near East and to Mesopotamia. These articles were designed to add up to the book you are now reading. Authors were asked to tackle a particular subject and to be intelligible and readable. They had to give a clear account of their presuppositions and intentions in order to put readers at their ease. The questions to be addressed were deceptively simple and beguiling. Where did these rather mysterious inhabitants of the country come from? How did people live and die there? What did these ancient ancestors eat and drink? What did they think of love, and how did they make love? How did they treat women? How did they cope with the worries, ills and misfortunes of existence? What meaning did they give to life and death? How did they persuade their gods to intervene in their affairs and problems? And to what extent did they influence our nearer ancestors, the authors of the Bible and the Greeks? These and many other facets were explored, each one allowing a glimpse of and entrance into the same vast system: they were itineraries, easy to follow, sometimes eccentric, often picturesque and always enriching, each in its own way leading to the very heart of that old country where our culture was first created.

I have assembled and arranged this lively collection of articles in an accessible form to offer readers the best introduction to the vast subject of ancient Mesopotamia. The neophyte is likely to develop a taste for it and will gain enough of an idea to want to tackle the forbidding but fascinating syntheses of the learned scholars. And I think even the initiate may derive some profit from this exploration of some little excavated nooks and crannies of this venerable civilisation.

Jean Bottéro

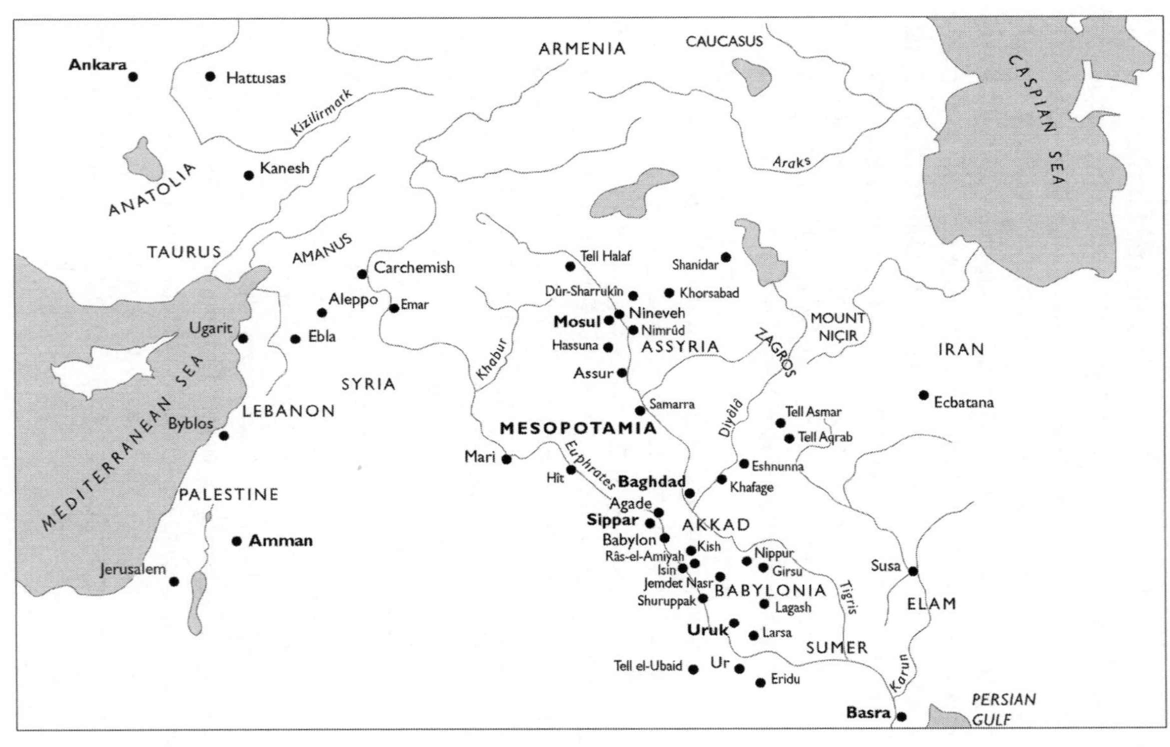

Ancient Mesopotamia in its geographical setting

Part I

Origins

CHAPTER 1

Did the Sumerians Emerge from the Sea?

Georges Roux

The origin of the Sumerians is one of those false 'great problems of history' arising from our passion for wanting to know everything. Its true interest is not easy to perceive. What matters to a historian is less the region of origin of a people than the texture of their lives, their political, social and economic organisation, and their contribution to the cultural heritage of humankind. Besides, it is not a new problem: it arose one hundred and fifty years ago, has caused much ink to flow and is still far from being resolved. Truth to tell, for some years now most scholars have been hardly concerned with it and would gladly have relegated it to the archives had not recent archaeological and geophysical discoveries resuscitated it in unexpected ways.

A Strange Language from Elsewhere

The problem of the Sumerians' origin presents a remarkable special feature: it goes back to an era when absolutely nothing was known about them – not even their name – or about the civilisation that flourished in Lower Mesopotamia in the third millennium BC, whose paternity was quite rightly attributed to them. In fact, the problem was first posed in purely linguistic terms.

At the cost of immense efforts spread over about a hundred years, scholars had managed to decipher texts written in cuneiform signs. At first, they brought their learning to bear on inscribed stones and bricks carried back to Europe by travellers who, since the seventeenth century, had been journeying through the East and had picked them up from the earth out of simple curiosity. Then they tackled the great inscription in three languages (old Persian, Elamite and Babylonian) which the king of Persia, Darius, had had carved a hundred metres above the ground on the rock of Behistun (Iran). Lastly, thousands of clay tablets were dug up during the very first excavations carried out in northern Mesopotamia by the Frenchman Paul-Émile Botta, at Khorsabad (1843–54), and the Englishman Austen Henry Layard, at Nimrud and Nineveh (1845–55).

By the 1850s, enough was known about inscriptions to be able to state that the great majority of them, coming from Assyrian cities as well as the still unexplored ruins of Babylon and its environs, had been composed in Assyrian or Babylonian. Those dialects were very close to each other, and both were related to Hebrew, Aramaic and Arabic or, in other words, Semitic. But the same could not be said of numerous inscriptions on bricks gathered in southern Mesopotamia, or of the second language on certain bilingual tablets (the first being Assyrian) from Nineveh. As that second language was written with the same signs as the Assyrian and Babylonian texts and, like the 'syllabaria' assembled by Assyrian schoolteachers for their students, gave the pronunciation of the signs, it was possible to 'read' it phonetically and even to make out its structure, but no one could understand it.

Indeed, people were in the situation in which most of us would find ourselves if faced, for example, with a Vietnamese text written in Latin characters. One thing was certain, however: that other language of Mesopotamia was neither Semitic, nor Persian, nor Elamite and, to continue the comparison, it differed as much from Assyrian or Babylonian as Vietnamese does from French.

In 1852, Sir Henry Creswicke Rawlinson – one of the great English pioneers of Assyriology – basing his view on the apparent grammatical structure of this mysterious language, ascribed it to the Scythians or the 'Turanians', a term which at that time embraced nearly all the peoples of central Asia. The following year, he suggested calling it 'Akkadian' (from the name Akkad, part of ancient Mesopotamia), and ventured to state that its pronominal system gave it particular kinship with Mongolian and Manchurian. It was only seventeen years later, in 1869, that the great French Assyriologist Jules Oppert proposed calling the language 'Sumerian', basing his choice on the title 'King of Sumer and Akkad', which Mesopotamian monarchs readily assumed. His reasoning was as follows: according to certain texts discovered in the meantime, the name Akkad seemed to be applied to the region of Babylon where most of the inscriptions were in Babylonian or a neighbouring, but slightly more archaic, Semitic language, which merited the name Akkadian.[1] The word 'Sumer' must therefore designate South Mesopotamia, exactly where there was a predominance of scattered bricks written in that other language which, in his opinion, had affinities with Turkish, Finnish and Hungarian.

Thus for the first time, together with the problem of the exact nature of this unusual language, there arose the

[1] Actually, Akkadian as such was not identified until later. Nowadays, the word 'Akkadian' is often used in the broad sense to designate the whole of the Semitic dialects of Mesopotamia (Akkadian, Assyrian and Babylonian).

question of the origin of the people who wrote it and, very likely, spoke it. And all this well before any of the numerous *tells* (artificial hills) of the land of Sumer had been excavated, or a single work of art from that region had been touched. Although Rawlinson and Oppert had suggested only linguistic 'affinities', a certain number of people were already wondering whether the Sumerians came from central Asia, the common place of origin of the Mongols, Manchurians, Turks and Finno-Ugrians. From this theory to its affirmation was just a step, and one happily taken by many journalists and popularisers of the time. But that theory, given hardly any credence nowadays, had a tough life, even among the experts. Joseph Halévy, a French epigrapher of great renown, fiercely maintained for a quarter of a century (1874–1900) that Oppert's 'Sumerian' was nothing but a secret writing, a sort of code invented by Assyrio-Babylonian scribes to conceal some esoteric knowledge. In the end, he bowed unwillingly before the unanimity of his colleagues.

Now, thanks to bilingual texts, to veritable 'dictionaries' on tablets left to us by Mesopotamian scribes, and to studies demanding as much patience as knowledge and imagination, experts can read Sumerian without too much difficulty. All the linguistic theories built up since 1852 (including the 'Caucasian' or even 'Indo-European' theories) have been abandoned. There is general agreement in thinking that although, by its structure, this language really belongs to the vast group of 'agglutinative' languages (whose area of dispersal extends from America to Africa, central Asia and Polynesia), morphologically it resembles no other known language, dead or living. Philology is therefore no help in resolving the problem of the Sumerians' origins.

By Sea or by Land?

Eight years had still to elapse between the brilliant 'invention' of the Sumerians by Oppert on purely linguistic foundations and their discovery, in the strict sense of the word, by another Frenchman.

In 1877, Ernest de Sarzec – the French consul at Basra – commenced excavations at Tello, the site of one of the most important cities in the land of Sumer, which had long been called Lagash but whose real name is now known to have been Girsu. Those excavations and, from 1899, the American ones at Nippur, some hundred kilometres north-west of Tello, yielded hundreds of texts written only in Sumerian, as well as temples, tombs, sculptures, vases, jewels, cylinder-seals and various objects of great interest. Having been unknown for so long (for, unlike the Assyrians and Babylonians, they appeared neither in the Bible nor in Greek authors), the Sumerians suddenly became real, almost alive. Not only did they enter history, but it was soon learnt that they had 'created' it, being the authors of the oldest known historical inscriptions.

But at the same time, the problem of their origin was posed in new terms, because these people were immediately perceived as 'foreign' to Mesopotamia, where they were nevertheless firmly entrenched. Not only did the Sumerians form a kind of linguistic islet in a vast Hamito-Semitic world stretching from Addis-Ababa to Babylon and almost completely surrounding them (their only other neighbours being the Elamites, to the east), but they had neither the same physical appearance nor the same clothing customs as the Assyrians and Babylonians, so it was believed. They were another people, another race. In 1906, the historian Eduard Meyer had insisted on this point. With the long-haired and bearded Assyrians with their long heads, plump hooked noses and fleshy lips, he contrasted the round-headed Sumerians and their prominent but thin noses, thin lips and shaven heads and chins. Besides, whereas the Assyrians wore long robes adorned with embroideries, the Sumerians were clad only in a coarse woollen skirt or, at the most, a kind of cloak draped over one shoulder, leaving the other bare. On all the evidence, these people had come from elsewhere and, added Meyer, had arrived in Mesopotamia after the Semites, whose bearded gods they had adopted. But *where* had they come from?

Other historians, like L. W. King and M. Jastrow, replied that the Sumerians could have come only from a mountainous country, for they used the same sign *KUR* for 'country' and 'mountain', and their temples included stepped towers (*ziggurats*), proving that their former places of worship must have been situated on mountain tops. Mesopotamia is encircled by mountains on three sides: the Amanus and the Lebanon to the north-west, the Caucasus to the north and the long chain of the Zagros which, to the east, separates it from the Iranian plateau. For preference, people turned to the last, because it was nearer to Mesopotamia than the other mountains, and the excavations carried out in the south-west of Iran (notably at Susa) had revealed an important and very ancient civilisation: Elam.

But although the Sumerians could easily have come from Iran on foot (or donkey-back), could they not also have come from other mountainous lands much farther away but still situated to the east: Baluchistan, for instance, or Afghanistan, or even the Altaï, in the central Asia that had tempted the linguists? In that case they would have come by sea, embarking on the Gulf of Oman after a fairly long land journey, then coming up the Persian Gulf. This 'maritime' theory relied fundamentally on the fact that the Sumerians seemed to have settled at first in the extreme south of Iraq, around the mouth of the Tigris and the Euphrates – rivers which, in antiquity, were known to have flowed separately into the Gulf, some 300 kilometres north of the present-day mouth of their common affluent, the Shatt el-Arab.

Furthermore, there was the legend reported by Berosus – a Babylonian priest living in the third century BC in a country Hellenised by Alexander's successors – who had written, in poor Greek, a history of his country entitled *Babyloniaca*, dedicated to the Seleucid monarch Antiochus I (281–260 BC). The work is lost, but fragments of the summary which the writer Alexander Polyhistor had made in the first century AD were preserved by the historian Flavius Josephus (his contemporary) and bishop Eusebius of Caesarea (in the fourth century). At the beginning of his *Babyloniaca*, Berosus recounts that originally the inhabitants of Babylonia lived 'without laws, just like wild animals'. But a strange being named Oannes, half-man half-fish, had emerged from the Erythrean Sea (a name given at that time to the Persian Gulf as well as to the Red Sea), 'in a place adjacent to Babylonia', and had lived for a time with those savages. 'He brought them the knowledge of letters, sciences and all kinds of techniques. He also taught them how to found cities, build temples, promulgate laws and measure plots of land. Similarly, he revealed to them how to work the land and gather fruits and, in general, gave men all that is connected with civilised life.' Then he dived back into the sea where, incidentally, he had spent all his nights, 'for he was amphibious'. Perhaps this fantastical story concealed a grain of truth? Could it be the reflection, distorted and wrapped in mystery, of a distant tradition according to which men from the sea landed one day to introduce civilisation into a still prehistoric Mesopotamia, which is precisely what the Sumerians had done?

Speculation had reached this point when the First World War broke out. Interrupted for six years, archaeological research in the Near East was resumed in 1920 and extended to many lands that had been little explored until then, notably Syria, Turkey and the Indus valley. In Mesopotamia excavations increased, became more scientific and, in the space of around forty years (1920–60), completely overturned our knowledge of the civilisations of the Euphrates and Tigris, together with many received ideas.

The Revelations of Eridu

At first, many other Sumerian cities other than Girsu and Nippur were explored, notably Ur and its celebrated royal cemetery (see p. 24) flowing with gold; the great town of Uruk, homeland of the hero Gilgamesh, which was to yield the finest proto-Sumerian temples and the oldest known texts; and the little town of Eridu, to which we shall return. Other important excavations apart from Sumer were Kish, Mari and the sites in the valley of Diyala (Tell Asmar, Khafâje, Tell Aqrab). These excavations revealed the profound influence exerted by Sumerian civilisation over the whole of Mesopotamia and well beyond. They completely demolished the notion of a Sumerian race, showing us Semites of Mari and the Diyala with shaven heads and woollen skirts, as well as a mixture of brachycephalic (short) and dolicephalic (long) skulls. They taught us that the relatively later *ziggurats* derived from platforms on which ancient temples had stood, simply to elevate gods above mortals. Lastly, epigraphers were able to establish, among a thousand other things, that the sign 'mountain' (*KUR*) was applied only to foreign countries, the land of Sumer being designated by the sign *KALAM*. In a word, theories carefully constructed on foundations whose fragility astounds us nowadays were seriously called into question.

But the greatest merit of those excavations was to bring

to light a whole Mesopotamian prehistory and protohistory which had been unknown until then. From the cave of Shanidar, in Iraqi Kurdistan in the Mousterian era (80,000–40,000 BC), to the dawn of history, in Sumer (around 2800 BC), a series of neolithic, then chalcolithic, cultures had followed one another between the Tigris and Euphrates, cultures which, for want of anything better, had been given the names of the sites where they had first been identified: Jarmo, Hassuna, Halaf, Ubaid, Uruk, Jemdet-Nasr. Each of those cultures had been characterised by specific elements, most typically pottery, first crude (Jarmo), then painted (Hassuna, Halaf, Ubaid, Jemdet-Nasr) and finally undecorated (Uruk). The distribution of these types of pottery was either relatively narrow (Jarmo, Hassuna, Jemdet-Nasr), confined to the north of Mesopotamia (Halaf), or extended to the whole of that region (Ubaid, Uruk). It was the pottery, allied to the remains of religious architecture, which showed us that occupation of southern Mesopotamia was far earlier than had been believed until then; and that revelation was due to the excavations of Eridu.

Compared with Ur, from which it was only some 15 kilometres distant, Eridu was never a great city, but it occupied a prime position in Sumerian tradition. In fact, according to the great *Sumerian King List*, published in 1939 by the American Sumerologist Thorkild Jacobsen, it was the oldest of all Mesopotamian cities, the one where 'royalty had descended from the sky' for the first time, well before the Flood. The names of its two sovereigns, Alulim and Alalgar, are cited by Berosus in a distorted and Grecianised form (Aloros and Alaparos) as being the 'first king of the country' and his son. Another noteworthy point: other texts clearly indicate that Eridu was situated 'on the shore of the sea'.

The British archaeologist Seton Lloyd and Iraqi Fuad

Safar, who excavated at Eridu from 1946 to 1949, brought to light a cemetery, a large building they called a 'palace' and the remains of a *ziggurat* constructed in the Third Dynasty of Ur (c. 2100–2000 BC). But beneath a corner of this *ziggurat* they discovered an impressive series of eighteen temples, built one on top of the other, which testified not only to a very long occupation of the site but also perhaps to a very ancient devotion to the same god. To judge by the many remains of fish offerings in each of the temples, the god could have been Enki, the Sumerian god of the waters, or at least his equivalent.

Pottery found there enabled the five uppermost temples to be dated from the beginning of the Uruk era (c. 3700 BC) and the six preceding temples to the Ubaid period (4500–3500 BC), but the deepest sanctuaries contained pottery that was painted rather differently from that of Ubaid. Ceramics of levels 14 to 12 were identical to those which the German archaeologists excavating at Uruk had already found at Qala'at Hajji Mohammed, near that city, while those from levels 18 to 15 – particularly elegant – had no known parallel. They were therefore christened 'Eridu pottery'. We now know that Eridu pottery was limited to a small zone in the vicinity of this site, whereas ceramics from Hajji Mohammed were to be found as far afield as Ras-el-Amiyah, north of Kish, 240 kilometres from Eridu. It is very important to note that Hajji Mohammed and Râs-el-Amiyah were not *tells* (artificial hills) but sites discovered by chance (a crumbling cliff on the Euphrates, the digging of a canal) beneath the present level of the Mesopotamian plain, as were the deep levels of Eridu. We must also note that Eridu pottery shows certain affinities with that of Halaf and, because of its stratigraphic position, like the latter may well date to about 5000 BC.

A Continuous Population

In very ancient times, therefore, the *whole* of Mesopotamia was inhabited by various peoples whose names and history will be forever unknown to us, because they have left us no texts or documents. It was not until around 3200 BC, in layer 4b of the Uruk culture levels, at Uruk itself, that the first clay tablets appeared, bearing archaic cuneiform signs. Unfortunately, these ancient texts (the oldest in the world) are solely formed of 'logograms' (drawings representing a word) and lacking signs with a phonetic value used as grammatic particles; so we cannot be sure if they are written in Sumerian. Furthermore, in 1943–5, the great Sumerologist Benno Landsberger demonstrated that genuinely Sumerian texts contain words that are neither Sumerian nor Semitic, notably certain names of towns and rivers, including the Euphrates (*buranun*) and the Tigris (*idigna*) and numerous names of occupations and everyday objects. It would thus seem that the Sumerians had borrowed these words from a people 'X' who had preceded them in Mesopotamia.

Despite all these discoveries, the problem of the Sumerians' origins still remained obscure. It was even becoming more complicated and was now accompanied by a chronological question: if the Sumerians had arrived in Mesopotamia before 3000 BC, as seemed probable, had they been the bearers of one of those prehistoric cultures, and which one? And where had they come from?

Scholars were perplexed. Generally speaking, the archaeologists (Seton Lloyd, Henri Frankfort), impressed by the continuity of culture evidenced by the superimposed temples of Eridu, were inclined to think that the Sumerians' arrival had coincided with the beginning of the Ubaid period (4500–3500 BC) or even of Eridu. The philologists

E. A. Speiser and S. N. Kramer, for their part, based their view on the fairly late appearance of writing; on a tradition in Sumerian literature of a 'heroic age' similar to that of other conquering peoples (Greeks, Germans and Hindus); and on the replacement of painted pottery (Ubaid) by undecorated pottery (Uruk) to date the Sumerians' arrival to the beginning of the Uruk period (c. 3500 BC), if not later. But their departure point was still just as mysterious: the many excavations carried out in the whole of the Near East as well as in India, Pakistan, Afghanistan, the Caucasus and central Asia between 1920 and 1960 had indeed yielded nothing which resembled, either closely or distantly, what we know of Sumerian civilisation. So we were left with the old theories. In 1951, the American Assyriologist Speiser concluded a long article by stating, without the slightest proof, that the Sumerians, entering Mesopotamia in the Uruk period, 'had come from the east, probably by sea, although their country of origin seemed to have been a mountainous region'. And speculating: Transcaucasia, Transcaspian, Upper Asia? In France, André Parrot alone inclined towards Anatolia, the traditional centre for plain pottery, as Iran was for painted. In his opinion, the Sumerians had come from the north, at the beginning of the Uruk period, following the Euphrates valley. It was an original theory but, like the 'maritime' theory, rested on no tangible proof.

What was known around the end of the 1950s about the Arabo-Persian Gulf on which the Sumerians were supposed to have sailed, like Vikings, before conquering Mesopotamia? Very little, in fact, apart from what certain texts said about it.

Those texts – royal inscriptions and administrative tablets, which were plentiful between 2300 and 1800 BC – mentioned vessels from lands called Dilmun, Magan and Meluhha, mooring in the river ports of Ur and even Agade, not far from Babylon, after wandering over the 'Bitter sea' (or 'Lower' or 'of the Rising Sun'), as the Gulf was then known. From Meluhha they had brought gold, the 'precious cornelian', ivory objects, various tree essences, while from Magan came the 'noble copper' and that beautiful black stone, diorite, in which Sumerian sculptors carved statues of Gudea, prince of Girsu, which can be admired in the Louvre. As for Dilmun, it seems to have been used mainly as a trading post through which these goods passed. We know little about what the Mesopotamians gave in exchange; probably cereals, hides, cloth, manufactured articles. In any case, it was a flourishing trade which Mesopotamian sovereigns – from Man-ishtusu, king of Akkad (c. 2269–2255 BC), to Sargon II, king of Assyria (721–705 BC) – seem to have been periodically tempted to monopolise by seizing those areas or extending their control over them. Those three lands can now almost certainly be identified. Meluhha was probably the Indus valley, where a very remarkable civilisation flourished at the end of the third millennium. It seems increasingly certain that Magan was present-day Oman, rich in copper ore and volcanic rocks; and there is agreement in recognising the ancient Dilmun as the island of Bahrain. But with the exception of this island, studded with thousands of tumuli – several of which had been excavated in 1906 and 1925 without yielding much – the entire west coast of the Arabo-Persian Gulf as well as Oman remained *terrae incognitae* for archaeologists in the 1950s.

Oil changed all that. Conferring wealth, then independence, on the coastal countries of the Gulf, it awoke in their rulers a strong enough national feeling for them to encourage, fund and even promote research into the distant past of these brand-new states. After Bahrain, excavated very successfully by the Danes from 1953, there followed the island of Failaka (belonging to Kuwait), Qatar, the United

Arab Emirates, the eastern provinces of Saudi Arabia and finally Oman. Several American, British, Danish and French missions are at work in this too long neglected part of the Near East, carrying out surveys, digging in *tells*, opening tombs. It is of course too early to try to sketch an overall picture of the results of this work, this genuine 'archaeological revolution' about which it is surprising that the public at large is not better informed, but three points have already emerged which are worth emphasising. First, in antiquity these regions appear to have been richer and more populous than they were before the great oil boom of the 1960s. Next, as early as the third millennium BC, Bahrain, certain parts of the Gulf coast and Oman had their own culture – sometimes modest, sometimes fairly impressive – and had close connections with Mesopotamia, eastern Iran, Baluchistan and the Indus valley. Lastly, commercial, and perhaps political, relationships with Mesopotamia went back to a far more remote period than was suggested by the texts, since pottery from Jemdet-Nasr (c. 3100 BC) has been found in the heart of Oman, and Ubaid pottery – even that of Hajji Mohammed – all along the coast of Saudi Arabia as far as Bahrain and Qatar.

Sumerians Below the Gulf?

We are also indebted to oil for other kinds of research, as into the domain of geology and geophysics for example, with occasional repercussions on the history, prehistory and archaeology of the Gulf and neighbouring countries. Of this research we will consider here only the underwater probes carried out in 1964–5 by geologists of the German oceanographic vessel *Meteor*, because they have a direct bearing on our subject. Indeed, these probes enabled us to confirm, and above all to date, what had already been known for a long time, namely that the level of the Arabo-Persian Gulf fluctuated considerably during the Pleistocene and beginning of the Holocene period, depending on the formation or melting of the enormous icecaps which, on four occasions, covered the entire north of Europe and America.

It was thus possible to establish that around 70,000 BC, in the warm period between the last two glaciations (Riss and Würm), the Gulf level was some 8 metres above the present level, which implies that water then covered a large part of the Mesopotamian plain. The level went down after that, as the climate became colder and the glaciers formed again, to reach its lowest point (–120 m) at the peak of the Würm glaciation, around 14,000 BC. The entire Gulf was then a large plain crossed by the Tigris and Euphrates (or the equivalent of the present-day Shatt el-Arab), which flowed directly into the Gulf of Oman. Then, as the icecap receded, the level of the Arabo-Persian Gulf rose again, very slowly at first, more quickly later. The head of the Gulf was situated east of the peninsula of Qatar around 12,000 BC; halfway between Kuwait and Bahrain around 10,000 BC; some 100 kilometres farther north around 8000 BC; on the latitude of Kuwait around 6000 BC; and in its present position around 4000 BC. One last rising of the waters, around 3000 BC, would seem to have raised the level by about 3 metres, enough to submerge part of Lower Mesopotamia, and it was the gradual alluviation by the rivers, which now had a weak flow, that caused the sea to recede, the town of Ur being situated some 20 or 30 kilometres from the shore around 2800 BC.

It is therefore possible to suppose that between 14,000 and 3000 BC, what is today the bed of the Gulf was a broad valley watered by one or two big rivers and their tributaries, with scattered lakes and, seemingly, habitable. One cannot help imagining that this valley, from a certain period yet to be pinpointed, could have been inhabited by the Sumerians, or at least their ancestors.

This hypothesis, which one scarcely dares to whisper, would have the advantage of resolving certain problems. It would provide a semblance of a rational basis for the legend narrated by Berosus. The fish-man Oannes would personify this people, withdrawing before the rising waters, literally 'coming out of the sea', to settle around Eridu, then in the whole of Lower Mesopotamia.

Next, if it is accepted that the Pre-Sumerians were the carriers of the painted pottery of Eridu, Hajji Mohammed and Ubaid (nowadays thought to be successive varieties of one and the same 'Ubaid pottery'), such a theory would be in keeping with the presence of this ceramic output in Qatar, Bahrain and along the north-west coast of the Gulf, as well as in the extreme south of Iraq.

Lastly, it would take into account a Sumerian concept whose *raison d'être* is far from obvious: that of 'Dilmun, the lost paradise', a concept doubtless referred to at the end of the oldest Mesopotamian account of the Flood (see Chapter 13), when Ziusudra, the Sumerian Noah, emerges from the ark, offers a sacrifice, is transfigured into a god and installed 'in the land of passage, the land of Dilmun, where the sun rises'. But the most explicit text in this regard is a long poem, quite well preserved despite a few lacunae, entitled the 'Myth of Enki and Ninhursag'.

An Unverifiable and Unnecessary Hypothesis

This bizarre and complex myth is in essence a myth of sexual creation, staged in Dilmun, with Enki (the god of the waters) and his wife Ninhursag (the earth-goddess) as protagonists. We see Enki make fresh water flow in Dilmun to bathe meadows and orchards, impregnate his wife and even, successively, his daughter and granddaughters, thus creating goddesses, and finally have his seed stolen by Ninhursag to produce eight probably magic plants. But he eats them and, cursed by the earth-goddess for this deed, falls gravely ill. However, Ninhursag, who had fled, returns, takes pity on him and creates eight healing deities (one for each part of his suffering body) to whom Enki assigns certain divine functions or allocates certain territories. Let us note here that Magan is given to the god Ninsikilla and Dilmun to the god Enshag (which may also be written Enzak or Inzak). The name Inzak can be read on inscriptions dating from the beginning of the second millennium, discovered at Bahrain and on the island of Failaka. But for our purposes, the most interesting part of the myth is the description of Dilmun that opens the story. To quote its last translator, Professor Kramer of Philadelphia, Dilmun is a 'pure', 'clean', 'shining' land, a 'land of the living' where neither illness nor death reigns:

> In Dilmun the crow does not utter its cry,
> The *ittidu* bird does not utter the cry of the *ittidu* bird,
> The lion does not kill,
> The wolf does not seize the lamb,
> The wild dog, devourer of kids, is unknown,
> He whose eyes hurt does not say: 'My eyes hurt',
> He whose head aches does not say: 'My head aches',
> The old woman does not say: 'I am an old woman',
> The old man does not say: 'I am an old man' . . .

In short, it is a dream country, a veritable paradise – as places often become in men's memory when they have had to leave them long, long ago, with no hope of returning.

Might the Sumerians (or at least their ancestors) have come from Dilmun, that is to say, the island of Bahrain or, in the broader sense, from the part of the Gulf situated between that island and Kuwait and now covered by water?

As attractive as the hypothesis of a 'prehistoric Sumer' sunk in the bottom of the Arabo-Persian Gulf may appear, it runs up against many objections – chronological, geological and archaeological – which render it scarcely credible. For instance, on the latitude of Bahrain, the bed of the Gulf was dry from 14,000 to 10,000 BC, a period corresponding to the upper Palaeolithic, and too far back to fit in with a protohistoric culture. Besides, according to the geographer Vita-Finzi, the rarity of fluviatile sediments at the bottom of the Gulf and the absence of a true delta at its entrance (probably because of the very strong flow of the river or rivers in those distant times) would have made it 'a depression generally deprived of water and containing some marshy zones'. Another noteworthy point: Eridu pottery (although the oldest) has not been found in Bahrain, Qatar or the Gulf coast, and most of the Ubaid pottery collected there is of a late date within the Ubaid period.

Moreover, the 'undersea' hypothesis is marked by a major flaw: it is *unverifiable.* For what could one hope to find nowadays, on the floor of the Gulf, of the reed huts and houses of mud and unbaked bricks which formed the ordinary habitat of the Sumerians and their predecessors? Also it is not *necessary* even to explain the myth of Enki and Ninhursag. We can easily imagine that the Pre-Sumerians, whether from east or west (of Mesopotamia, that is), were able to stay and create colonies or trading-posts along the Gulf coast and at Bahrain, then abandon them or lose them to other peoples. Later on, the Sumerians would then have transposed their myth of a Paradise lost to those distant lands 'where the sun rises', as the Hebrews who had settled in Canaan placed theirs in the Garden of Eden, between the Tigris and Euphrates.

Up to the present, nothing has revealed an ethnic movement from east to west across the Gulf. On the other hand, the hypothesis of a Mesopotamian 'origin' seems increasingly probable and deserves to be examined.

In my view, the chief merit of the numerous excavations carried out on the protohistoric sites of Iraq during the past twenty years has been to confirm that the Sumero-Akkadian civilisation – like all civilisations, ancient or modern – was an amalgam of various elements melted together in the same crucible, poured into the same mould. The appearance of each of those elements – whether we are talking of techniques, arts or architecture – can henceforward be localised in time and space and, though it is indisputable that some have been borrowed from neighbouring countries, the majority, in Mesopotamia itself, have such deep roots that they can be considered indigenous to that region.

Thanks to those excavations we now know that the most ancient prehistoric cultures of Mesopotamia were to some extent contemporaneous and that there was no hiatus between them, because the transition from one kind of pottery to another, for example, was almost always gradual. Besides, it is extremely likely that the replacement of the painted pottery of Ubaid by the unpainted of Uruk had been due to a technical innovation, the potter's wheel, allowing mass production; and there is no longer any reason to suspect a sharp change of population. Of all these cultures, only that of Halaf seems to have been imported, 'ready made', into Mesopotamia, probably from eastern Anatolia or Armenia, but its limited spread, gradual appearance and disappearance suggest a peaceful infiltration rather than conquest.

Where is the 'Cradle of Origin'?

Recent archaeological researches have also revealed a new protohistoric culture that must be inserted between the culture of Hassuna and those, contemporary with one another, of Halaf in the north and Eridu (Ubaid I) in the south, which carbon 14 enables us to date to about 5500 BC. This culture has the name Samarra, as the very elegant painted pottery that characterises it was discovered as early as 1912 in a cemetery underlying the medieval level of this town. But its type-site is Tell es-Sawwan (the *tell* 'of the flints'), situated on the left bank of the Tigris, not far from Samarra, and excavated by an Iraqi mission between 1963 and 1969. The epicentre of this culture appears to correspond to the Middle Tigris, between Mosul and Baghdad, but Samarra pottery is found on the Middle Euphrates and the Khabur (to the west) and the foothills of the Zagros (to the east).

The inhabitants of Tell es-Sawwan – mainly farmers and stockbreeders – seem to have been the first in Iraq to practise a primitive form of irrigation, utilising the floodwaters of the Tigris to water their fields of wheat, barley, oats and flax. They were also the first in that region to surround their town with a moat and a wall. Their houses, which were spacious and built of unbaked bricks, contained not only beautiful Samarra pottery but also vessels skilfully carved in translucent marble. Their tombs, situated beneath their dwellings, yielded terracotta or alabaster statuettes, standing or squatting and mostly of women. Some of the terracotta figurines had eyes made of a disc of clay cracked 'like a coffee bean' and very elongated skulls – eyes and skulls very similar to those of the Ubaid culture figurines. On the other hand, the eyes of other terracotta or alabaster statuettes were big, wide open, encrusted with shell and surmounted by thick eyebrows in bitumen. Not only the eyes but the very attitude of the people (arms bent at the elbow, hands joined in front of the chest) and their pointed headdress bear an astonishing resemblance to those of archaic Sumerian statuettes which date to 2800–2500 BC. The archaeologist Joan Oates made another noteworthy discovery at Choga Mami, east of Baghdad: clay figurines with coffee-bean eyes similar to those of Tell es-Sawwan, as well as pottery of a transitional style between Samarra pottery and that of Eridu (Ubaid I) and Hajji Mohammed (Ubaid II), all three, moreover, equally present in their pure form on the same site.[2]

Tell es-Sawwan and Choga Mami thus offer us a remarkable example of cultural continuity between the 'Samarrans' and the 'Ubaidians' and even, so it would seem, the Sumerians of historic times. I do not think that one can conclude from this that the 'Ubaidians' were 'Samarrans' who had emigrated to the south, or that the 'Ubaidians' were indisputably the ancestors of the Sumerians, but these discoveries can only reinforce the hypothesis that the Sumerians were a part of the diverse population who had long been settled in Mesopotamia and had doubtless mingled and merged over the centuries, as our own ancestors did.

If we follow this theory, the origin of the Sumerians would be lost in the mists of time, for we do not, and never shall, know anything precise about the movements of the Neolithic and Palaeolithic populations who succeeded one another in the Near East, Europe or Asia. The deep desire to find a 'cradle of origin' for the Sumerians, even to the point of searching the sea bed or constructing theories on foundations that fall apart when closely examined, is to feed on illusion or, as Frankfort put it so well, 'to chase a daydream'.

[2] Archaeologists excavating at Tell el-Ouelli, near Larsa, have discovered not only the four classical levels of Ubaid, but also a level christened Ubaid 0, which has certain points in common with the culture of Samarra. Under this last level, they have been able to make out even deeper levels, but difficult to explore because of the water table. Lower Mesopotamia was therefore populated much earlier than was believed until now.

CHAPTER 2

The Great Enigma of the Cemetery at Ur

Georges Roux

During the 1920s, two sensational archaeological discoveries were talked about worldwide: the tomb of Tutankhamun, in Egypt, and the royal cemetery of Ur, in Iraq. Both discoveries were made by Englishmen and both concerned royal burial places – or were regarded as such – remarkable for the extreme richness and great beauty of their grave furnishings. But there the similarity ended.

In the Nile valley, there was a single tomb – that of a well-known young pharaoh, who had reigned from 1361 to 1352 BC; a hermetically sealed tomb cut out of dry rock, so that the sovereign's embalmed body and the treasures surrounding him had all been perfectly preserved. By contrast, in the valley of the Euphrates, no fewer than seventeen tombs were found – dating back to the third millennium, dug into ground that was often damp – and their occupants were far from being all identified. They were skeletons that time had reduced to dust, and precious objects that could be saved only by technical expertise. Moreover – and this was a unique phenomenon in Mesopotamia and extremely rare in the Near East – accompanying nearly all the distinguished dead were the bodies, sometimes very numerous, of members of their retinue or court. On the one hand, therefore, the plain evidence, historical simplicity and clarity; on the other, uncertainties, an aura of mystery, the horror of the hecatombs. *Tod und Nebel*, death and mist; without a doubt, the greatest and certainly the most disturbing of the enigmas in the whole of Mesopotamian history.

Ur in Sumer

Situated in the south of Iraq, some 200 kilometres north-west of Basra, the ancient city of Ur – Abraham's homeland – was born around 3000 BC out of a large prehistoric village, and was continuously inhabited until about 200 BC. Together with Uruk and Lagash, it was one of Sumer's three great capitals, lands that its kings dominated twice during the third millennium. Even today, the ruins of Ur are the most beautiful and eloquent in all Mesopotamia. Although the Euphrates, which once flowed in the shadow of its walls, is now some dozen kilometres away, its enormous *ziggurat* (staged tower) still dominates the 'sacred precinct' and its temples, and a walk through the narrow and twisting alleys of its popular districts recalls a visit to Pompeii, almost the only difference being that the Ur region is older by eighteen centuries.

After some explorations and probes, the first of which go back to 1854, the Ur excavations began in 1918. Soon interrupted for want of money, they were resumed in 1922, funded by the British Museum and the University of Pennsylvania, and regularly kept up over twelve years under the direction of Sir Leonard Woolley. In 1922, the *ziggurat* and the great rectangular platform surrounding it had been partly exposed, but the boundaries of this sacred zone remained uncertain, notably in the south-east sector. Woolley therefore set to work on that sector, having dug a large trench. He then found himself (although he did not know it till later) between two supporting walls of the sacred esplanade: one had been erected by the kings of the Third Dynasty of Ur (c. 2112–2004 BC), probably following an older wall line, the other constructed by Nebuchadnezzar II (615–562 BC); both had been mostly destroyed (Fig. 2.1). From this trench many clay vessels emerged, as well as beads of cornelian, lapis lazuli and even gold, sure evidence of the presence of tombs. Excavating a cemetery, above all in Mesopotamia, is always technically difficult and, as Woolley's labourers and the archaeologist himself lacked experience, he had the admirable sense to close the workings and not return until four years later. The celebrated 'royal cemetery' of Ur was thus excavated between 1926 and 1932, at a rate of three or four months a year.

In fact, the beads and pottery discovered in 1922 had come from tombs datable to the dynasty of Akkad (c. 2334–2154 BC), which were the shallowest; it was subsequently found that the whole bank of detritus at the foot of the oldest wall in the sacred zone was literally bristling with superimposed and entangled burials, more than 2500 of which have been explored. Most often, they were simple graves where the dead lay, sometimes wrapped in a mat, sometimes resting in coffins of wood, plaited reeds or ceramic, accompanied by a few pots, bowls and personal articles such as weapons, modest jewellery or sometimes a cylinder-seal.[1] The tombs named 'royal' and situated lower,

[1] Small cylinders (1–8 cm) generally of stone, pierced lengthwise so that they could be worn on a cord round their owner's neck. They are carved with motifs and scenes that vary according to the period and, in their detail, from one cylinder to another. When rolled on damp clay they drew a little bas-relief border which authenticated the document (contract, for instance) or the object (jar-stopper) to which they were applied. The comparative study of cylinder-seals (*glyptics*) provides interesting information and can be used to give approximate datings.

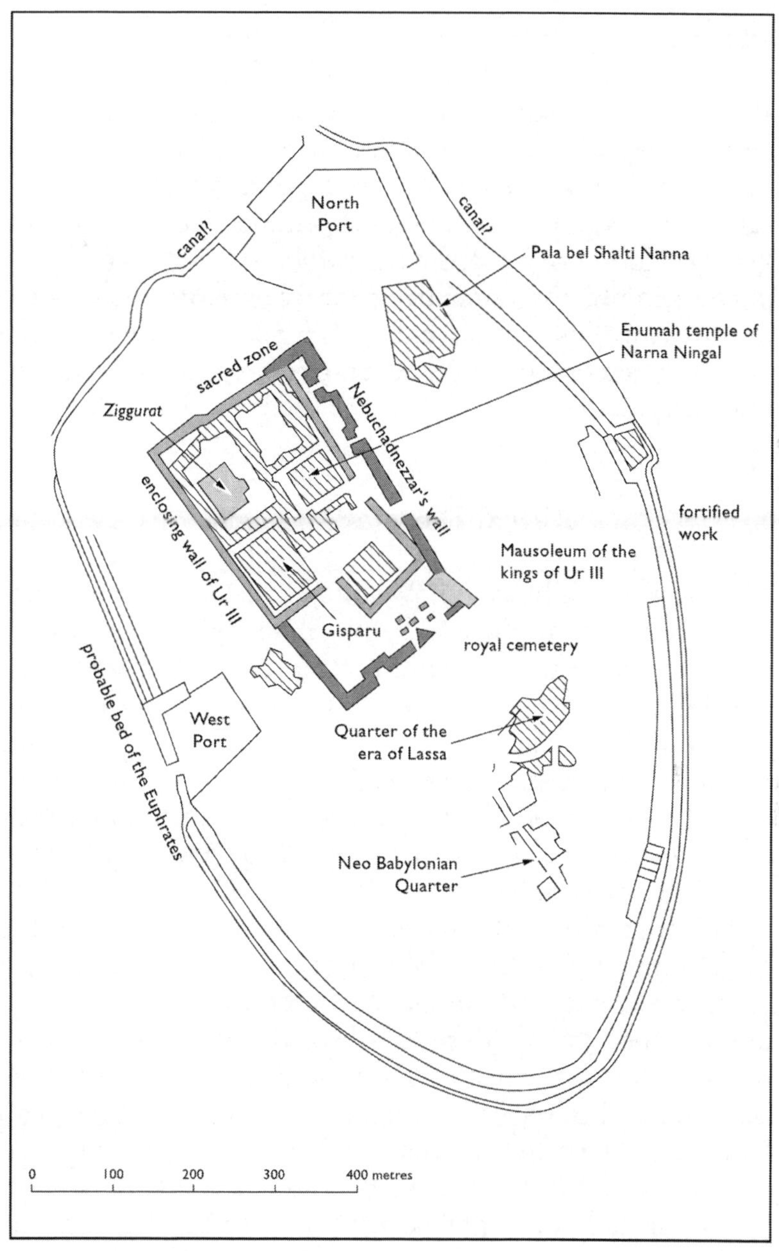

Fig. 2.1: The town of Ur (from L'Histoire, *no. 75, p. 60)*

were recognisable by three distinctive features: in general, they comprised a vaulted tomb built of stones or bricks at the bottom of a square or rectangular pit (wide and deep) which was reached by way of an inclined plane ending in a vestibule; their grave goods were especially rich and plentiful; and most of the graves contained several bodies. Beneath these, other ordinary tombs were buried deeply in the ground. By comparing the seals from the vaulted tombs with those from tombs lying above and below, the 'royal cemetery' of Ur could be dated to about 2600 BC (Fig. 2.2).

Buried Kings and Queens

The sixteen tombs which Woolley called 'royal' fell into two categories: on the one hand, six fairly vast pits whose vaulted tomb was not found (or had never existed), christened 'the death pits' by him; on the other, ten pits containing a vault with one or several chambers. However, to this list must be added a seventeenth burial tomb (tomb 755), similar to those of ordinary mortals, but containing such riches that it could not have belonged to anyone but a king or prince, or so it would seem.

The first difficulty one encounters when studying the 'royal cemetery' of Ur is the identity of the presumed royal personages who had been buried there. First – and this is notably the case with the 'death pits' – it was not always possible to distinguish the 'principal' corpse from the 'secondary' bodies surrounding it (those of people who had been sacrificed so that they could accompany the corpse). Second, the skeletons were generally in a very bad state and could not be studied with all the scientific rigour desirable in such instances, so that the sex of the principal corpse could be established only by observing the

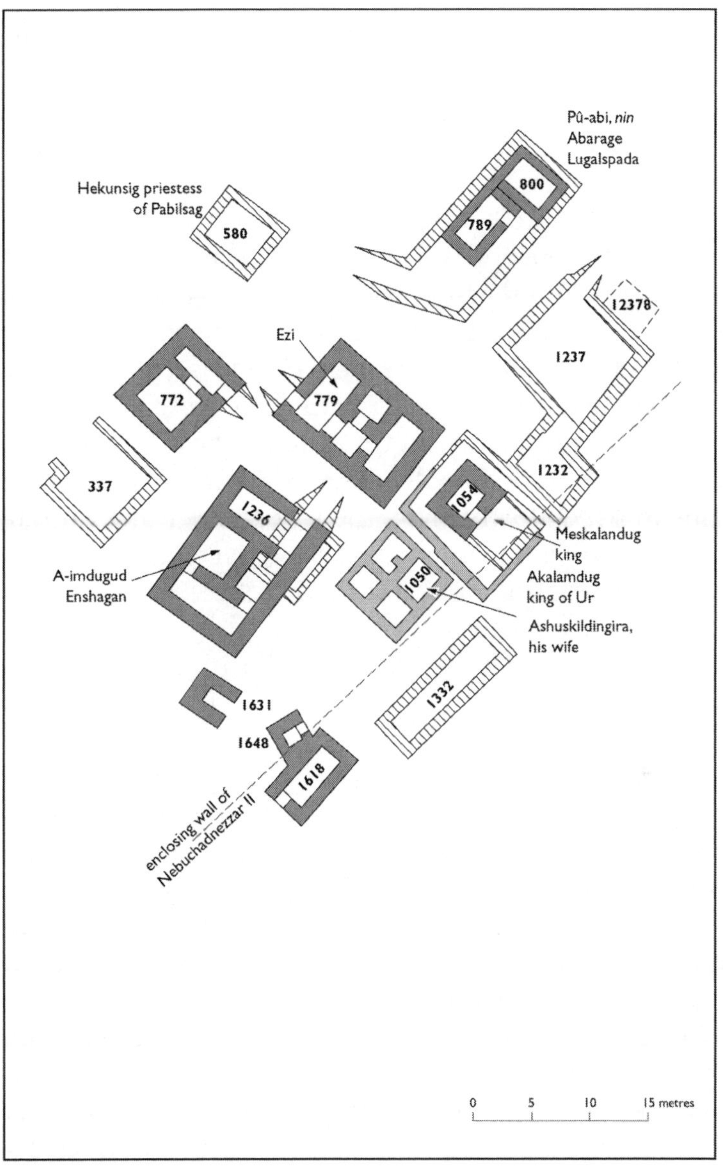

Fig. 2.2: The royal cemetery of Ur. The tombs with hatched edges are the 'death pits'; tomb 755 (Meskalandug, no title) is not shown on this plan, it underlay part of tomb 779; the inscribed seals found in the tombs are indicated (from L'Histoire, *no. 75, p. 61)*

jewels it was wearing, the ceremonial headdress on its head or the articles accompanying it. For this diagnosis, it has recently been suggested that the cylinder-seals found in the tombs should be used: scenes of fights between animals or heroes and animals would be characteristic of men's burials, while so-called 'banqueting' scenes (sometimes reduced to two people drinking from the same vessel with straws) would indicate women's burials. It is an ingenious method, but it is not always known whether the seal in question belonged to the principal dead person or a member of the entourage buried with the corpse.

The inscriptions carved on some of the cylinder-seals or metal vessels have the advantage of revealing their owner's name to us. Unfortunately, the Ur cemetery yielded only a few still legible inscriptions, and very few of them give us any information about the title or office of the individual concerned. The longest and most explicit of them is on a lapis lazuli cylinder found on the floor of tomb 1050. It reads 'Akalamdug, king of Ur, Ashusikildingira, his wife (*dam*)'. However, it is not certain that this sovereign of Ur still rested in the vault, which had been completely pillaged in antiquity, its 'principal body' having vanished. This cylinder might have been stolen from elsewhere and lost there by the looter; moreover, like many laconic inscriptions of that period, this one may mean that the cylinder had been dedicated to Akalamdug by his wife and that, in fact, it had belonged to her.

Another cylinder-seal bears the inscription 'Meskalamdug, king (*lugal*)', without specifying of which city. It came from tomb 1054, which comprised two vaults, one on top of the other, separated by several layers of beaten earth on which lay funeral vases and a few human bones. The lower vault contained the skeleton of a woman, accompanied by some beautiful gold articles, and the more modest upper vault – from which the inscription came – held a coffin with the skeleton of a man and two gold daggers. It would therefore seem that a king (probably of Ur) had himself interred above his wife, who had predeceased him.

However, the same name, Meskalamdug (which means 'the hero who is good for the country'), but this time without any other title, is found on a lamp and two gold bowls discovered in tomb 755 – the ordinary-looking tomb mentioned earlier – which contained, among other marvels, the famous gold 'helmet', a very beautiful gold dagger with a silver sheath, numerous vessels in precious metals and – unexpectedly – women's jewellery. In the same tomb a copper vase was found inscribed with the name Ninbanda and, as *nin* is a title applied to both queens and priestesses, it was deduced that this Ninbanda was the wife of Meskalamdug. But why, then, was her vase in this eminently masculine tomb? And which was the true burial place of king Meskalamdug: the upper vault of tomb 1054 or the coffin in the small pit 755? Or should we be thinking of two kings, or a king and a prince bearing the same name, also highly possible?

The fifth important piece of writing was carved on the cylinder-seal of a woman called Pû-abi ('Word of my father'), who was expressly designated as *nin*.[2] This time the cylinder was in place, on a level with the skeleton's shoulder, and the tomb (numbered 800) was at once revealed as one of the richest with, notably, the *nin*'s splendid headdress with leaves and rings of gold, a profusion of gold tableware, a superb lyre and a sledge-chariot adorned with lionesses' heads in silver. Five soldiers and twenty-three 'ladies-in-waiting', also superbly attired, surrounded their mistress. Two other inscribed cylinders, one

[2] For a long time read in Sumerian SHUB.AD (Shubad), this name must now be read in Akkadian *Pû-abi* (Pû-abi), the two interpretations having nearly the same sense. This *nin* of Ur was thus of Semitic origin, which confirms the merging of the two populations of Mesopotamia at the dawn of its history.

with the name Lugalsapada, the other with Abarage, were found in the same tomb: people wanted to see Abarage as Pû-abi's husband, and vault 789, next to tomb 800, was attributed to him. But nothing indicates that he had been a king, and what was his seal doing in his wife's tomb?

Of the four remaining inscriptions, all on cylinder-seals, only one is explicit: that of 'Hekunsig, priestess (*nin*) of the god Pabilsag', discovered in a 'death pit' (580). A cylinder with the name A-imdugud and another with the name Enshagan (from tomb 1236), like that of Ezi (tomb 779), tell us nothing about the social rank of these men. Let us note, however, that A-imdugud's was of gold, which is quite rare, and that vault 1236, which had unfortunately been looted, was the largest in the cemetery.

Thus, of the noteworthy occupants of these seventeen tombs identifiable by inscriptions, we have only one king of Ur (Akalamdug) and his wife, another king (probably of Ur; Meskalamdug-King), two *nin* (queens or priestesses; Pû-abi and Ninbanda) and Hekunsig (priestess of a minor god). in other words six persons among five tombs, to which we must add the untitled Meskalamdug of tomb 755, who could have been a prince. Of the sovereigns or important personages buried in the twelve other tombs known as 'royal' – or the nine others, if we are absolutely determined to consider Abarage (vault 789 and tomb 800) and A-imdugud (vault 1236) as kings, despite the absence of formal evidence – we shall, alas, never know anything at all.

By analogy with the first two rulers of the First Dynasty of Ur (c. 2560–2420 BC), Mesannepadda and A-annepadda, Meskalamdug is often regarded as the father and predecessor of Akalamdug ('the father good for the country'), but that is only a probability. We must also note that not one of the kings in the Ur cemetery figures in the *Sumerian King*

List,[3] which would seem to indicate that they never reigned over the whole of Sumer. If that is so, these kings would probably have had to content themselves with the kingdom's own territory, that of the 'city-state' of Ur, which was of modest size. But Ur was a great port on the Euphrates estuary, and it is highly likely that it derived its wealth – dazzling in these tombs – from a very old, active and fruitful transit-trade which made Ur's fortune for many centuries: with the rest of Mesopotamia, Syria and Anatolia by river; with Bahrain (Dilmun), Oman (Magan), eastern Iran and perhaps even the Indus valley (Meluhha) through the Arabo-Persian Gulf.

The Victims

Whatever their sex, title or office, the 'top people' for whom these tombs were intended were, generally speaking, accompanied by other men and women whom they had dragged into death with them and who, for that reason, were called 'the victims'.

Some of these victims lay inside the vault, near the 'principal' corpse, but the majority were found in the pit itself, around the vault, in the narrow vestibule or even on the access ramp. Their number varied considerably from one tomb to another, mostly because many of the skeletons had fallen away to dust or had been scattered by grave robbers. This was doubtless the case for tomb 1236, devoid of any bodies; tomb 1631, which contained only its chief

[3] Reconstituted by T. Jacobsen (*The Sumerian King List*, Chicago, 1939) from about fifteen different tablets, this list gives the dynasties and their kings who reigned over the land of Sumer from the distant time when kingship descended from heaven up to the reign of Damiq-ilishu (c. 1816–1794 BC), king of Isin. The beginning of the list is largely mythical; the remainder should be used with caution, notably because certain important dynasties, like that of the kings of Lagash, are not shown. However, the three dynasties of Ur in the third millennium are quoted.

occupant; and the pit that was the last resting-place of the priestess Hekunsig, where only the skeletons of three draught-oxen were found. Six tombs, including that of Meskalamdug-King, yielded only a few victims (from two to eleven).

By contrast, the *nin* Pû-abi was surrounded, as we have seen, by a numerous entourage, and her presumed husband, Abarage, by sixty-three people of both sexes. Akalamdug's tomb held fifty-three skeletons on three different levels: twelve lying on the ground above the vault, one in a reed coffin slightly lower, and forty in a pit beneath the vault. But the palm must go to pit 1237, nicknamed 'the great death pit' by Woolley, which contained no fewer than seventy-four victims: six soldiers and sixty-eight women, including four lyre- or harp-players, and sixty-four 'ladies-in-waiting'.

Noteworthy is the absence of any child's skeleton, or any indication of a wife's voluntary immolation to be with her husband, and the predominance of women, even in the tombs presumed to be those of men. Furthermore, the 'victims' were not wretched slaves, but bodyguards with their leather helmet, large shield and lance; drivers and grooms next to chariots drawn by oxen or onagers; female musicians and ladies of high rank, to judge by their finery. Those accompanying Pû-abi, for example, wore a head-dress of gold leaves like that of the *nin*, although less elaborate, and like her, necklaces of gold, cornelian and lapis lazuli – in several rows – as well as large gold ear-rings in the form of a crescent moon. Respect for the hierarchical order was apparent in pit 1237, where twenty-eight women wore gold ribbons in their hair, and the other thirty-six wore silver ribbons.

There is no doubt at all that the victims were not killed but voluntarily poisoned themselves (or fell into a coma) when in the tomb by drinking a toxic beverage – opium or hashish have been suggested. The skeletons bore no trace of violence or blows from blades; their adornments were not even slightly disarranged, as would have occurred had the bodies been carried; and the latter were aligned in perfect order. Woolley described the 'great death pit':

> The men lay to one side (of the vault), near the door. The women's bodies were laid out in regular rows crosswise on the ground. All were lying on their side, their legs slightly bent and their hands slightly drawn near to their face, and so close to one another that their heads rested on the legs of the women in the next row above [. . .] After the drug had taken its effect, whether that was sleep or death, someone would enter the tomb to put the finishing touches to the arrangement of the bodies.

At that point, it would appear, the harps or lyres were placed on the bosom of the musicians, and the little lethal goblets, of terracotta or metal, near the victims; the draught animals were put to death, and the entrance to the tomb was sealed. Then the great pit was gradually filled with earth, which was stamped down every so often, and containers of offerings – sometimes the bodies of other victims – were laid on these successive floors. While this was being done, a pottery tube was embedded in the ground, just beside the vault, for the purpose of libations. Lastly, the whole was crowned with a small commemorative building in unbaked brick. Each of these actions, each of these stages in the completion of the tomb was most probably accompanied by rites and incantations which no text so far has enabled us to know.

How splendid and poignant those funerals must have been, beneath the dazzling sun or leaden sky of the east, nearly 5000 years ago! A few soldiers, at the head, preceding the carriages bearing the body of the dead man or woman, together with his or her most precious treasures;

next, the musicians plucking the strings of their lyre or harp; lastly, the long procession of women, young for the most part, wearing long-sleeved red garments (shreds of material were found), adorned with sparkling headdresses and multicoloured jewels, probably very pale under their make-up, and perhaps singing. And all around, the massed crowds, silently staring at all those people walking slowly towards death at the bottom of a deep, dark pit, carpeted with mats. But in whose honour was that hecatomb, that great collective suicide? Who *were* these personages whose natural death called for the voluntary sacrifice of so many others? What was the purpose of that atrocious ritual which inspires horror in us but was then perhaps regarded as a great festival, a cause for rejoicing?

If the victims, and probably the spectators, of these terrible funerals knew the answers to those questions, up to now no text has been able to provide the information, and we can only construct hypotheses.

The first, proposed straightaway by Woolley and generally accepted since, is that these were kings and queens of Ur, buried with part of their court. However, for Sumerians, life beyond the grave was a dismal affair, in dust and half-light, with no hope of paradise, resurrection, reincarnation or attainment of divine rank, and scarcely more pleasant for rulers laden with rich gifts. How could it justify such collective suicides? To answer that objection, Woolley supposed that these kings and queens had been regarded as gods or demi-gods during their lifetime. Besides the inscribed cylinders of the 'royal cemetery', where *nin* was systematically translated as 'queen', he based his argument fundamentally on the unchallengeable fact that all tombs with human sacrifices discovered throughout the world were those of monarchs or great war leaders. The Sumerians of Ur would simply have been conforming to a tradition followed by other peoples, and not only in antiquity.

Although attractive at first glance, that theory did not sit well with the results of the excavations carried out by Woolley himself. In the first place, it is far from certain that all the distinguished occupants of the 'royal cemetery' of Ur had been kings or princes, as the parallel would require. It is not impossible, on the other hand – and we have seen why – that almost all the vault tombs and the 'death pits' were the burial places of kings' wives (like the wife of Akalamdug) or priestesses (like Pû-abi and Hekun-sig). That would explain the predominance of women among the victims, whereas in all the other civilisations, only male slaves or servants, ministers, officials and soldiers were sacrificed. Moreover, not one of the names of kings on the seal inscriptions is preceded by the sign of the star which reads *dingir*, 'god' in Sumerian, and characterises deified kings in Mesopotamia.

Up to now, only two other cemeteries with human sacrifices are known in that country: one at Kish, a town situated not far from Babylon; the other at Ur itself – but they are very different from the cemetery known as 'royal'. In cemetery 'Y' at Kish (datable to around 2700 BC), three pit tombs contained only chariots, the animals that pulled them, the driver and groom. As for the cemetery known as that 'of the Second Dynasty of Ur', at Ur, it comprised only five pit tombs, relatively poor in grave goods and totally anonymous; the 'victims' (if that is what they were) were buried separately, individually, in the earth infill of the pits. These tombs, dated to between the end of the Akkad dynasty and the beginning of the Third Dynasty of Ur (that is, roughly between 2160 and 2100 BC), are certainly very close to the splendid mausolea of the kings of that dynasty, well known from their inscriptions, but are clearly distinct from them. Because of its richness and the number and sex of its 'victims', Ur's 'royal cemetery' is therefore unique in the whole of Mesopotamia and in all periods.

In the immense literature left to us by the Sumerians, Babylonians and Assyrians, there are only two texts which may be considered as perhaps alluding to the Ur funerals. The first is a passage from a Sumerian poem translated and published by Professor Samuel N. Kramer under the title *The Death of Gilgamesh*. It depicts the semi-divine and largely mythical Gilgamesh, king of Uruk, presenting the goddess Ereshkigal, sovereign of the Underworld, with gifts offered by various members of his entourage, whom he names: his wife, his son, his concubine, his musician, his valet, his servants, his major-domo and the officials of his palace. Let us remember, however, that none of the attested or presumed kings of the Ur cemetery seems to have been buried at the same time as his wife or concubine, and that no child's skeleton was found. Similarly, let us note that all the staff mentioned in this poem were males, and there is nothing to indicate that they were with Gilgamesh at the moment when he was offering the presents to the goddess. In other words, it may well have been a matter of funerary offerings made to Gilgamesh by his entourage at the time of his own funeral.

According to another hypothesis, the high-ranking personages buried in the 'royal cemetery' of Ur were kings and priestesses who had taken part in the rite of sacred marriage. In this ritual ceremony, which was very ancient and illustrated by a fair number of often beautiful texts, the king personifying the god of the flocks, Dumuzi, had carnal union with a priestess playing the role of Inanna, the great Sumerian goddess of love. Through a phenomenon of magical transference, it was believed that this union would ensure the fecundity of livestock, the fertility of the soil and, consequently, the wealth of the land of Sumer.

Several arguments challenge this way of looking at the matter. None of the texts relating to the sacred marriage makes the slightest allusion to the death of the one-night husband and wife, their funerals or their life beyond the tomb. Moreover, one would have expected them to be buried in adjoining vaults, which is the case at Ur only for the tomb of Pû-abi and the (presumed) grave of Abarage, for whom there is no evidence that he had been a king. Lastly, it is hard to understand why this fertility rite should have entailed, sooner or later, the death of so many young women, probably priestesses or 'novices', some of whom could have been candidates for the role of Inanna.

Other people have attempted to regard the kings of Ur's cemetery not as regular sovereigns, but 'royal substitutes'. Here we approach another custom peculiar to Mesopotamia, a country where magic and divination have always played a predominant role. When predictions concerning the future of the king and country were too gloomy, some individual – usually of low birth – was chosen to take the king's place temporarily, put to death after a while and given a solemn burial. He was to some extent the scapegoat on whom were heaped the sins which had provoked the gods' anger.

I think this theory should be rejected. By definition, it can apply only to men, and takes no account of the presence of queens or *nin* among the dead of Ur. And then, what a waste of all those victims, all those treasures, for some unfortunate who was eliminated once he had fulfilled his purpose! Finally, the stratagem of the royal substitute was attested for the first time only in the first half of the second millennium, and was repeated on several occasions only among the Assyrians a thousand years later.

We are left with a fourth theory, brilliantly defended for some years by the British archaeologist P. R. S. Moorey: the collective burials of Ur's 'royal cemetery' were specific to that town and connected with the worship of its tutelary gods, the Moon-god Nanna and his wife, Ningal. We must remember, in fact, that in every period the cult of the

Moon-god at Ur was always led, not by a high-priest, but by a high-priestess, usually the daughter of the reigning sovereign. The 'clergy', probably mostly female, perhaps lived with the high-priestess in a sort of cloister, a vast building with many rooms, situated on the sacred esplanade and known as *giparu*. This theory would take into account the predominance of women, among both the 'principal bodies' and the 'victims', and at the same time the unique nature of Ur's 'royal cemetery'. Besides, it has recently been proved that Pabilsag, the god who had Hekunsig for his priestess, was the brother of the god Nanna. The second text that is more or less connected with these funerals is a beautiful prayer to Inanna, in which a 'mourning harp' occurs, and one (or several) people 'ready to die at the sound of the sacred song'. The author of this prayer was none other than Enheduanna, daughter of king Sargon of Akkad (c. 2334–2279 BC) and, because of that, high-priestess of the Moon-god at Ur.

Moorey's explanation is extremely seductive, but presents a major flaw: we know very little about the cult of Nanna and Ningal at Ur; all the author's arguments are indirect, and these few words in Enheduanna's prayer are not sufficient to be absolutely convincing.

Thus, more than half a century after its discovery, Ur's 'royal cemetery' still keeps its secret; but *nil desperandum*. The thousands of towns and villages still buried in the Mesopotamian *tells* probably have many more surprises in store for us. One day, perhaps, in some chance excavations, other cemeteries with human sacrifices – or, better still, tablets covered with cuneiform writing – will be able to tell us who all those dead people were, surrounded by so much gold, and will solve this baffling enigma.

Part II

Everyday Life

CHAPTER 3

The Oldest Cuisine in the World

Jean Bottéro

Animals do not cook, and the need to modify food before ingesting it is, like laughter, exclusive to humankind and just about as old. Every society, every culture, in harmony with the preferences and aversions of its members, their natural surroundings, their economy and even their traditional interpretation of the universe around them, has always decided upon a choice of its food and developed a routine system of ways of handling it and rules for preparing it to suit particular tastes – in other words, an original cuisine. But which is 'the oldest in the world'?

If it is posed in the absolute of our past, such a question makes no sense, since no one can answer it. From our interminable prehistory, only material vestiges remain – food residues, utensils, fireplaces – but nothing tells us exactly how these were used. Only written evidence can give us some idea of the 'method of use'; of recipes which make up the whole cuisine. And as the appearance of writing is no earlier than the third millennium, it is only from that period that we can get to know the oldest systems of tastes and traditional procedures that effectively transformed raw materials into dishes adapted to those tastes and immediately consumable.

Until now, the oldest preserved collection of cookery recipes was the celebrated 'Culinary Art' (*De re coquinaria*) compiled in the fourth century AD from the work of Apicius, the famous and extravagant Roman gourmand and gourmet, the contemporary of the earliest years AD. Thanks to him, 'the oldest cuisine' known was therefore that of the Romans.

Before that, some Greeks, especially in Magna Graecia, had also composed some culinary lists. The very first whose memory remains with us was a Syracusan named Mithekos, who must have lived around 400 BC. But all those works were lost, apart from a few short quotations, for the most part preserved in the surprising gastronome's and scholar's 'bible' written by Athenaeus of Naucratis, around the early third century AD, under the title 'The Banquet of the Learned' (*Deipnosophistai*).

To go further back in time and widen the field of investigation, people happily cite 'the Phoenicians', forgetting that we do not have the slightest written evidence about them on this subject; and 'the Bible', in which it would be hard to find a single word concerning culinary technique as such. The same must be said of the Hittites, who date back to just before the middle of the second millennium, and the Egyptians, still older; their diet is fairly well known to us, and we know that both had developed a style of cooking but, apart from some vague general hints, we do not have a single 'recipe' to give us a sufficiently distinct idea of it.

There remains Mesopotamia. It was the seat of an early civilisation, original and archaic, which had been formed starting from the fourth millennium at the latest; one which around 3000 BC had been the very first to invent writing, and had subsequently survived and developed, through many ethnic and political ups and downs, until shortly before the dawn of the Christian era, continuously spreading its sphere of influence over the whole of the Near East. *A priori* it would seem unimaginable that such a cultural system, so rich, complex and refined in every field, should have failed to perfect not only a special range of consumable goods, but also an entire technique and art for preparing and cooking them. In fact, among the half-million written documents – not to mention a huge amount of archaeological odds and ends – which we have discovered relating to that long history, and of which we have managed to decipher the two languages used to write them, Sumerian and Akkadian, we have ample material at our disposal to transform the assumption into a certainty – although the very uneven distribution of our voluminous dossier, in both time and place, does not enable us to establish a chronological sequence.

From Writing to Cooking

First, we are able to establish an impressive inventory of the goods that formed the ancient Mesopotamians' everyday fare: cereals, various vegetables, fruit – chiefly of the date-palm, but also apples, pears, figs, pomegranates and grapes; bulbs and roots; 'truffles' and mushrooms; seasoning herbs; meat from large and, mainly, smaller livestock, pork, game, birds – with the exception of poultry, which arrived later – and their eggs; sea and freshwater fish; turtles, crustaceans, shellfish and, of the insects, at least locusts; milk, 'butter' and other fats, both animal (lard and so on) and vegetable oils (sesame and olive); manna (a sugary exudation) from various trees, and honey to sweeten their food; mineral products (salt, ashes?) to intensify the flavour. All these indigenous ingredients were so varied that, as far as we know, the Mesopotamians never imported from abroad, so to speak, in spite of the intensity and geographical extent of their trade even before the third millennium.

But although they contented themselves with their native products, they went out of their way to treat, transform and prepare them in a great variety of ways. First, they knew how to preserve them: by drying not only cereals and vetches (beans, lentils), but various vegetables and fruits (especially dates, grapes and figs), and also meat and fish, which they had perhaps learnt to smoke and which they commonly preserved in salt ('salted' fish, beef, gazelle). They also knew how to conserve and 'candy' some fruit, in honey, and pickle fish, preferably in oil. They had perfected a pickling brine, for use both in cooking and as a condiment, for fish, crustaceans or locusts, which they called *shiqqu*, similar to nuoc-mam (a spicy sauce made from raw fish) or pissalat niçois. They used lactic fermentation to concoct 'soured milks' and cream cheeses. Just to mention in passing, some of these procedures were already culinary: it was enough to prepare the relevant foods for immediate consumption.

Similarly, a whole technique for treating cereals had been developed: these were malted and crushed with a millstone (in a 'grinding trough') to make different kinds of semolinas and flours, which could be rendered coarser or finer by sifting. From malt they brewed beer, the country's national drink, but they also knew wine, which came from the north and north-west. With the flours they prepared thick pastes and doughs that could be eaten just as they were, or preserved by drying, or fermented – which greatly increased the possible ways of serving this basic breadmaking constituent. Inseparable from their cuisine, in a civilisation that knew nothing of the independent 'bakery' of our times, breadmaking had been perfected even before the beginning of the third millennium, as had beermaking.

As for fire, the ancient Mesopotamians had well and

truly domesticated it. They did not merely expose their foodstuffs to flame or glowing embers to grill or roast them; they also used intervening agents to modulate the cooking heat – for example hot ashes, or shards placed on the embers. They used vertical clay cylinders, fiercely heated internally, on the inner walls of which they plastered flat rounds of unleavened dough to cook them, as is still commonly done today in the East, where even the name of this oven (*tannûr*) is derived from the one used by the old Mesopotamians (*tinûru*). Even before the third millennium, they had perfected 'domed ovens', which allowed less fierce cooking (the accumulated heat of the walls and floor) and in a moist atmosphere (steam produced by the food to be cooked), thus ensuring the cooking of fermented doughs and leavened bread. Another way of employing fire for cooking, which they especially seem to have put to widespread use and refined, was indirect cooking in a liquid medium – perhaps fat (although to date we have no indubitable proof), and mainly water. For this purpose they had even set aside two principal types of container: one, preferably in pottery, the 'cooking-pot' (*diqâru*); the other in bronze, the 'cauldron' (*ruqqu*). It is likely – as we shall understand better further on – that each was allocated to a particular type of cooking; perhaps fast boiling in plenty of water for the 'cooking-pot', and a kind of simmering, in reduced liquid, for the 'cauldron'.

Archaeologists have unearthed many remains of a very abundant range of kitchen utensils, and our texts provide us with the names of several containers and culinary utensils of all kinds.

These are all data which enable us, *a priori* to some extent, to assume that very diversified techniques and almost infinite combinations of treatments for preparing food were used in that ancient country: in short, an authentic 'cuisine'.

Other written evidence considerably reinforces and fleshes out such a theory. For example, making a detour by way of a small satirical text, we learn that they knew how to 'stuff a gut', apparently with meat: from which it is but a step to attributing to those extraordinary Mesopotamians something akin to a distant foretaste of one of the most glorious inventions of man's culinary genius – delicatessen.

But without a doubt, the most impressive work was a sort of encyclopaedia, in two columns, in which can be found – catalogued by name, Sumerian on one side, Akkadian opposite, and carefully classified into main categories – all the components, natural or artifical, of the universe that the Babylonians could contemplate all around them. The entire work was conventionally divided up over twenty-four tablets, each with about 400 rubrics. The last two, comprising some 800 entries, were set aside for the 'food' sector. They represented only a choice, however, and other similar 'dictionaries' as well as documents on practice and literature add enough at least to double this respectable nomenclature of food and drink, leaving us to imagine a pretty gargantuan 'menu'.

For instance, we can pick out eighteen or twenty varieties of 'cheese', and even though they possibly all represented a single, and to some extent 'elementary', kind of cheesemaking (cream cheese), such a diversification implies a remarkably demanding taste and a skilful technique. The catalogue of 'soups' – in the widest sense, understanding by this dishes obtained by cooking in water, called *tu* in Sumerian and *ummaru* in Akkadian – lists at least a hundred different ones. 'Breads', the essential product of local cuisine and a basic food, has almost 300 items, which for such an elementary comestible presupposes both a real 'gourmandise' and an overflowing culinary imagination – as much for the variety in materials (this or that flour; leavened or not; with oil, milk or beer; sweet, flavoured with this or that spice; containing such and such fruits, and so on) as for shape (every size, from the 'very big' to the 'minuscule'; every kind of thickness and length; every sort of shape, including those, somewhat humorous, in the form of a heart, a head, an ear, even a woman's breast!). And since we are on the subject of the care given to the presentation of the foodstuffs, let us remember that in the Palace of Mari (around 1780 BC) no fewer than fifty different types of moulds were found, which are very likely to have been used to give various dishes agreeable appearances to please the guests' eyes before enchanting their tastebuds.

It was the same aesthetic bias which conferred on the person in charge of the kitchen the Akkadian title *mubannû* or 'embellisher'. We do not know what this title – *muhaldim* in Sumerian, 'Akkadianised' into *nuhatimmu* – means in itself, but we find it attested since the early years of the third millennium. And as the craftsman is inconceivable without the craft, we must conclude, after all we have just noted, that in the dawn of historical time a culinary art and technique existed in Mesopotamia that was as complex and refined as everything else we have been able to find out about this astonishing, opulent and exotic civilisation.

A Wealth of Ingredients and Flavours

We have been able to go a little farther than the simple discovery of Mesopotamian cuisine, already surprising enough, but still superficial and somewhat detached. Assyriologists in fact knew two of its recipes.

The more ancient one, datable to the beginning of the second millennium, has not been passed on to us in explicit terms; we can merely deduce from the name of the preparation and the lists of ingredients which, in various administrative documents, are recorded as having been supplied to the preparer. The name – in Akkadian *mersu*, in Sumerian ninda.ì.dé.a – implies by its root sense a 'mixing' or 'stirring'. The ingredients are: flour; sometimes water, milk or beer, but preferably oil or, maybe, 'butter' to moisten it; then dates or other dried fruits (grapes, figs, apples), as well as different kinds of pine kernel (?), for the filling; lastly, no fewer than four aromatic seasonings – nigella (?), cumin (?), coriander (?) and, something that may rather surprise us, garlic! The identification of many concrete and precise data, starting with a number of plants, is well-nigh impossible, or purely conjectural. Hence the question marks above; and they will be encountered on more than one occasion in what follows. Returning to our recipe: sometimes honey was added, and the 'mixing' or 'stirring' of the mixture seems to have been done for preference in a 'cooking-pot'.

In its final, therefore edible, state, it was presented as a 'bread', which presupposes that it was cooked in an oven. The entire procedure brings to mind the picture of a kind of cake, a preparation which in itself suggests a liking for good food. But the most striking thing is the number of ingredients, especially the four flavourings, no less than the many operations imposed by the elaboration of and variations on the same basic formula according to the liquid used to moisten it and the fruit, or fruits, used to fill it. No one can deny that it had something subtle and refined about it, whatever the final taste may have been.

We get the same impression from the other, more recent, recipe (the sole manuscript dates to c. 400 BC), but communicated to us by its form, although it is not fully detailed, or in the slightest way placed in any culinary context whatsoever. Here is the translation, slightly adapted to our own cookery rituals:

> Take some fennel [?]; watercress [?]; dodder (Arabic: *kuchut*) [?] and cumin [?], all (in seeds) roasted. Bring six litres of water to the boil (previously flavoured, by infusion [?]) with (raw) mustard; add fifteen grams of cucumber [?]. Cook until reduced to one litre, then strain. Lastly add the meat of the sacrificed animal to be cooked.

The way it is set out is remarkable: it matches the presentation of Apicius, even our own. Here again, four flavours are combined to give the liquid an aroma; one of them is even given in two forms, natural and roasted – a preparation required for the other three, revealing the quest for a notably subtle taste. A fifth component, a vegetable (?), is added after the first boiling. Cooking is extended to reduce the initial volume to a sixth; in other words, a heavy concentration of the liquid is called for, which will thus become smoother and more flavoursome. But – and this is a fresh sign of refinement – it is not used until 'filtered', that is to say, for its flavour alone and cleared of everything that may have been used to impart it.

Lastly, the meat is cooked only when the broth has been prepared; seeing how little of it remains, very probably it was used less as a 'court-bouillon' than as a 'sauce' and would be still further reduced during the cooking of the meat, which would acquire its flavour while imparting its own taste to the liquid. We could do no better ourselves. Even the style of the recipe has something familiar for us. But it begins to become equally evident that the *nuhatimmu*, who prepared such dishes, were both the technical experts and the artists of a high-class cuisine.

A recent discovery, as yet unpublished, will show us in a rather surprising way how far we are from exaggerating when referring to ancient Mesopotamian cookery as 'cuisine'.

In a collection of cuneiform documents belonging to Yale

University in the United States and long awaiting publication, there are three tablets which had at first been taken for pharmaceutical prescriptions but which, on examination, proved to be well and truly collections of cookery recipes.[1] Written in Akkadian, they are datable to about 1700 BC and, for such a distant era, immediately reveal a cuisine of such richness, refinement, consummate technical know-how and art that we would certainly never have dared to imagine so advanced nearly 4000 years ago.

The infuriating effect of the habitual curse of these venerable dried or baked clay tablets means that not one of the three is intact. One in particular, the shortest (53 lines), is cruelly devastated and no longer offers us anything but a few short decipherable fragments here and there. It is enough, however, to reveal clearly that it is closely connected with the other two which, happily, and despite the lacunae which too often for our liking interrupt the flow and the sense, are much more complete and coherent. The better-preserved lists twenty-five formulas in seventy-five lines; twenty-one whose essential basis is meat, and four with vegetables. They are short – two to four lines each. Their style is very concise, recalling that of our own works which are the preserve of professionals (such as A. Escoffier's *Culinary Guide*) and which keep to the essentials of ingredients to be used and methods to be adopted, in a 'specialist' and ultra-laconic manner. The other tablet is far more ample but also, unluckily, more mutilated. In its original state it comprised about 200 lines, but at best set out only seven recipes, which is to say that these are explained in infinitely more detail. All relate to the preparation of various 'birds': poultry or birds in general.

[1] Here I should like to give my warmest thanks to my colleagues and friends W. W. Hallo (Yale), F. Köcher (Berlin) and J. van Dijk (Rome/Amsterdam), thanks to whom I learned about these tablets and was able to study them even before their official publication.

Supreme Refinement, Technical Expertise and Art

In the tablet with the twenty-five recipes, all have a constant base of water and fat, most often cooked in 'the cooking-pot', that is by boiling for a long time; but on two occasions, however, and for a kind of 'braising' (?), the 'cauldron' was used. The difference between the first twenty-one and the last four is that, while in all cases meat is part of the composition of the dish, the latter add a vegetable, except perhaps the last, where there appears to be no meat. The variations are created by the basic ingredients, the different methods prescribed for the cooking and presentation of the dish, and the many condiments which give variety to the flavour. Cropping up in all the recipes, sometimes even in double doses, are the alliaceous plants, especially the well-known trio of garlic, onion and leek, which seem to have delighted the palates of those old gourmets. But there are also plenty of others, which we do not always manage to identify with any certainty: mustard (?), cumin (?), coriander (?), mint (?) and cypress berries, for example; *shuhutinnu* and *samidu*, which must have been alliaceous (again!); and others, such as the *surummu*, about which we are not even capable of making worthwhile conjectures. Various cereal products – semolinas, flours, barley (?) malted (preferably compressed into little cakes) – were used to thicken liquids and give them smoothness. And sometimes, for the same purpose, milk, beer or blood were also added. Salt was used but, so it seems, not systematically, some dishes appearing to acquire their flavour only from their ingredients and seasoning herbs.

Each recipe begins (like our own!) with its title: the name of the dish – taken from its essential component or its presentation – constantly preceded by the generic term *mê* (lit., 'water', but actually something like 'stock', or rather, 'broth' (since the entire content of the dish and not just the liquid was clearly to be consumed), perhaps even 'sauce' – it all depends on the volume and smoothness of the liquid in its final state, which we do not know). There is thus a 'broth' of meat, deer, gazelle, kid, lamb, mutton, pigeon and 'birds called *tarru*'; but also, a broth of 'leg of lamb' (?) and one of 'spleen'; similarly a 'dodder' broth, and others, 'salty', 'red', 'clear' and 'sharp' (?). Twice the name seems to have been taken from the foreign origin of the dish: an 'Assyrian' broth, coming from the northern part of the country, and an 'Elamite', borrowed from the neighbouring Elamites who occupied the south-western corner of Iran. In the last instance, at the end of the recipe, we are even given the name of the dish in its original language: *zukanda*. For the last four recipes, the title is provided merely by the name of the main vegetable: for example, 'turnips' (this is the only one we know how to translate for certain).

It seems that additions were often made to the basic meat – which might be a whole animal (a pigeon), or several (the *tarru*) or a piece of meat, often not specified but sometimes clearly designated (a leg of lamb (?)) and, very frequently, offal (the spleen and various internal parts). A piece of meat was nearly always added to vegetables. Sometimes it was not specified but supposedly known to the professionals, and may have been mutton. But the Akkadian verb showing its presence is ambiguous: *izzaz* may mean 'must be present' in the dish, or 'must be divided', 'cut into pieces'. One or two indications make me, for the time being, incline to the first meaning, for example the fact that at the end of more than one recipe commencing precisely with that *izzaz* applied to the meat, one finds the phrase 'to be presented to the knife' in order to suggest that the work of the chef is finished and that, before being tasted by the guests, the dish must be 'cut into pieces' – which used to be the task of the 'écuyer trenchant' (or squire who cut the meat) in olden days.

Some Recipes

To give a more precise idea of all this, here are a few of the recipes. One of the simplest: 'Meat broth. Take some meat. Get the water ready. Add some fat. Some . . . [the word is lost], leek and garlic pounded together, and plain *shuhutinnu*'. This one is richer:

> Red broth. No meat necessary. Get the water ready. Add fat. Pluck (heart, liver and lungs), tripe and belly. Salt, cracked malt, onions, *samidu*, cumin, coriander, leek, *surummu*, pounded together. Before putting on the flame ['in the cooking-pot'], the meat will have been steeped in the blood set aside [from the animal sacrificed for the dish].

Already this is more complicated than the first, but the terse style of the text is remarkable; it keeps to the essentials and never specifies either quantities or cooking times, which are left to the discretion of the cook, implying that he must have, as we say, 'known his job'.

Here is another, in which we see that the chefs knew how to use various ways of cooking to enrich the flavour:

> Kid stew. Sear the head, feet and tail [before putting in the pot]. Add meat. Get the water ready. Add fat. Onion, *samidu*, leek and garlic; blood; soft cheese [?], all to be pounded together. Next an equivalent quantity of plain *shuhutinnu*.

In another 'broth' whose name ('with crumbs'?) may have been derived from the final operation, once (a first?) cooking has been completed, it is necessary, 'before removing (the cooking-pot from the fire), to sprinkle the contents with the sieved crumbs of a crushed cereal-cake', obviously to give it a binding agent. 'Pigeon stew' is made as follows: 'Open the pigeon into two halves; meat is also necessary. Get the water ready. Add fat. Salt, cracked malt, onion, *samidu*, leek and garlic: all herbs to be soaked in milk [before putting them in the pot]. To be presented for carving.' One of the longest recipes is for '*Tarru* broth' (perhaps wild pigeons, quail or francolins – of the partridge family; at all events, small). Besides these birds, 'fresh haunch of lamb [?]. Get the water ready. Add fat. Truss ['tie'] the *tarru*. Salt, cracked malt, onion, *samidu*, leek and garlic, pounded together with milk'. Once the *tarru* are cooked 'in the cooking-pot water', they must be crushed and put (to braise) in a cauldron with stock taken from the cooking-pot, before returning everything to the cooking-pot (for a final boiling). 'To be presented for carving.' Lastly, here is a vegetable recipe; *tuh'u*, the one used as a base is unknown to us.

> [In addition] some haunch meat [?] is necessary. Get the water ready. Add fat [. . .] salt; beer; onion; rocket [?]; coriander; *samidu*; cumin and beetroot; add [just as they are] to the cooking-pot. Then pound leek and garlic together and add. Let all blend and reduce to a pulp, to be sprinkled with coriander and *shuhutinnu*.

I must also quote the other, longer, tablet, whose recipes are far more minutely detailed. However, their syntactic complexity and, given that we have never seen those ancient cooks at work, the difficulty we experience in trying to 'realise' and understand the successive stages in their methods, plus the number of words and technical terms whose precise meaning eludes us, together with the annoying interruptions and breaks in the text are all obstacles to both decipherer and translator. For various passages, my interpretation is only provisional, and I shall have to return to them more than once, in accordance with working habits, gleaning the opinion of my colleagues, before I can be more certain. All part of the job . . .

The shortest recipe is not far removed from those quoted above. It involves *kippu*, a type of bird unknown to us:

> If *kippu* are to be cooked in a broth, they are to be prepared like *agarukku* [doubtless other 'birds' that we are equally unable to identify, but the recipe for which must have preceded this one on the tablet, or at any rate have been well known]. They are first split open, rinsed in cold water and placed in a cauldron [to braise or fry quickly to seal]. When the cauldron is removed from the flame [after braising or sealing], a little cold water is added and a sprinkling of vinegar. Then mint and salt are pounded together and rubbed into the *kippu*, after which the liquid in the cauldron is strained [?] and mint is added to this sauce, in which the *kippu* are replaced [to cook for a moment, after they had been removed to be rubbed with the minted salt]. Lastly, a little cold water is again added and [to complete the cooking] everything is poured into a cooking-pot. To be presented for carving.

Noteworthy are the changes of receptacle, probably corresponding to a change in the method of cooking; and also the cooking by stages – all indications of a skilled technique.

Here is a much longer recipe (forty-nine lines, as compared with eleven for the last one). As it has more lacunae and is very complicated – at least for us – while the lack of punctuation (which is unknown in cuneiform) makes things no easier, it would be better to paraphrase somewhat in an attempt to give at least a sufficiently clear picture, but one that is not at all guaranteed for a number of details. In the present state of our knowledge, this is all we can gather from such a new, isolated and unexpected document. The beginning is lost, but we can understand that 'little birds' are being prepared, at that time designated by their name. The dish seems to have been prepared in several stages. First of all, there is the preparation of the ingredients: 'Remove the head and feet; open the body to remove (with all the rest) the gizzard and the pluck. Split and clean the gizzards. Rinse the bodies of the birds, and dry (?)'. A preliminary cooking must then take place: 'prepare a cauldron, in which the birds, gizzards and pluck are placed, and put on the flame' (with or without liquid or fat? We are not told; the procedure was doubtless customary in the 'trade'). Then (after a first exposure to heat, braising or sealing?) remove the cauldron from the flame. There then followed a second cooking period: 'Rinse a cooking-pot with fresh water; pour in milk and put on the flame. Remove the contents of the cauldron [birds, gizzards and pluck]; dry all; remove the non-edible parts; salt, and put into the cooking-pot, adding fat to the milk in it. Also add rue, previously cleaned. When it comes to the boil, add a mince [?] of leek, garlic, *samidu* and onion' (four alliaceous plants!), but, the text specifies: 'without overdoing the onion'. 'And add a little water.' During the cooking, the ingredients necessary for the presentation of the dish had to be prepared. 'Rinse crushed wheat, soak in milk and incorporate, by kneading, seasoning-brine (*shiqqu*), *samidu*, leek and garlic, with enough milk and oil to obtain a sufficiently malleable dough, which should be exposed for a moment to the heat of the fire [?]. Divide it into two balls.' Here the text suffers from many tiny cracks which make its interpretation very conjectural.

By and large, this is what we can make out: one of the balls would be for making unleavened bread. The one to be used is left for a short time in a cooking-pot to rise (?) (which would suggest that a raising agent had been introduced in the meantime). Then it is taken up again to be used in setting out the dish for presentation at table: 'Take a dish that is big enough to hold [all] the birds: line it with the prepared dough, taking care that it slightly overhangs the edges of the dish [. . .] To cook, place all on the stove.' When the pastry is cooked, the dish is removed and sprinkled with a final mince of three or four alliaceous ingredients, including the inevitable onions and garlic. 'Arrange the cooked birds on the mince-sprinkled pastry, and put the gizzards and pluck on top. Pour the sauce over the entire dish. Cover with a lid of cooked pastry and send to the table.'

Haute Cuisine and Popular Cookery

Any commentary is useless; and although this or that passage remains uncertain or obscure, the texts speak for themselves, and eloquently. Here are a number of operations for the preparation of one and the same piece of food which, in reality, it would have been enough to expose willy-nilly to the flame if the only intention had been to cook it. For example, the regulated use of several methods of cooking and different utensils, each adapted to its own special role; combinations of foodstuffs, especially seasonings, frequently more than one and probably regarded as complementary (some dishes call for more than a dozen and several are regularly paired), all with the plain intention of seeking complex flavours and a particular taste, neither that of the raw food nor that of each added ingredient, but something different and, so to speak, superior, which results from all the rest. Also, the extreme attention paid to the presentation, to satisfy the eye before delighting the palate. These are all features which, on the part of the diners, respond to a genuine concern that should unhesitatingly be described as gastronomic; and on the part of the practitioners, to a technique, a 'profession' and an art which are complex and well-tried.

We are therefore dealing with what may be called a high-class cuisine which, by its elegance and refinements, easily reminds us of that of the ancient Romans, the Chinese, the Near Easterners, the Italians and, of course, the French. The only thing is that it exceeds them in age by over fifteen centuries.

Looked at from another viewpoint, although those three modest tablets alone have managed to linger on to our day, from all the evidence they were just the flotsam from an enormous shipwreck; you have only to read them closely in the text to find unequivocal signs of the use that must have been made of different, and very probably written, sources. Not to mention that it is hard to visualise those ancient cooks confining their ingenuity and ambition to making 'twenty-five stews' and some dozen dishes with a bird base, deliberately neglecting the other meats, vegetables, fruits, fish and all the other innumerable foodstuffs that formed their diet. This is just all that has lasted, to date, of a genuine culinary literature. But Iraq's soil is very rich in future finds, and they may still astonish us! Whether or not the combined hazards of the preservation of ancient documents, excavations and retrieval allow us to complete it one day, at least we have recovered one or two chapters of the oldest known 'cookery manual' in history; and its great age is truly venerable. The cuisine into whose secrets these *membra disjecta* have introduced us is well and truly, and by far, the oldest-known great cuisine in the world, and the ancient Mesopotamians are the oldest gourmets identifiable amid the mists of our distant past.

To be absolutely fair, dotting the i's, and crossing the t's, this conclusion must be toned down by two or three comments.

First, we must never forget the vast distance that separates these very ancient people from our own horizon, our mental outlook, our way of being, seeing, understanding and feeling things. It would be an irritating anachronism to judge these culinary tablets with the same eye that we use for judging our own cookery manuals. In theory, the latter are meant to be read by everyone; each is the work of an authority who wishes to spread his or her knowledge, and they are first and foremost didactic. Today, everyone can read and even in Apicius' time, or that of Mithekos of Syracuse, the number of literate people was large, albeit far more restricted than these days; to learn a couple of dozen alphabetical characters was more or less within everybody's scope. In ancient Mesopotamia, the system of writing – not at all alphabetic but simultaneously ideographic and syllabic, with several hundred signs each having several possible values – was terribly complicated and, if it was to be mastered, called for many years of exercises and studies which could be tackled only by an elite or members of a professional body as restricted as those of lawyers or doctors nowadays. To write, and consequently to read, was a profession, the speciality of a limited number of 'scribes' through whom everything written had to pass and all of whom, as a general rule, first worked for government representatives. Cooks, illiterate like everyone else, would scarcely have had the idea of composing 'books' for other cooks, no less 'illiterate' than themselves, or for a limited public of scribes who were busy with quite different matters from being informed how to create dishes, and even less for a completely non-existent 'public at large'.

Our tablets, therefore, cannot be considered as didactic; they are essentially administrative and normative. They would have been 'written' by order from above, to record and lay down 'what was done in the kitchen', as other tablets (also in our possession) recorded and laid down what was done at court, according to etiquette; in the temple, according to the liturgy; in the offices of doctors and apothecaries, in keeping with practice; among certain technicians, according to traditional formulas and procedures. Rather than a culinary *manual*, our texts represented a culinary *codex* or, perhaps, *ritual*: they codified contemporary practices, the outcome of age-old habits, enriched (but still capable of requiring further enrichment) by constant improvements and inventions.

Furthermore, it should be obvious to everyone that this cuisine, 'ritualised' and set down in writing, was essentially the one used at the Palace (or Temple). Such refinements and elegance, such a complex technique, calling for considerable appliances and installations and many ingredients – some of which at least were evidently precious and expensive – could hardly be performed except by true specialists (the *nuhatimmu*) and were viable only at the expense and in the service of the great in this world – or the next. The wretched peasants and 'workers' who formed the majority of the country's population, with meagre resources, ground down by forced labour, servitude and debts, as we learn from the documents, can scarcely be imagined with enough time and means to prepare or afford the sumptuous 'broths' or 'dishes of birds' we have discovered in the tablets. There was therefore in Mesopotamia – as elsewhere, both then and now – an *haute cuisine*, reserved for the upper classes (and the gods), and ordinary cooking for most of the population. We have just encountered, and sung the praises of, the *haute cuisine*.

But everyone knows that in any given society and culture, imagination and taste are contagious. So for my part I am convinced that even the 'humblest housewives in the smallest households', if this expression may be used, knew how to concoct dishes, relatively speaking, that were as tasty and imaginative, if not as varied or complicated, as those with which the Palace *nuhatimmu* busied themselves. For, apart from the *haute cuisine* which was the affair of the *nuhatimmu* – rather as our 'chefs' are those in the large restaurants or grand houses – among the general populace the run-of-the-mill cooking was 'women's business' for the Sumerians and Babylonians, with their reduced and poor means, their tiny ovens and very modest range of utensils. And I have never accepted the picture my colleagues persist in painting – perhaps because they lack imagination and have never in their life poked their nose into a kitchen – of a Mesopotamian people reduced during thousands of years, like sad ruminants, to masticating everlasting and dismal 'porridges' and 'gruels'. Even though – as they were unable to write – it is highly likely that we shall always be ignorant of their everyday fare, recipes and culinary customs.

Lastly, let me say quite plainly that it is virtually impossible for us to execute these recipes of Mesopotamian *haute cuisine* we have discovered, deciphered and read. The exact and concrete meaning of certain obviously technical terms and the 'tricks of the trade' they suggested to those using them elude us and risk doing so forever, since in order fully to understand and be able to imitate an action – even if it is not very complicated – one must have seen it performed. Every cuisine, like every technique, is made up of 'knack and know-how'. We must not forget that ancient Mesopotamian civilisation, its languages and writing, which died well before the Christian era, subsequently disappeared completely from human memory for two millennia, and we have had to reconstruct them in their entirety. Such a break in tradition is a terrible handicap for the historian, which is why we are all too often at a loss to identify a number of goods, ingredients and condiments, actions and articles which appear in these recipes. And even when we manage 'roughly' to pick out one here or there – it must be an alliaceous plant! it must be a milk product! – we are never sure that we have picked the right one. Everyone knows that in good cookery it would be catastrophic to substitute an explosive Munster cheese for an easy-going soft white cheese, although they are both milk products . . .

Finally, although we find ourselves obliged to celebrate the old Mesopotamians as the oldest-known gourmets and gastronomes, it is clear that their idea of good fare and taste was a million miles from our own. To give just a few examples: their devotion to fat (mutton fat) with which they so generously basted all their dishes; their veritable mania for alliaceous plants, in combination and as if reinforced; the perhaps secondary role that salt appears to have played in their diet; and other indications which, rightly or wrongly – *de gustibus non est disputandum* – seem to us deucedly off-putting. I shall therefore never amuse myself by trying out their recipes; and although I consider them to be the first inventors and practitioners of gastronomy and a high-class cuisine, I would not advise trying to incorporate their culinary tradition, just as it stands, into our own.

In any case, it would be useless; modified, adapted, elaborated and enriched, their cuisine has happened to come down to us in what we today would call 'Turco-Arabic' cookery, delighting palates from Greece to deepest Iraq and offering us plenty of treats on the spot. It is likely that, polished and domesticated over the centuries, its substance harks back as far as the ancient 'chefs' – *nuhatimmu* – of Sumer and Babylon.

CHAPTER 4

The Oldest Feast

Jean Bottéro

From the kitchen to the 'dining-room'. Nearly all the recipes in what is today considered the oldest-known cookery compendium – dating back to around the seventeenth century BC – end with a phrase denoting the final stage of the duly prepared dish: 'to be sent to the table', or more often, 'ready to serve' – lit.,'to be presented to the knife', at that time the sole implement available to the consumers for tackling their food. The role of the 'chef' now over, enter the guests.

To hazard a glance at the second act of the show and spy on the new actors about to dispatch what has been more or less artistically prepared for them, we find ourselves somewhat ill-provided. We do not even know whether a regular setting for meals existed, or what it was; it is possible that the ancient Mesopotamians did not know what a 'dining-room' was, their 'tables' being trays brought to the diners wherever they ate – bedroom, divan, hall or garden. Among our half-million cuneiform tablets, we do not possess the slightest account – ordinary, colourful or solemn – of a feast or even a simple meal. We therefore have to proceed obliquely, and we are not short of 'indirect' evidence, even if it is less loquacious than we could wish. Besides scattered allusions, notably in correspondence or literature, we have a prodigious mass of administrative items among which a fair number have to do with food, and thus suggest several, sometimes unexpected, conclusions concerning its consumption.

Surprising as it may seem, we also have plenty of religious literature. Those people had resolutely conceived their gods on the model – exalted and superlative, it is true – of their own personalities and society. When speaking of them they could hardly fail to see themselves mirrored in the gods, transposing and magnifying in them what they knew about themselves. So, myths, sacred chants and liturgical rituals, when we know how to read them, commonly tell us more about their authors than their subjects. We shall see this again in later chapters, in connection with love and sex for example. In this way, therefore, we manage to create as good a picture as can be expected of the fare in that venerable Mesopotamia, the probable homeland of the oldest identifiable 'civilised people' in our past.

In kitchen matters – as in most other areas of life – it is the ordinary people, those whom we nowadays call the 'working masses', who are the most successful in eluding us. Not only was this majority of the population incapable of telling us about themselves by means of the complex writing used at that time, but the well-read were not keen to make them the subject of their works. We glimpse them mainly in the endless lists drawn up by the administration, in which the rations allocated as payment to workers and those liable to obligatory labour were recorded. But distributions were made only of the basic foodstuffs for their means of subsistence: mainly cereals, oil and beer; rarely meat or fish. The rest – vegetables, fruit and seasonings – they had to procure for themselves, and there is no indication of the ways in which they dealt with it all for their everyday diet, or their eating habits or table manners.

The common rule seems to have been two daily meals: one 'in the morning', the other 'in the evening'. The latter was probably the main meal, since the Sumerians designated 'meal' in general with the same word as 'twilight' (*kin.sig.*), whereas in Akkadian the term referred only to 'consuming' (*naptanu*). But the wealthy in that world, at least, doubled those sittings with two 'little meals', also in the morning and evening.

Bearing in mind their modest means, or rather, their chronic poverty and enforced labour, the ordinary people – 'the silent ones of the country' as a Sumerian proverb would have described them – could hardly have a beanfeast every day. There was always something lacking explains a similar proverb: 'When a poor man has bread, he has no salt, and when he has salt he has no bread; if he has some seasoning, he has no meat, and if he has meat, no seasoning.' Assyriologists, perhaps impressed by the above mentioned lists of cereals that were distributed, were ready to imagine these populations doomed to daily and everlasting porridges gloomily masticated as if by a herd of melancholy ruminants. However, there is no lack of evidence to show that such sombre theories reflect some gastronomic allergy on the part of their advocates rather than the actual state of affairs.

Of course, the common expression used to designate a meal was 'bread and water'; but this was a metonymy, probably based less on this fundamental nourishment than on the first acts that it governed: 'eating and drinking'. It should not be used as a reason for picturing those multitudes of people reduced to nibbling depressing crusts dunked in water in order to survive. Not only (as I suggested in Chapter 3) was the gastronomic elegance evidenced by the ancient *haute cuisine* recipes inevitably contagious, but the great local treatise on oneiromancy[1] – which listed and categorised common dreams, following a logic which is harebrained to our eyes but at the time was held to be infallible, to draw conclusions concerning the dreamers' future – included a big chapter devoted to dreams about food. And the number and variety of dishes (the majority completely real and duly attested) which people believed they had eaten in their dreams composed an enviable menu. We also have several good reasons to believe that – apart from a few exceptions – such fare in all its variety was, like dreams, well and truly accessible to all and sundry.

Those who lacked the wherewithal could always get themselves invited by the better-off. A story, both good-natured and satirical, tells how 'a poor wretch from the town of Nippur', with an empty belly and a groaning urge for a good meal, dreams of getting himself invited by the mayor, offering as his share a sheep that he counts on obtaining through selling his last rags and tatters. But as he manages to raise only enough to buy an old nanny-goat, the magistrate, scorning such a derisory gift, sends the poor wretch packing. The latter gets his revenge three times, in amusing but stinging fashion. As in all places and in all ages, the pleasures of the table were thus within reach of everyone, even if the more modest subjects could not eat their fill as much as the wealthy and the 'officials'.

It is perfectly clear that it was first and foremost the wealthy, the beneficiaries of the *haute cuisine*, who enjoyed sumptuous and frequent banquets – to say nothing of the gods, a great part of whose worship was concerned with

[1] The ancient Mesopotamians were passionately interested in divination and had perfected a method that was especially theirs. They extracted the various possibilities of the future from a multitude of phenomena of all kinds, of which they had drawn up long lists in the form of 'treatises', each specialised by its principal subject (see Chapter 11, i.e. 'A Long Tradition of Divinatory Schools'). One of these, of which large fragments remain, dealt with dreams.

the servicing of their table. Of this we have overabundant evidence. From Mari, for instance, we still have several hundred calendar tablets (c. 1780 BC) bearing the list of provisions supplied, day after day for several years, mainly by shops selling cereal products, oil and dried fruits, but also by 'butchers', for the daily fare of the king, who seems to have had a very comfortable life.

Yet the humblest individuals could participate in many of the festivities; one more occasion for them to have a good meal. In the story of the Flood (see Chapter 13), the Babylonian Noah, king Atrahasîs (lit., 'Supersage'), on the advice of his protector god Enki/Ea, having made his subjects build and fit out his 'Ark', invited these workers to a great banquet to reward them and, without their being aware of it, grant them one last joyful moment before the brutal arrival of their fatal destiny. However, their host, anxious and ill at the thought of the imminent catastrophe, took hardly any part in the fun:

> So they ate copiously
> And drank abundantly!
> He, however, did nothing but come in and go out,
> Never remaining seated or even squatting,
> So desperate and sickened was he! . . .

On more than one occasion the feasts given by rulers, especially for their staff and troops, are evoked for us. These 'great banquets' were often accompanied by distributions of reward-presents, perfumed unguents for a *toilette* that would be worthy of the ceremony.

Unfortunately, we do not have the menus for these 'blow-outs', but at least we still have the breakdown of the eatables consumed during one of the most enormous feasts in history, which by far outstrips the celebrated banquet given on 22 September 1900, by Émile Loubet, president of the Republic, in the Tuileries Gardens for the 20,000 mayors of France.

A great rejoicing was held around 870 BC in the Assyrian town of Kalhu (known today as Nimrud, some 25 kilometres south of Mosul, in Iraq), to inaugurate the sumptuously rebuilt palaces. King Assurnasirpal II (883–859 BC) invited (if it has not been over-exaggerated, as was the weakness of composers of inscriptions to the glory of kings) no fewer than '69,574' guests for ten days, including – rather like Atrahasîs, after the construction of his 'Ark' – the 40,000 or so of his subjects who had been needed for the work, plus the staff of his court and a number of 'VIPs' from nearly all the corners of his realm. It was, in short, 'a housewarming' for the new capital and its installations.

A stele, found on the site in 1951, supplied us with the details of this monstrous 'eat-in': some 50,000 items of cattle and smaller livestock, farmyard animals and game; 10,000 fish; the same number of eggs; to say nothing of the sumptuous catalogue of vegetables, fruits and various condiments, by the bushel, and dairy products, by the basket; and to wash it all down, 10,000 earthenware jars of beer and an equal number of goatskins of wine – bread and water probably not being taken into account in this extravagant enumeration. We are told nothing of the battalions of cooks who must have had to busy themselves with such a Pantagruelish orgy. Detailed study of the picture, however, enables us to guess that the guests did not all receive uniform treatment, and that there were seemingly several menus depending on the social rank or political importance of the participants. Whatever these disparities may have been, the king, ending the account of this memorable event, could flatter himself that after ten days of masticatory celebration he was able to send home 'satisfied and happy' all the fellow-trenchermen at this gigantic feast.

For, then as now, although in the first instance a meal provided the sustenance and comfort indispensable to life itself, at the same time it brought joy – 'the feeling of life', as good philosophers understand it – made people happy and immersed them in a kind of bliss. Contributing to this were not only the abundance and variety of the food served, the company of the guests and what we call the communicative warmth of the banquets, but also the almost obligatory accompaniment to everything the moment a simple meal bordered on a feast: alcoholic drinks.

In that country, where wine had been known from the very earliest times (see Chapter 5), the fermented 'national' drink was nevertheless beer, with a cereal base and prepared – following refined techniques – in over thirty ways, if we are to believe the texts; 'white', 'russet', 'light', 'dark', 'cloudy', 'sweetened with honey' and 'flavoured' with many aromatics, sometimes 'diluted' but often 'strong'. Several people at a time would happily drink it, sucking it out of the jar through tubes which were provided at their lower end with a kind of grille to filter impurities. The sole known specimen in that country of what we would call a 'drinking-song' is dedicated to beer, and perhaps composed – suggests its translator – for the inauguration of a tavern. It ends with these glorious lines:

I will summon brewers and cupbearers
To serve us floods of beer and keep it passing round! What pleasure! What delight!
Blissfully to take it in,
To sing jubilantly of this noble liquor,
Our hearts enchanted and our souls radiant!

When a God Has Had a Drop too Much

Beer was an obligatory accompaniment to a banquet, to the point where, to designate it, the 'Akkadians' (using *qerîtu*) merely emphasised the number of guests 'invited' to participate in the feasts, but the Sumerians stressed the 'beer poured' (*kash. dé. a*). Its presence makes us imagine those ancient rejoicings to be more or less a model for our own, with their plentiful food, of course, but also their 'libations', their toasts, the merry and sometimes thunderous hubbub, light-years away from a formal and hieratic ceremonial. The danger was that good food, intoxicating drinks and mutual warmth might rapidly go to people's heads. Without going as far as brawls and 'revolts against the established order', which our documents sometimes pinpoint, sang-froid was easily lost. This is what an old myth in Sumerian tells us about the god Enki.

The most intelligent and ingenious of all the gods, Enki had discovered and perfected all the prerogatives of a refined civilisation: institutions, manners and techniques, which were imagined as being materialised in certain precious talismans, from which emanated the matching 'powers', and which he guarded jealously in his temple-city of Eridu.

One day Inanna, the supernatural patroness of the town of Uruk, came to visit him – apparently as a courtesy but doubtless also because he was 'turned on' we might say by the intoxicating and enchanting goddess. He offered her a feast of her own choosing, in the account of which, as often happened, drink was pushed to the forefront:

At the sacred table, at the celestial table,
He welcomed the holy Inanna!
And Enki, side by side with her, in his Temple,
Sang the praises of beer and gulped down wine,
Their goblets full to overflowing,
Vying with each other in toasts to Heaven and Earth,
Savouring, without haste,
goblets as deep as boats! . . .

'The beer drunk, the wine appreciated', the by now rather tipsy Enki was overcome with that tender and ostentatious generosity which often rises with the alcohol fumes. He suddenly decided to offer as a gift to Inanna – who was too cunning to have asked for anything or to have allowed herself to lift her elbow immoderately – his complete treasury of cultural values. Thus endowed, and without asking for any more, the goddess hastily loaded her boat and made for her home town. Scarcely had she departed when, 'the effects of the beer having worn off', Enki feverishly looked everywhere for his talismans, which he did not even remember having put at the disposal of his guest. His page reminded him; and Enki sent him with all haste in pursuit of Inanna to retrieve his treasures – too late! That was how, so the explanation goes, Uruk had gained access to the great civilisation borrowed from Eridu.

Like most of them, this myth is ambiguous. Certainly, it shows the transmission of the cultural prerogatives in the guise of an accident due to the effects of an over-indulgent banquet; but at the same time it takes its place in a whole series of similar accounts, according to which the great decisions about the universe, nature and culture had been taken by gods at table, the latter clearly being regarded as the proper background for the principal deliberations and resolutions of the divine community.

For example, it was at the end of a feast celebrated in honour of the 'invention' of men by this same Enki, where those assembled were similarly 'merry', that the goddess Ninmah proposed a kind of tournament. During this match, he had to assign a 'destiny' to – in other words, find a worthwhile role, a real usefulness for – various specimens which the goddess would draw from the same human 'mould', but with some serious manufacturing flaw, like broken vessels: the blind, the paralysed, the hermaphrodite, barren women . . . It goes without saying that the god played and won. That is why those blind from birth were musicians and bards; those whose sex was doubtful had their place in the ranks, then popular, of homosexuals and transvestites; women incapable of bearing children were made for prostitution, and so on. In the end, however, Enki discountenanced Ninmah by proposing, in his turn, such a monster – inert, amorphous, devoid of reaction, strength or speech – that she was unable to find any useful occupation for it whatsoever. This was the case of beings who were totally malformed and disadvantaged from birth, of which various passages from medical and divinatory treatises in fact give us a picture.

The Feasts of the Gods

The importance of the banquet, the regular setting for a plenary meeting of the members of divine society, is even more manifest in the famous *Epic of Creation*. When, confronted with the mortal danger to which 'Sea' (Tiamat) – their monstrous and formidable ancestress – exposes them, the gods want to deal with the situation, they meet at the banqueting table. Replying to the appeal of the chief of their line, who has summoned them,

> All the great gods, assigners of destinies,
> Having entered the presence of Anshar, were filled with joy
> To find themselves all assembled, and embraced one another.
> After holding confabulations, they took their places at the banquet!
> They ate their 'bread' and drank their beer:
> They filled their drinking-straws with the heady sweet drink!
> Thus taking in the intoxicating beverage, they felt relaxed,
> Without the slightest care, their souls in bliss!

They then decided unanimously to invest their champion, the young god Marduk, with full powers to wage war against their terrifying enemy. When she was defeated, and her victor had created the World from her remains, and with the additional invention of human beings, Marduk found the means of ensuring for all his fellow gods an idle, blessed life provided with all they wanted through the labour of those creatures; and when the gods, in gratitude, had built the splendid edifices of Babylon and its temple for him, there was a fresh banquet, given this time by Marduk, during which the gods completed his investiture, making the strongest and wisest of them their supreme Sovereign and the Master of the World, for all time.

Here, in the magnifying mirror of mythology, there appears a new role for the solemn communal meal: it is not only the setting for refreshment, gastronomy, rejoicing, relaxation and pleasure, it is also the occasion for fellow-diners to take major decisions about their own interests. In our feasts we have retained the first of these functions, physiological and psychological, so to speak, but we have lost almost all awareness of the other function, social and above all 'political'. Here is another reason for us to pause a moment, for on this point things went pretty far in ancient Mesopotamia.

It is likely that the 'political' significance is fairly subtly concealed, in our inexpert view, in the majority of the official and public feasts mentioned above, but perfectly noticeable to their participants, who perceived things much better than we can. For the sovereign to assemble his subjects, or at least a representative selection of them, at one and the same 'sitting', to share his own meal, was both to display and create or strengthen the cohesion of all in a single 'body', a single state. It was also a way of demonstrating and consolidating his power over them: not only did his guests eat the same food as himself – in other words, were united in the same life derived from the same food-stuffs – but their presence together, the good things they were sharing and their common happiness tacitly announced their approval of the sovereign from whom they received these benefits; confirmed his authority over all of them and the entire population they represented; and renewed, if you will, his investiture. To complete the picture, a few rituals underline the liturgical context of such a demonstration: thus connected with a moment in the worship of the gods, the king's banquet – filled with all this meaning – received the approbation and sanction from 'on high' at the same time as that of his subjects.

This especially is the likely significance of a strange and mysterious ceremony that has caused a lot of ink to flow and much foolishness to be printed: hierogamy, or sacred marriage – the carnal union of a god and goddess, in the form of their statues and by a kind of play of marionette statues in a recent period, but portrayed and replaced, in earlier times, by the king and a priestess. It was neither more nor less than a necessary complement to royal investiture or, according to the probable custom, to its formal annual renewal. By virtue of this formality, the king, whose 'marriage' placed him henceforward in a position to ensure his lineage and the dynastic perpetuation of his supreme authority in the land, truly became the king outright – the perfect representative of that 'royalty descended from the heavens', as it was known, and sent by the gods among men for their greater mutual profit. The wedding night was necessarily followed by a great banquet, nominally served to the divine and royal couple, but in which the population took part with much joy, as if the better to unite around their newly invested, or reinvested, sovereign.

Examined closely, the 'political' function of the public banquet, when all is said and done, was only the result of the extension to 'national' solidarity of the fundamental role played by the meal in family cohesion – the primary cell, basic unit and model of the whole social organisation. On the subject of the family meal we are better informed. Directly or not, a fair number of texts of various kinds prove to us to our heart's content that all the high points in family life were marked by feasts reserved for the whole extended family, and that alone.

Solemn Meals for Marriages

The major episode in family development was marriage. In such an exclusively patriarchal society, a woman had to leave her own family to go and live, until her death, in her husband's 'house' and among his family, who paid the bride's parents a compensatory sum fixed by the contract of agreement between the two family groups. As long as things were only at the contract stage, the marriage was merely provisional. It became effective upon the 'entry' of the 'fiancée' into the house that from then on would be hers. And this 'passage' was sanctioned by a banquet whose cost was met by the husband's family. The contracts – and we have a fine collection of them – have little to say on the matter; their purpose was to emphasise the legal and economic conditions of the agreement, and not the ceremonial of the festival. But some 'codes of laws' go a little bit further, and we have found a rather charming myth which tells us much more.

It narrates how the great god Enlil had fallen in love with a very pretty daughter of the gods, who was a stranger in his town. At first he had taken her for a loose woman, and had therefore merely proposed sleeping with her; she had haughtily rebuffed him. Realising his mistake, very embarrassed and all the more infatuated with her, Enlil sent his *chargé d'affaires* to ask her parents for her hand in marriage, according to the rules. As soon as his envoy returned to tell him of the family's consent, the first concern of the happy future groom, in raptures of joy, was to send not only a rich ritual present of jewels to his beloved but also, to her family, the wherewithal for preparing an enormous and ostentatious banquet.

The news, says the text, 'was a great relief to Enlil, And filled his heart with great joy . . . He therefore gave orders . . .' to assemble and send herds of animals on foot:

Quadrupeds, from goats to asses,
which grow freely on the steppes
And frequent the High Lands,
A multitude were chosen: . . .
Beefy bulls, with massive horns, lowing;
Cows with their calves;
Wild cattle with large horns,
Led on precious leashes;
Ewes with their lambs; goats with their kids,
Cavorting and butting one another;
Stocky kids, with long beards,
Pawing the ground with their hooves . . .
Sheep worthy of the royal table . . .

Then, as a splendid supplement to this already sumptuous array of meat:

Full fat cheeses; spiced cheeses; sheepsmilk cheeses . . .;
Milk products of every kind . . .;
White honey, hard honey; the finest pastries [?] . . .;
Dates; figs; juicy pomegranates . . .;
Cherries [?]; plums: nuts; pistachios and acorns . . .;
Massive bunches of early grapes;
Exotic fruits on their stems . . .

It was a right royal feast!

The meaning of such a wedding feast is very clear, if we can just get under those people's skin. By consuming their own foods provided by her husband's family, the new wife became incorporated into it, drawing life from the same sources. The meal was therefore not merely a rejoicing, or a prestige-enhancing expenditure, but the particularly effective sign – the proper 'sacrament' – of the union of husband and wife by the wife's introduction into the husband's family. From then on she would be truly a part of it, just like all the other members.

Apart from the occasion of marriage, when, for one reason or another, it was a matter of enlarging the family by adding an outsider through adoption, a meal taken by the adoptee among and with his new 'kith and kin' similarly consecrated that incorporation.

Even the simple sale of property was sanctioned in a similar way. It must be understood that, above all in the archaic period, the ancient Mesopotamians had a special feeling about land. Landed property in itself, from which the family group derived its subsistence and life, was just as much a part of the family as people; it was a noble, essential possession, we would say 'sacred', and thus inalienable. A logical and sincere procedure – or a simple subterfuge to get round the strictness of the prohibition – when one came to the point of having to yield land to an outsider, the purchaser had first to be incorporated into the selling family, achieved by having a communal meal. This happens to be mentioned, mainly in the early period (third to second millennium), in the terms of the contract. Here, for instance, is the text of a fairly late example (c. 1780 BC):

> Ili-pahallu [the seller] has sold to Yarim-Addu [the purchaser] 180 square metres of developed land; and [in counterpart] Yarim-Addu has sold to Ili-pahallu 85 grammes of silver . . . In the presence of X, Y and Z [here the names of a dozen people acting as witnesses to the conclusion of the deal]: they have eaten and drunk together . . .

Family Banquets with the Dead

The family banquet, a solemn repast eaten communally, was therefore something quite different from a mere intake of food or simply an occasion to gather together and enjoy one another's company; taken as a whole, it was the conscious sign and agent of family solidarity. There was even one kind which, from all the evidence, had no other aim than to affirm and maintain such solidarity, to the point where it was not only kept solely for relatives but extended to all kin, including the deceased. It was known as *kispu*, an Akkadian term whose root meaning referred to 'sharing the same food' – a cardinal element of the rite.

This solemn meal was celebrated at regular intervals, usually on the last day of the month, when the Moon's disappearance evoked death and thereby made thoughts turn to those who had passed on. It seems to have taken place for preference in the 'sacred' part of the house; the wing of the 'icons', under the floor of which – in accordance with an ancient custom – the family dead were interred. It was believed that, besides the bones of the dead, and in a mysterious but undoubted relationship with them, there existed what was called the 'phantom' (the 'shade', 'spirit' or 'soul' of our own folklore) – a kind of indistinct, hazy, insubstantial double of what the dead person had been like in life, rather as seen in dreams. Placed under the ground by the obligatory rite of burying the body, this phantom reached what would from then on be his own and final 'home': Hell, a sort of immense underground cavern covering the same area as our world. All the dead were gathered there, under the rule of the infernal gods, after being governed on earth by the gods of the heavens. There they led a somnolent, dull, parsimonious and mournful life. Although they no longer had the same need for daily and plentiful food and drink as they had felt in their prime on earth, they still required a little, now and then, to feed their meagre survival. The *kispu* repast – to which they were invited, their place marked, and in which they mysteriously came to participate – partly provided for that need, and it was a sacred duty of those still living to celebrate it with more or less solemnity and splendour, depending on their individual means.

Naturally, the royal family did not fail in this. We have even found a tablet, dated to the penultimate king of the First Dynasty of Babylon, Ammî-Ṣaduqa (1646–1626 BC), which seems to be consecrated to it. It gives a long inverted family tree of the king's ancestors, going back to the lineages which had preceded his own, and ends with this apostrophe:

> O phantom-members of the Amorite Dynasty; those of the Hanean Dynasty; those of the Gutian Dynasty . . ., you and all the phantoms of the soldiers who fell in terrible wars in the service of their sovereign: those of the princes and princesses, and of all of you, from East to West, who no longer have anyone to care about you, come, take your part in this feast, and bless Ammî-Ṣaduqa, the king who offers it to you!

Is it not moving to see those ancient dead thus addressed – not only the monarchs, but their troops and all their subjects, especially the most abandoned among them? Is it not striking to see them all equally invited by the sovereign to a banquet prepared for them to ease their pitiable hunger and thirst? But, above all, gathering them all together around the same fare, which the living ate with them, in this way affirmed and maintained their belonging to an immense and united 'national' family, which even death could not shatter.

'Would to God!'

The gods, too, celebrated the *kispu* on their own account, with the same intent and the same meaning; and as they had no dead, their 'brothers' in Hell stood in for them. But these, entrenched in their subterranean residence, could not come in person – to the feast that was held in Heaven – or so it was believed and therefore had to send a representative to receive their share and bring it back to them. For what mattered was not their physical presence around one 'table', but the consumption of one food. Nothing better suggests the profound meaning of the rite, which was based not on pleasure enjoyed communally but on life derived from one and the same source, consequently identical and indissolubly binding together all the participants.

We have a very curious myth, whose starting-point is precisely the invitation given to the underworld gods and their queen Ereshkigal to this celestial family banquet:

> One day, on the point of their ritual feast,
> The gods sent a messenger
> to their sister Ereshkigal [in Hell]:
> 'We ourselves are unable to come down to you,
> And you cannot come up to us!
> Therefore send someone to collect your portion of the fare!'

But when the messenger arrived, one of the gods of the heavens, out of mischief or just a passing whim, refused to greet him like all the others. This was a very serious offence which Ereshkigal, when told about it, wanted to avenge by ordering the culprit to appear before her; after many captivating vicissitudes, this would end in marriage – a 'money match' according to one of the versions of the myth, a passionate love match according to the other, both versions equally anxious to explain how a god, at first placed in Heaven, had ended up as Sovereign of Hell.

On earth as in heaven, among both gods and men, the eating of food in those far-off times also had a 'mystic' and 'sacred' value. It is found again in the Bible, and if something of it remains with us today, it is through religion. Of course, the early Christians' *agape* (or love-feast) and the eucharistic celebration of 'bread' and 'wine' – in other words, the communal meal – have in the meantime acquired new references and enriched significance. But they are still 'sacred' repasts, and the vision and practices of the ancient Mesopotamians must have played a part in their oldest history.

Outside this field, and since our 'business lunches' are no longer much more than celebrations of economic victories or exercises specially intended to make adversaries give in gracefully, the banquet – even within the family – has scarcely any value in our view except for reunions, meetings, displays of prestige, stuffing oneself, gastronomical and oenological exploration and, above all, having fun. And the bawdy Rabelais is forever its best eulogist: 'Would to God' says Pantagruel to his fellow-diners, in the course of one of those good free meals whose colourful accounts spangle the four or five immortal books – 'Would to God that each of you had two pairs of hawk-bells on your chin, and I had the great chimes of Rennes, Poitiers, Tours and Cambrai on mine, to see what an aubade we would produce when we champed our chops!' (II, xxvi).

CHAPTER 5

An Ancient Vintage

André Finet

In ancient Mesopotamia, among the oldest 'civilised people' in the world, alcoholic beverages were part of the festivities as soon as a simple repast bordered on a feast. Although beer, brewed chiefly from a barley base, remained the 'national drink', wine was not unknown. We find it mentioned early in the third millennium, and its success was always undeniable throughout the whole of Mesopotamian history.

In the eighteenth century BC, it was a common topic in the archives of the palace of Mari, the brilliant metropolis of the Middle Euphrates. These texts, which throw light on the political and social life of the kingdom and its neighbours, also provide useful evidence about eating habits. We lack direct information about the life of the ordinary people, and it does not seem very likely, *a priori*, that it copied court life. Nevertheless, wine figures among the travel provisions allocated to foreign messengers and much later – but that may only be due to the chancy nature of our documentation – itinerant traders would offer it in the streets.

In the time of Mari, the main grape-growing regions extended outside the kingdom, to the north and west. Even today, they are found in the Anatolian south, at Nizip or Gaziantep, as in western Syria, around Homs or Aleppo.

Viticulture is just as much a matter of tradition as favourable soil or climate. The town of Carchemish on the Euphrates – on the present-day Turco-Syrian border and the outlet for the produce of Anatolia and the foothills – was by its geographical position the most important port of the Upper Euphrates and a very well-patronised market. It was the capital of an independent kingdom, in friendly relations with Mari.

If Carchemish was the key city of the north, the port of Emar – on the great loop of the Euphrates, where the river leaves the north–south direction to go eastwards – was the centre of trade with the west, that is, the land of Yamhad and its capital, Aleppo, Canaan and Mediterranean coastal ports such as Byblos and Ugarit. In the time of Zimri-Lim (1775–1760 BC), the town of Emar was one of the king of Aleppo's possessions. As at Carchemish, besides grain, wood and wine were also loaded. Canaan's vintages were renowned; according to the Bible, the region of Samaria was surrounded by vineyards, and the land of Moab had an abundance of winepresses. The Gibeon vintage was famous in the eighth to sixth centuries BC; excavations at El Jib/Gibeon have revealed a very important wine-making centre, with presses, fermentation vats and wine-stores at a constant cool temperature. The eighty-three warehouses discovered could have held some 100,000 litres. On this point Herodotus confirms the importance of the western regions; according to him, the Babylonians had no vines, and Phoenician wine was taken there by the boatload.

There were numerous varieties of wine, but it was not until the first millennium that these were given names, sometimes taken from their vineyard. Most often, wine (*karânu*) is mentioned without any qualification. When it is determined, it is chiefly 'red' wine. There are few mentions of 'white' wine, but this may be because of our ignorance of the precise meaning of certain adjectives. There is 'first quality' wine and 'ordinary' or 'second choice' wine. There is 'light' wine, that is, 'white' or 'rosé', or perhaps 'young'. The same adjective describes wine used for ritual offerings: in this instance it is translated as 'pure', which signifies that it is suitable for liturgical use or, quite simply, that it has not been diluted with water.

There is 'new' wine and 'old' wine; the latter would have been a wine allowed to age to develop its qualities – which was also done for some beers. There is 'sweet' wine and 'sweetened white' wine, naturally or by the addition of honey or fruit extracts. There is 'bitter' or 'sharp' wine, probably made so by the incorporation of the juice of certain plants. There is 'strong' wine, probably with a high alcohol content. And there is 'good' wine, like that destined for Mari by the king of Carchemish, or the one which, a thousand years later, Sargon's soldiers would draw by bucketsful from the reserves of the palace of Ulhu. Are we to understand by this a wine of superior quality reserved for the royal tables or, less probably, a wine 'sweetened' perhaps with honey?

The dispatches of wine from the north to the palace of Mari were often accompanied by jars of honey; but what accompanies is not necessarily complementary. In fact, the wine was 'treated' by incorporating various ingredients intended to alter its taste or density – water, honey or some sugary exudation, essences of aromatic types of wood. As well as being diluted, it was also decanted, doubtless to eliminate sediment, and blended.

The wine reserves of the palace of Mari were laid down in one or more storerooms: the jars were placed in a wooden rack intended to hold them and keep them separate. This was known as a *kannum*, and gave its name to the wine-cellar, called the 'room with the *kannum*'. Besides the usual jars (*karpâtum*), holding slightly less than ten litres, perhaps there were also vats of larger capacity. All the palace stores were under seal, and only the top officials had access to them. The wine stocks were especially precious, judging by a passage from the *Annals* of Sargon II of Assyria who, in his 714 BC campaign, meticulously looted the palace of an Urartu vassal: 'I entered his wine-store which was part of his secret treasure.' In the mountains of Armenia, the king of Urartu had turned the Ulhu region into a land where it 'rained' fruit and wine. Sargon caused terror there, forced his way into the royal residence, and his soldiers 'drew good wine in goatskins and pails, as if it were river water'. Archaeological excavations have brought to light large wine-stores at Karmir-Blur near Erevan.

At princely tables, they drank wine cooled with ice. Wine and ice were placed in the store, *nakkamtum*, just before consumption. The ice was collected in winter in the mountains of the north, and perhaps also hardened and compacted snow, but certainly hailstones when a sudden storm hit the country.

They then had to be kept and their surveillance ensured, while porters were assembled to collect them as quickly as possible and transport them to a place where *shaqû*, 'cupbearers', 'wine-waiters', would take delivery of them and place them in this or that store. All this work called for rapid execution, apart from much improvisation. There were specialists to share the tasks, and the means of transport – jars, goatskins or sacks – were sufficiently well-tried to be reliable. It seems incredible to us today that, with these rudimentary means and a far from propitious climate, the Mesopotamians were able to carry ice for 200 kilometres!

The ice for immediate use, taken from the reserve to be placed in the goblets, was kept in iceboxes. These icehouses (*bît shurîpim*) have been found at Hattusas, the capital of the Hittites, in the heart of Anatolia, and at Qatara, in the north-west of present-day Iraq. These two areas had frosts in winter that could sometimes be long and severe; but where that was not the case, in the kingdom of Mari, texts mention three ice-houses. They were brick buildings buried with drainage pipes to extract the water. In short, a construction very similar to the ice-houses that could still be found, in the nineteenth century, in the parks of châteaux and large country houses.

It was mainly on the occasion of festivals and banquets that strong drinks were taken. The guests drank straight from the jar, with the aid of a hollow stalk. Many monuments evoke drinking with a straw, and some representations associate it with erotic scenes; where these show the coupling of a man and woman, some people believe they can recognise the annual rite of the *hieros gamos*. This 'sacred marriage' between the king and a priestess taking the place of a fertility goddess is well attested in literature; it was thought to ensure general prosperity for a year. Partaking of strong drink prepared them for lovemaking or boosted weakened energies. Others see nothing 'religious' in these representations; they are merely an image of happiness in a civilisation where even the most deviant sexual act was subject to no taboo (see Chapter 6).

Libations Offered to the Gods

People also drank from goblets; to clink drinking vessels was a sign of happiness. The conclusion of an agreement or the 'signing' of a contract was sealed in the same manner. Similarly, everyone propitiated his own personal god or goddess by offering the first pickings of the meal. Everywhere, the deities in the pantheon were receptive to libations of good beer or wine. In 714 BC, when Sargon II set about the methodical looting of the temple of the god Haldia, amongst the booty was 'a large bronze vat with a capacity of 80 *mandâtu* [unknown but certainly large measure], with its great bronze stand, which the kings of the land of Urartu filled with wine for libations during the performance of sacrifices before the god Haldia'. At the end of the second millennium, a wish was expressed for the Cassite king of Babylon: 'that my lord may imbibe life, when he drinks the bitter wine of Tupliash, the remains of the offering to the goddess Ishtaran, who loves thee'. The wine of Tupliash was a renowned vintage harvested in the region of Eshnunna, east of the Tigris.

The Mesopotamians also knew fruit-based wines. It is difficult to identify them, as we do not fully understand the vocabulary. The wine *amurdinnum* may well have had the dark fruit of wild blackberries as its base; others are merely names to us. A date-based drink was made, the *shikar suluppî*, which some Assyriologists hold to be a variety of beer. Dates were called *ana shikari*, 'for the fermented drink', perhaps because their over-ripe state destined them for it. A date alcohol is still made in Iraq, the date 'arak', in the same way that in the Dörtyol region of Turkey an orange 'arak' is made. Intoxicating drink brings euphoria; there were drunks in the streets. In the Epic of Gilgamesh, when Enkidu curses the courtesan who has awakened him to civilisation, he wishes 'that the drunkard may soil your festive garments with his vomit [?], that the sot and the boozer slap your face!' At a time when the use of wine was widespread enough for it to be offered by itinerant sellers, a correspondent of king Assurbanipal (668–627 BC) puts him on his guard. The sovereign has just promoted three soldiers; now, 'these men are drunks and, if he has had too much, a man carrying a dagger does not turn away from anyone coming towards him'. Like Aesop's language, the vine is the best and the worst of things. We learn that certain Jewish circles, around the time of Jesus, made it the tree of the knowledge of good and evil, with its forbidden fruit.

CHAPTER 6

Love and Sex in Babylon

Jean Bottéro

Just like the imperatives and rites of eating and drinking, love and the sexuality that governs it are inherent in our deepest and primal nature. Of necessity, therefore, each culture has reserved a privileged place for them in its system, presenting them in its own way. Any more than we know how our prehistoric ancestors dealt with their cuisine, we shall never know how they made love or, above all, how they valued it; the images they have left us are ambiguous and not easy to interpret. Only written information, and in plain language, could provide us with detailed knowledge.

Together with ancient Egypt, the Mesopotamia of antiquity is the oldest country to have known and used writing. Between 3000 BC and the start of the Christian era it left us a monumental pile of items – something in the region of half a million tablets, covering many 'literary genres', from the most finicky apothecaries' accounts to the wildest creations of the imagination. It would be very surprising if, among this gigantic jumble which has been rummaged over by Assyriologists for a century, we did not come across something to give us some idea of the sexual and amorous life of the ancient inhabitants of a country where, between the fourth and third millennium, the first great civilisation worthy of the name was born.

Although the Mesopotamians were unaware of many of our 'taboos' about sex and its practices, unlike our contemporaries they at least did not care to flatter themselves unduly, at any rate in writing, about their preoccupations, abilities and prowess in this field. It all seemed far too natural to be worth talking about. Even in the most personal part of their literature, their correspondence, they seem to have retained a strange modesty about their most intimate feelings. We find not the slightest declaration of love, no effusion of sentiment or even tenderness. Such impulses of the heart surface rarely, and are suggested rather than openly expressed. As, for example, in a letter in which the queen of Mari, around 1780 BC, hopes that her campaigning husband will come home as soon as possible, 'tranquil and satisfied', and invites him to wear the woollens she has prepared for him and is sending by the same messenger. Or in the desperate note of a young wife who, around the same period, informs her husband of the death, in the seventh month of pregnancy, of the baby she was carrying 'in her belly', and tells him of her own fear of dying, through illness or grief, abandoned by all, far from the husband she yearns to see again very soon.

If therefore, among their literary heritage, we cannot hope to come upon much of what love – sentiment, passion or simple amusement – may have unleashed in the way of personal experiences, happiness or drama, there remains a great deal that allows us a glimpse of how those ancient ancestors understood and practised love and many of the pleasures and pains it could bring to their life. All the more so because they envisaged their gods as a superlative version of their own society, and many pieces dealing with these lofty personages give us information that is as good as, if not better than, if ordinary mortals had been the subject. Some examples follow further on.

In Mesopotamia, amorous impulses and capabilities had traditionally been channelled by collective constraints with the aim of ensuring the security of what was held to be the very nucleus of the social body – the family – and thus to provide for its continuity. The fundamental vocation of every man and woman, his or her 'destiny', as they said, referring matters to a radical wish on the part of the gods, was therefore marriage. And

> the young man who has stayed solitary [. . .] having taken no wife, or raised children, and the young woman [who has not been] either deflowered, or impregnated, and of whom no husband has undone the clasp of her garment and put aside her robe, [to] embrace her and make her enjoy pleasure, [until] her breasts swell with milk [and] she has become a mother

were looked upon as marginals, doomed to languish in an unhappy existence.

Marriage, which was normally monogamous, took place at a very early age, and was arranged by the parents of the future couple when the latter were still children, sometimes even before their birth, although they might not meet until the girl was nubile. It was then that she left her family 'to be introduced into her husband's paternal house', where she would live until her death, unless she proved barren and unable to fulfil her essential function; in which case the husband could reject her. Nothing gives a better understanding of the extent to which matrimonial vocation and union were first and foremost 'subservient' to the constitution of the family, the procreation and rearing of children, and the survival of the community.

That this institution was not enough to exhaust, so to speak, all amorous possibilities may be seen first by the right accorded to every man – according to his fancy and, principally, his economic means – to take one or several 'second wives' or concubines into his household. But we see it mainly from the number of 'chance mishaps', conjugal experiences and dramas pinpointed here and there in those manuals of jurisprudential casuistry that have wrongly been termed 'codes of laws'; in items of legal procedure and divinatory treatises, where omens and the future for which they were responsible dealt almost entirely with the 'already experienced'. There we find men who 'in the middle of the street' threw themselves on women to seduce or rape them; or who slept with them in secret, whether or not they were married women, at the risk of being surprised by the husband, father or other embarrassing witnesses. We find women gallivanting around and setting tongues wagging; others reputed to be 'loose'; others who deceived their husband, shamelessly or on the sly, through the good offices of indulgent women friends or go-betweens; still others who 'up to eight times' left their home, or turned prostitute; and finally, some who went as far as getting rid of a husband who was in the way by denouncing him, having him murdered or even bumping him off with their own hands.

When discovered, these crimes were severely punished by the judges, including the use of the death penalty: those of men in so far as they did serious wrong to a third party; those of women because, even when secret, they could harm the cohesion of the family. To say nothing of the fact that, in this country where the culture was fundamentally patriarchal, the man, as of right, was the absolute master of his wife, his servants, cattle and possessions. Such an automatic position, common to both ancient and modern Semites, seems in fact to have been fairly toned down in Mesopotamia, not only because of a more liberal conception of the feminine condition (see p. 112ff.) – perhaps inherited from the archaic influence of the Sumerians – but also because in those times, as always, no one ever really succeeded in preventing women from doing as they pleased and, tacitly, leading men by the nose.

The gods themselves did not escape such misadventures. In a Sumerian myth, the god Enlil espied the young goddess Ninlil, swooped upon her, violated and impregnated her, whereupon the other gods, disgusted by his misconduct, banished him – which did not prevent his starting all over again! Inanna, daughter of the god An, was raped by her father's gardener, according to another Sumerian myth, whereas in its Akkadian version it was she who shamelessly solicited him, and in very crude words, and when he resisted changed him into a frog. In the famous *Epic of Gilgamesh*, in Akkadian, the same goddess similarly offers herself without a blush to the hero who has returned in glory from his expedition to the Forest of Cedars; but he, not wishing to fall into the clutches of this shameless hussy, throws in her face the list of all the many lovers she has abandoned and mistreated after making love to them.

'Free' Love

This sort of situation explains why, as well as the love that was 'subservient' to the needs of society, there was room for what I have called 'free' love, freely practised by each for his or her own pleasure. So that it should be to no one's harm or detriment, it was provided by 'specialists' engaged in what we would call prostitution. Given the tastes and ways of looking at things of the period and the country, according to which love was not necessarily heterosexual, these employees of 'free' love were professionals of both sexes. But unlike what happens in our own times, there is a strong likelihood that their services were highly tinged with a religious element. In these roles, not only did they take part in liturgical ceremonies, especially in certain sanctuaries, but they had been given as patroness and model the goddess called Inanna in Sumerian, Ishtar in Akkadian, the most notorious in the pantheon, where she had the title of 'Hierodule' – a divine religious prostitute. We may already have gained some idea of the licence that such a role allowed her.

Judging by the many designations for them that we know – although the majority do not tell us much – female and male prostitutes appear to have been divided into various categories or corporations whose differences and specialisations we have no means of discerning. To go by its designation ('Ishtarians'), one would appear to have been more closely connected to the person of Ishtar; and another ('consecrated'), in more direct contact with the religious world. Among the men, some must have been not only homosexual but also transvestite, some – we have invented nothing! – even having women's names, or – if we can believe an astonishing oracular text – playing the part of wives and even mothers.

There were many of these officiants of 'free' love, especially around certain temples. The good Herodotus (I, 199) was mistaken; surprised to see so many of these poor creatures auctioning their services, he concluded it was a matter of 'all the women in the country' being obliged by a 'shameful custom' to take part at least 'once in their lifetime'. They were treated as marginals, relegated to the fringes of the social areas of towns, around the ramparts, and appear to have had hardly any protection against ill treatment, snubs and contempt. A myth in Sumerian suggests the reason: in short, each one had 'failed his or her specific destiny' – women, to have a single husband in order to give him children; and men, to take the male role in lovemaking.

Such a disparaging judgement on those engaged in the service of 'free' love did not prevent the latter, as a human activity, from being held in the highest regard, reputedly an essential prerogative of what we would call a sophisticated culture. Another myth in Sumerian explains it without beating about the bush, and we have the proof in the story of Enkidu, the future friend and companion of Gilgamesh, at the beginning of the *Epic* that bears this hero's name. Born and raised in the steppe with wild beasts for his only company, a sort of powerful brute and 'beautiful animal', he discovers true love – no longer brutish, but with a real woman, expert and lustful – thanks to a prostitute who has been sent to tame him:

> She let fall her scarf
> And revealed her vulva, so that he could enjoy her.
> Boldly, she kissed him on the mouth ['took his breath']
> And threw off her garments.
> Then he stretched out on top of her,
> And she showed him, this savage,
> what a woman can do,
> While he fondled and petted her. (I, iv, 16ff.)

After 'six days and seven nights' of embraces, he was completely under the spell of this enchantress and ready to follow her anywhere. She then made him leave his native steppe and animal companions, who in any case now fled from him, and took him to the town where thanks to her he 'became a man' in the fullest sense of the word, cultivated and civilised. It was 'free' love that, from a state of nature, introduced him to culture. How better to show to what extent one of the privileges of early civilisation was valued, this possibility of giving free and full play – if necessary with the help of 'experts' – to our innate amorous capacities?

Needless to say, to our knowledge there was no explicit

ban, no inhibition – conscious or not – to restrain the exercise of such a prerogative. Making love was a natural activity, as culturally ennobled as food was elevated by a cuisine. Why on earth should one feel demeaned or diminished, or guilty in the eyes of the gods, practising it in whatever way one pleased, always provided – self-evident in such a disciplined society – that no third party was harmed or that one was not infringing any of the customary prohibitions which controlled daily life. For instance, on certain days of the year (the sixth of the month of Tashrit – September–October – to name just one), lovemaking was inadvisable or prohibited; we know not why. And again, certain women having been somehow 'reserved' for the gods, totally or partly, it was a serious misdemeanour to sleep with the first or have a child with the others. These restrictions aside, not only did the practice of lovemaking pose not the slightest problem 'of conscience', but, as long as they were asked according to the rites, the gods in person were quite ready to contribute to its success.

Prayers for Success in Love

We have a certain number of prayers and pious exercises 'to [favour] the love of a man for a woman' or 'of a woman for a man', and even 'of a man for a man' the expected counterpart, 'of a woman for a woman', does not appear in the list but we are aware that sapphic love was obviously not unknown). There were other prayers, 'to seduce a woman', 'to manage to make love' (lit., 'to laugh', one of those many synonyms full of imagery, in every erotic language, to describe the union of the sexes); others 'for the case when a man has not yet reached the point of sleeping with a woman'; still others 'so that a woman may let herself be seduced', and so on.

Here is one 'to get a woman to desire [lit., "cast her eyes on the penis of"] a man':

> The most beautiful of women invented Love! Ishtar, who delights in apples and pomegranates [fruit reputed to be aphrodisiac], created Desire. Rise and fall, love-stone [probable erotic term, relating to the erect member rather than to a simple stimulant]; go into action at your best! May Ishtar preside over our coupling! To be recited three times over an apple or a pomegranate, which the desired woman must be made to bite: at once she will yield, and you can make love.

Perhaps even more eloquent are other similar procedures, kinds of spell, but nearly always secondary to the aid implored from the gods and which, for this reason, it is better to consider as 'sacramental' rather than 'magic' – many have been found touching all sectors of individual and social life. One catalogue, part of which is lost, listed at least seventy; but we have recovered hardly more than about thirty, often very fragmented. All were placed on the mouth of the partner ('the woman', not 'the wife'!), its purpose being to ensure that the lover, 'going strong' to the end, might thus give her all the physical pleasure she had the right to expect from their coupling. For the man, this ability unfailingly to take his woman to orgasm, was called *nish libbi* in erotic language – lit., 'lifting the heart', a transparent metaphor.

Such 'prayers' are quite remarkable. Addressed to the gods and goddesses, they emphasise the compatibility of pleasure and religious feeling. They also testify that in a society so apparently 'macho', as we say today, in the matter of lovemaking woman was really man's equal; she had just as much right to pleasure as he, and was neither an object nor an instrument but a real partner – and it is worth stressing this. Lastly, the content itself of these devotions is especially spicy: it allows us to enter, so to speak, into the intimacy of the couple in action. We find an ardent woman, her passion unleashed and a little crazed, talking wildly and howling with pleasure and desire. These are excellent documents of amorous life. Here are two prayers, the first accompanied by 'reinforcing' manipulations, the second composed of cries alone, but how eloquent!

> Take me! Don't be afraid! Grow as hard as you can! By command of Ishtar [the goddess of Love], Shamash, Ea and Asalluhi [the gods who commonly presided over the 'sacramental' rites]! These words are not mine but Ishtar's own, goddess of Love! [the usual way of emphasising the supernatural origin and thus the infallibility of the rite] Gather some hairs taken from a rutting goat, some of its sperm, a few hairs from a rutting ram . . .; mix all together and place it on the loins of your lover, after reciting the above prayer over it seven times.
>
> Become aroused! Become aroused! Grow hard! Grow hard! Be aroused like a stag! Be as hard as a wild bull! [. . .] Make love to me six times like a moufflon! Seven times like a stag! Twelve times like a cock partridge! [all animals renowned for their sexual vigour] Make love to me because I am young! Make love to me because I am on fire! Make love to me like a stag! And I, under the protection of the god Ningirsu [who must have had a certain authority in this chapter which is not attested elsewhere], I will allay your passion!

Making Love

Since we find ourselves in the 'alcove', let us stay here a moment, because of a rather unexpected and very evocative document; it is a chapter of a large divinatory treatise.

Passionately interested in 'deductive' divination, the ancient Mesopotamians worked on the principle of regarding as an omen almost everything unaccustomed, fortuitous or singular that could be seen in the world, nature and men's lives.

With the rules of hermeneutics which they had painstakingly worked out, they were confident that they could 'deduce' the good or bad future in store for those affected by such circumstances. One of the many works they had devoted to it collected together the hazards of daily life: all the unforeseen incidents, uncommon encounters, that an individual could come across from one day to the next in the various areas of his existence. And one of the sections in this monumental collection (in its original state, unharmed by the injuries of time, it comprised 110 tablets, which must have represented between 10,000 and 15,000 presages and oracles) was assigned to sexual and conjugal relations. The whole beginning of tablet 104, which has reached us nearly complete – following 103, of which only scraps remain – specifically studies amorous relations. It was obviously not concerned with banal and invariable routine aspects – not a word is breathed, for example, of universally adopted and most common 'positions' – but with the most unusual flights of fancy, or accidents that might occur during amorous frolics.

It could happen, for instance, that an eccentric setting was chosen for these, instead of keeping to your favourite place, 'the bedroom'. You might take it into your head to 'make love on the roof-terrace of the house'; or 'on the threshold of the door'; or 'right in the middle of a field or orchard'; or 'in some deserted place'; or 'a no through road'; or even 'in the middle of the street', either with just any woman on whom you had 'pounced', or with a prostitute. You could also, with this aim in mind, alone or with your partner, go to a 'tavern', which played the dual role of 'watering-hole' and brothel. Various unusual 'positions' could be adopted: 'standing'; 'on a chair'; 'across' the bed or the partner; 'taking her from behind' or even 'sodomising her'; or 'with her astride you', even 'preferring to take the female role'. Homosexual love could be enjoyed, in which case you either sodomised 'someone from your own circle' – in other words, a non-professional – or 'one of your own domestics' or 'your servants', if you did not resort to a qualified homosexual; or yet, you could prefer so resolutely 'to submit to other men' that you could end up by passing for a professional yourself.

Furthermore, there were erotic dreams: a man could have one just after making love and even experience a violent ejaculation; or, in bed with his wife, he could dream about her constantly desiring him (lit., 'looking at his member'). The treatise on oneiromancy (or divination by dreams), portions of which have also been found, completes the picture on this point. The man in question might dream that he was making love to the goddess Ishtar in person or a priestess (forbidden); to the queen of the country; to the king's daughter; his own daughter; his own sister; and, in the homosexual world, to a god; to the sovereign, to an eminent personage; a young man; and even, in the last analysis, to a corpse!

It is remarkable that, in these documents or elsewhere, we have never found the slightest allusion to the sexual use of the mouth, so one may wonder whether fellatio and cunnilingus – well known in other areas at that time, for instance in Egypt – may have been the object of a particular aversion or customary prohibition. In contrast, sodomy was common, with women as well as men. Not only do many figurines testify to the practice, but texts speak of it openly. As well as in the above passage from tablet 104 of the treatise, it reappears at least four times in the remains of tablet 103. We even find the practice chosen as a 'contraceptive': in a treatise on divination by the state of the entrails of sacrificed animals, a priestess is mentioned who 'had herself sodomised to avoid falling pregnant'. As far as we know, they were not aware of other means of avoiding conception: the 'stones for not conceiving', like those 'in order to conceive', 'to have a child' or 'prevent childbirth', were a matter of 'magic' or 'exorcistic' therapeutics.

Medical texts add a few touches to this picture of sexual life. Sacrilegious – and therefore bringing bad luck – intimate relations are listed: with women 'reserved for the gods'; or incestuous, with close female family members, mother or sister; sexual relations with pregnant women near to delivery date. Also reported are illnesses that the patient must have contracted, apparently by contagion, 'when he was in bed with a woman', in other words, when making love with her; and venereal afflictions, which were called 'illnesses of coitus'. Such was the case, for example, of what we would call urethritis: 'When the patient experiences sharp pains in the penis, spontaneously loses sperm when urinating, no longer achieves erections and is unable to make love, and has a constant discharge of pus from his penis – he is suffering from urethritis [lit., "discharge"].'

Two or three passages – rather moving because the portrait they depict is still familiar to us – even describe 'lovesickness':

> When the patient is continually clearing his throat; is often lost for words; is always talking to himself when he is quite alone, and laughing for no reason in the corners of fields [. . .]; is habitually depressed, his throat tight, finds no pleasure in eating or drinking, endlessly repeating, with great sighs, 'Ah! my poor heart!' – he is suffering from lovesickness.

The text which, except in some specific ailments, is concerned with the male sex only, for once adds this comment, which I cannot help but find touching: 'For a man and for a woman, it is all one and the same!' (see p. 119).

Sentimental Love

This goes beyond simple eroticism and introduces us to the domain of love as a feeling. On this count, the 'technical' documents consulted on tablets 103 and 104 are hardly any help to us. It is in literature, above all in poetry, that we are more likely to find echoes of those sighs, those raptures, that flame, that sweetness, that tenderness, sometimes those storms and that fury, which portray the deep-seated attachment to 'the other one', the irrepressible need one feels for him or her. It is the true love of the heart, which may certainly arouse eroticism but does not really need it in order to grow; and, in any event, sustains and turns it into something noble on the scale of man himself.

'Profane', or non-religious, poems and love songs are rare in what has been recovered of great Mesopotamian literature. The only almost complete piece in our possession – about 150 lines, two-thirds of which remain – is, however, absolutely remarkable. Composed about 1750 BC in an archaic and ultra-concise Akkadian, with a particular and often obscure vocabulary full of features which, after thirty-eight centuries, elude us, it is divided into short 'strophes' which make up the elements of a dialogue between two lovers. At least it is clear that it is all on the level of feelings and the heart alone: there is not the slightest allusion to sex, not the slightest eroticism in the speech! Its theme is simple: the lover suspects her beloved of having a weakness for another woman. She complains; she cries out her love, which naturally flowers into a jealousy that is both tender and vehement. But she says she is convinced that she will win back this fickle man through her loyalty! Here, taken at random from the strophes, is how she expresses herself:

I shall remain faithful to you,
May Ishtar-the-Sovereign be my witness:
My love will prevail,
And that evil tongue [her rival!] will be confounded.
Henceforward I shall cling to you
And I shall reward your love with mine! [. . .]

But no, she does not love you! May Ishtar-the-Sovereign
confound her
And may she lose sleep, as I do,
And spend nights overwhelmed and cast down with
despondency! [. . .]

Yes! I shall embrace my darling:
I will give him kisses
And will never stop devouring him with my eyes! Thus I
shall win the day over my rival;
Thus I shall recover my beloved! [. . .]

For it is your charm that I seek,
I am thirsty for your love!

Confronted with these moving and ardent declarations, the lover is not shown in a good light: like all men in similar situations – and, as may be seen, since time immemorial – he contents himself with denials, bad temper and rebuffs, which by no means discourage her:

Don't say anything!
Don't talk so much! Why talk when you have nothing to
say! But no, I tell you no lies!
Really, one might as well gather the wind
As expect anything serious from a woman! [. . .]

More than you, I think over
Your former wiles!
But we have well and truly awoken [from our dream]!
And yet in my heart
I have not the least tenderness for her [still the rival!] [. . .]

Therefore do not believe what people tell you:
That you are no longer the only one I have eyes for! But if you would have the truth,
Your love at present, for me,
Is but trouble and quarrels! [. . .]

Nevertheless, conquered in the end by the faithfulness, tact and tenderness of the woman who loves him, he returns to her, as she had hoped:

Yes! You are the only one who matters!
Your face is as beautiful as ever! It is as it used to be,
When I held you close to me
And you rested your head on me! I shall never call you anything but 'Enchanting',
And 'Wise' shall be your only title, for me!
May Ishtar be my witness:
Henceforward your rival shall be our enemy!

This, I repeat, is a unique document, and it is of real interest that it was devoted in this way to exalting the pure and disinterested love of a woman, at the same time casting some shadow on her beloved's feelings for her. Many other similar poems or love songs – though obviously not all along the same lines – were written and circulated, even if luck has not preserved them or archaeologists have not yet brought them to light. We have proof in a catalogue from the end of the second millennium BC, which gathered together almost 400 of them, by 'title' (in other words, their first few words), of which almost a quarter remain. As these 'titles' are eloquent enough by themselves, here are a few, giving a fair picture of amorous sentiments:

> Sleep, begone! I want to hold my darling in my arms!
> When you speak to me, you make my heart swell till I could die!
> Ah! How I would wink my right eye at you . . .
> Here I am, in love with your charms!
> I did not close my eyes last night: Yes, I was awake all night long, my darling!
> O joy! The day has brought me nothing but good news!
> A woman, who is not as good as I, has taken it into her head to supplant me . . .
> It is tonight! This evening!
> How charming she is! How beautiful!
> She seeks the lovely Garden of pleasure that you are going to give her!
> So it is you, my sweet, who prefers my charms!
> O my little bird! My turtle-dove! You moan like one who laments!
> It is he, the gardener of the Garden of Love!
> That girl, her heart leads her to amuse herself!
> Since I slept body to body with my darling! . . .

With these chants and songs of tenderness, joy and passion, clearly for the use of young men and women at the age of passing fancies and love affairs, the same catalogue mingles others which introduce a devotional hue into the sector of amorous poetry:

> Rejoice, Our Lady! Utter cries of happiness!
> O, Wisest of the wise: you who take care of humans!
> I am the most formidable of the gods!
> I would sing of the very-strong divine King, the omnipotent King!
> Who, then, would be my Queen, if not you, Ishtar? . . .

The fact is that the majority of the poems and love songs which have been preserved for us revolve around the goddess who was seen as both the supernatural protectress and model of 'free love' – Inanna/Ishtar.

'Let me go! I must go home!'

Imagined as being patterned on men, the gods therefore each had a wife, even concubines; they founded families, had children. On this level, everything carried on peacefully, and we know of neither myths nor legends which – as with the Greeks – reflect the conjugal storms and difficulties among deities. Certain solemn rites, best attested during the first millennium BC, celebrated their weddings around their cult statues: bathed, perfumed, splendidly arrayed, then carried with great pomp to a room in the temple known as the 'nuptial chamber', they spent some time side by side, supposedly consummating their union, which was celebrated by banquets and rejoicings of the whole populace gathered around them.

But the gods also practised 'free' love. Above all, it was the totally independent Inanna/Ishtar, devoid of any conjugal or maternal attachment, dedicated entirely and solely to her infatuations and passions, who inspired a quantity of stories and songs on the subject. She was reputed to have had many affairs, but the one that was remembered most vividly, and regarding which an impressive mythological and lyrical documentation has come down to us, was her first: her 'youthful love' with Dumuzi (in Sumerian)/Tammuz (in Akkadian), probably an archaic ruler, who had been heroised much earlier and entered the ranks of the gods. He was thought to have been a shepherd and, so the story goes, Inanna had at first hesitated between him and the farmer god Enkimdu – probably the echo of a well-defined social and economic situation, which completely escapes us because it lies so far back in time, in this country where farmers and stockbreeders (the principal agents in the production of local resources) must have long been rivals. Then she chose the shepherd, as a sort of duo with chorus, composed in Sumerian, reminds us:

INANNA: And as for me: my vulva, my rounded mount,
Who then will plough it?
My vulva, the Queen's, my moist glebe,
Who will plough it?
CHORUS: O Sovereign Lady, the King will plough thy field!
Dumuzi, the King, will plough it!
INANNA: Well then, plough my vulva, O thou whom I have chosen! . . .

Another piece, also in Sumerian, describes her dreaming in anticipation of her love:

When I have bathed myself for the Lord, for Dumuzi,
When I have adorned my flanks,
Covered my face with cream,
When I have made up my eyes with kohl,
When his seductive hands clasp my loins,
When, lying close beside me, he kneads my creamy and delicious breasts,
When he places his hand on my precious vulva,
When his member, like a ship's prow, brings life to it,
Then I, too, will caress him for a long time [. . .]
He will put his hand in mine, his heart against my heart:
What sweet repose to sleep with his hand in mine!
What sweet pleasure to clasp his heart to mine!

Another, in the same language, depicts her impatiently awaiting the visit her lover is to pay her in her parents' house, since she was supposed to be still a young girl:

Inanna took a bath and rubbed herself with fine unguent,
Put on her splendid royal Robe
And placed a lapis lazuli necklace round her neck.
After which, she waited anxiously [. . .]
Then, Dumuzi opened the door
And slipped into the house like a moonbeam! [. . .]
Mad with joy, he gazed at her,
Enfolded her in his arms, kissed her [. . .]

There were times, too, when she furtively left the house, like an amorous teenager, to go to meet her beloved beneath the stars, 'which sparkled as she did', then to dally beneath his caresses and suddenly wonder, seeing the night advance, how she was going to explain her absence and lateness to her mother: 'Let me go! I must go home! Let me go, Dumuzi! I must go in! / What lie shall I tell my mother? / What lie shall I tell my mother, Ningal?'

And Dumuzi suggests an answer: she will say that her girl companions persuaded her to go with them to listen to music and dance . . . We could really believe we were in the present day!

The love affairs of Inanna and Dumuzi were also celebrated in liturgy, especially at the turning point of the third and second millennia, to the best of our knowledge. This 'sacred marriage', the union of the two supernatural lovers, was both pictured and enacted; not, as would happen later, in the form of images of the gods, but by a real night of love between the sovereign of the country, representing Dumuzi, and a 'priestess' taking the place of Inanna. We have retrieved a whole dossier on this subject, and in 1953 archaeologists excavating at Uruk even unearthed the necklace of one Kubatum, 'beloved of the king Shû-Sîn' (c. 2030 BC), who we believe played the role at least once. For such occasions, special songs or stories were composed; they are sometimes still captivating, despite the inevitable clichés in them. One example at least has been preserved for us in its entirety, and recalls the Song of Songs in the Bible. It really belongs here because, datable to the same king Shû-Sîn, it may well have been on the lips of the charming Kubatum:

O my love, dear to my heart,
The pleasure you give me is sweet as honey!
You have delighted me! I am all a-tremble before you!
How I wish you had already carried me off to your bedroom, my lion!
Let me caress you, my darling!
My sweet darling, I want to plunge deep into your delights!
In the small bedroom, full of sweetness,
Let us enjoy your marvellous beauty! Let me caress you, my lion!
My sweet darling, I want to plunge deep into your delights!
You have taken your pleasure with me, my darling:
Tell my mother, therefore, so that she may offer you sweetmeats!
And tell my father: he will give you presents!
Your soul, I know how to enliven your soul:
Sleep here, my darling, until daybreak!
Your heart, I know how to make your heart swell:
Sleep here, my lion, until daybreak!
And you, you, since you love me,
Please lavish your caresses upon me, O my lion!
My divine Sovereign, Lord and protector,
My Shû-Sîn who rejoices the heart of the king of the gods, Enlil,
Please lavish your caresses upon me!
This little nook that is sweet as honey, place your hand upon it, I beg you:
Place your hand upon it as you would on a material that is pleasant to touch,

And close your hand upon it, as you would on a material
voluptuous to feel!

From tenderness to passion, from gentleness to sensual delight, the lovemaking of Inanna and Dumuzi, in the end, is merely the projection on to a supernatural screen of the transports that trouble men's hearts and flesh. It portrays not only the love life of our ancient ancestors in Mesopotamia, but our own, because we can still be stirred by these lustful and tender scenes, these murmurs and cries of passion, immortalised in such beautiful 4000-year-old poems!

Those people were so well versed in the secrets of the heart that they had already realised that great loves always end badly. Their myths recount in detail how Inanna/Ishtar, when all was said and done, basely abandoned her lover, condemning him to death and dispatching him to the Kingdom of the Shades, where one day she had incautiously lost her way, obtaining her freedom from the dusty Gaol only on condition that she was replaced by a substitute. A whole series of elegies, discovered almost in their entirety, bewailed the anguish and tortures of the unhappy Dumuzi/Tammuz, pursued by the infernal henchmen demanding their prey. And as if to put the last touches to this picture of Love, they emphasised the heroic sacrifice made by Geshtinanna, the poor rejected lover's sister, who offered to share his sojourn in the Empire of the Dead! Thus true love, unselfish and noble, was contrasted with the showy, but fragile and deceptive, intoxication of passion.

CHAPTER 7

Women's Rights

Jean Bottéro

When it comes to feminism, the ancient Semites (see p. 246ff.) and their descendants have a rather poor reputation. Around the end of the first century AD, Diodorus of Sicily could not have written of them – as he did of the Egyptians in his *Bibliotheca* (I, 27, 2) – that 'women rank before men'. The Bible reflects quite a different picture, in short, 'antifeminist'. When the Preacher declares, 'One man among a thousand have I found; but a woman among all those have I not found' (Eccles. 7: 28), he prepares us to be less surprised by the discovery, in the oldest account of the Creation (Gen. 2: 4b–3), that the first woman was not only responsible for the first sin – the original cause of all our ills and misfortunes – but extracted in the first place from the body of a man; in other words, radically dependent upon and inferior to him. Given this state of affairs, why should biblical Hebrew, in order to designate the 'husband', resort to any other term than 'owner' (*ba'al*), *alias* 'lord-and-master' of his wife (Exod. 21: 3), like all the rest of his possessions (20: 17)?

The Koran takes the same tone, deciding straightaway that 'men are superior to women, Allah having preferred them' (Surah 4: 39). Hence, up to the present day, that inflexible 'machismo', those padlocked harems and those veils imposed upon wives so that, when they are out, no one other than their 'lord-and-master' (*ba'l*, the same word as the Hebrew *ba'al*) may see their face. When I was working with German archaeologists on the excavations at Uruk, in the south of Iraq, in the heart of the desert, the wives of our guards and servants, all Bedouin, did not wear veils like townswomen. But, unless we wanted to be guilty of a mortal insult towards our friends – their husbands – there was simply no question of our speaking to them or even noticing their presence if our paths happened to cross. One day a colleague gave me a lift back to Baghdad in his car, and we were accompanied by one of our friends and his wife. The three of us chatted, to kill time on the long trip, but even he did not utter a word to his young wife, although we knew how fond of her he was. And, when midday came, it would have been unseemly for us to share our food with her, though her husband personally was happy to help us tuck into it.

It is pointless to give more examples of these customs and laws: having a fair acquaintance with ethnology, and being aware of the extreme diversity of cultures, we are certainly capable of realising that some hold such an attitude towards our female companions, but it increasingly clashes with our sensibilities and egalitarianism. Even though more than one among us may feel a bit 'Semitic' on this point, when being perfectly frank he would perhaps agree that it was out of authoritarianism, egotism and vanity, but would hesitate to take pride in such an absolute principle and so firm a conviction.

What was it like in Mesopotamia, where the oldest-known Semites appear, whom we generally refer to as 'Akkadians'? Probably as early as the fourth millennium they found themselves in symbiosis with the 'Sumerians', another ethnic group of unknown origin and completely different culture and language. From their coming together was born that early and ancient hybrid civilisation, in which it is immediately obvious that the more inventive and go-ahead Sumerian element left a deep, indelible imprint.

Ethnically more vigorous, however, the Akkadians absorbed their partners during the third millennium and alone remained responsible for the maintenance and development of their sumptuous cultural system, until its disappearance shortly before the Christian era. Given such a considerable lapse of time, I will offer here only a panorama of the feminine condition in Mesopotamia.

First, let us set apart the slaves – the booty of war or in servitude for various reasons – who by definition were totally dependent on their masters, although the latter appear to have treated them fairly humanely, and more like domestic servants. If we are to believe the voluminous files and especially the legal picture of the basic relationships between the sexes, women's circumstances at first appear not far removed from those revealed in the Bible and, later, the Koran. In such a strictly patriarchal culture, the wife's subjection to the husband leaps out from everywhere in our copious business documents and legal sources.

For a man, marriage was (in Akkadian) 'to take possession of one's wife' – from the same verb (*ahâzu*) commonly understood for the capture of people or the seizure of any territory or goods. It was the husband-to-be's family who initiated the matter and who, having chosen the girl, after an agreement paid her family a compensatory amount (*terhatu*) – in short, a transaction which necessarily brings to mind a form of purchase. After this, the girl thus 'acquired' – generally well before she became nubile, and while waiting she would stay as if in storage with her parents – was removed from her own family by the matrimonial ceremony and 'introduced' (*shûrubu*) into her husband's family where, barring accident, she would stay until she died. The husband (*mutu*) had 'proprietary' rights over his wife, as over the rest of his property, personal estate and buildings: *bêlu*, the exact Akkadian equivalent of the Hebrew *ba'al* and the Arabic *ba'l*.

Once settled in her new status, all the jurisprudence shows us the wife entirely under the authority of her husband, and social constraints – giving the husband free rein – were not kind to her. In the first place, although monogamy was common, every man – according to his whims, needs and resources – could add one or more 'second wives', or rather, concubines, to the first wife. It was up to her to keep the upper hand over the others; her agreement in choosing them might even be asked, especially when, if she had not borne children, her husband took another to do so in her place and in her name, because the maintenance of the family line was the fundamental aim of marriage.

But, alone or with her female companions, the woman owed total obedience to her *bêlu*; it was her duty to remain in the house 'submissive and without leaving the premises', attending to household chores and bringing up the children, thus contributing, from her modest corner, to the smooth running of the home. When disagreements or brutality occurred, there was no question of her asking for divorce, which as such was unknown; the only outcome was repudiation, which was in the power of the husband alone. Nothing better reveals the inequality of their reciprocal condition than the following clause, inserted around 1700 BC in a marriage contract:

> Henceforth, if the wife should say to her husband: 'I no longer want you for my husband!', she is to be thrown into the water with her hands and feet tied. On the other hand, if he should say: 'I no longer want you for my wife!', he is to

pay her [by rejecting her thus, a premium – fairly comfortable for the period! – of] 80 grammes of silver.

The Woman in the Home

The woman who wanted to leave her husband could proceed only indirectly, and at her own risk and peril: either by making herself unbearable – but the husband was free to keep her all the same, and, if he sent her home, she would go empty-handed; or she could refuse all sexual relations – but then enquiries would be made among the neighbours about the respective conduct of man and wife. If the husband was in the wrong, she was free to go back to her family, together with her dowry; but if it was established that she had been 'disobedient, a manhunter [lit., "a woman who went out of the house"; to leave her fireside corner was at once to lay herself open to suspicion!], breaking up the home and bringing discredit on her husband', 'she was thrown into the water' without further ado (code of Hammurabi, § 141; c. 1750 BC).

While the husband's escapades were punishable only if they seriously harmed a third party, those of the wife were castigated without mercy. Lovers caught unawares were bound together and thrown into the water (the same code, § 129), or the husband was granted permission to have them killed or mutilated; for example, by 'cutting off her [his wife's] nose' and by 'making him [her lover] a eunuch' (Medio-Assyrian laws, A, § 15; second half of the second millennium BC).

Monopolised in this way by her husband and 'parked' in the home, it was obviously difficult for a woman to play any public role – economic or, still less, political. The crafts reserved to fill her spare time were all connected with her household tasks, sedentary and keeping her in the shadows: milling flour, cooking or preparing culinary specialities, spinning or weaving. In the majority of prestige professions, here and there we may find an instance of a female; even fewer when the knowledge and practice of writing were called for, as even among men these were the preserve of a professional elite. Women scribes or copyists, exorcists or experts in 'deductive' divination could be counted on the fingers of one hand, and cases of women as the truly well-read or authors of literary works are still more exceptional.

Not to mention those who, married or not, were pledged to some strictly religious duty and those – apparently so numerous that the excellent Herodotus (I, 199; around 450 BC) believed they all had to go through it at least once in their lifetime (see p. 95) – who by chance, after a matrimonial failure, gave themselves up to a 'pleasure' profession: tavern-keepers, singers or dancers and, more generally, prostitutes. Because of their job, these women too lived a life apart, humiliated and wretched, if we are to believe the destiny promised to their prototype in the *Epic of Gilgamesh* (VII, iii, 6):

> Never will you build a happy home!
> Never will you be introduced into the harem!
> Beer froth will stain your fair bosom,
> And drunks will splash vomit over your finery!
> You will live in solitude,
> And your station will be in the recesses of the ramparts!
> Drunks and sots will thrash you as they please!

In short, this was what may be called the 'general rule', the normal state of almost all women, the common feminine condition, the outcome of the fundamental parameters of the mental outlook of those times. Women *per se*, if not regarded as a separate species, were assigned a role that was to some extent ontologically – thus personally, economically, socially, politically – inferior and subject to men. The same legal documents that best disclose this situation nevertheless show a different picture provided that we read 'between the lines'. They then become testimonies to a whole range of practices and ways of life which, simply because they were commonplace, needed to be rectified since they were shocking or dangerous in one way or another. The condemnation of adultery, like that of theft or bearing false witness, necessarily presupposes that these practices were frequent enough to merit a wish to call a halt to them.

In addition to these texts, thousands of echoes from daily life remain; administrative documents, correspondence, literary works and still other sources, starting with those enormous divinatory collections in which – especially in the earliest – the future predicted by oracles was the reflection of a mundane and well-known past. These copious archives allow us to see, not the regulated and enclosed life – organised by the collective conscience to bring it into line with some axiom of the culture, worked out and imposed by women's natural 'superiors' – according to which women must be kept in the dark by men, but the spontaneous and ordinary daily life, which had nothing to do with such restrictive and corrective maxims.

What do we see, then? That, failing the liberty in principle denied them or bargained for, women had or took, *de facto*, enough liberties for their lives and status to be just as tolerable, balanced and enviable as in other cultures that were quite unaware of such excessive and discriminatory constraints.

In fact, in Mesopotamia as elsewhere, every woman had up her sleeve two reliable trump cards to stand up to any representative of the so-called 'strong' sex, even to dominate him, in spite of all the customary or legal constraints: first, her femininity; then her personality, spirit and character. And it was up to her to make use of these to swim against the opposing current of the contemporary 'mind-set'.

By her sexual attraction, she could fascinate and conquer men (see Chapter 6), their prestige, power and wealth, and in this way constitute a formidable danger: 'Woman is a real pit, a cistern, a ditch [into which one falls], An iron dagger that cuts a man's throat!' the author of the *Pessimistic Dialogue* (51f.; first half of the first millennium BC) makes his phlegmatic and mocking 'valet' say. For love has always existed and has always created havoc: 'If the patient is overcome; if he only talks to himself and laughs without reason; or if his throat is tight, with distaste for food and drink, if he utters "Ah, poor me!" and falls to sighing: he has the lovesickness!' the old doctors had already discovered (*Treatise on Diagnostics*, p. 178ff.: 6f.; see p. 103). And the same passage from the *Epic of Gilgamesh* that first allotted a gloomy and painful destiny to the public woman, as if to make amends later extolled her redoubtable power over men:

The greatest will be madly in love with you!
While still a mile away from you, each will slap his thigh [with impatience]!
At two miles, he will start to shake his head [with nervousness]!
. . You will be covered with gold and fine gems . . .
Precious rings will be hung from your ears . . .
And every man will be prepared to abandon for you
His own wife, even were she the mother of seven children!
(VII, iv, 2ff.)

As for the married woman, provided she had a little 'guts' and knew how to make use of her charms, employing all her guile, she was no less capable of making her husband toe the line. Our dossier sets out for us a rather amusing picture of conjugal life, no longer in accordance with the imperturbable rigour of the law, but following the tumultuous realities of daily existence, and in this picture the supposedly 'strong' party is often the underdog. Here we see the unfortunate husband not only as the victim of the outbursts and rages of a shrew who could go as far as 'to burn down the house by setting light to the conjugal bed', but also as the impotent witness of his wife's 'departures' (we would call them escapades), when she would run away from him to seek elsewhere what she reckoned she could not find at home, 'thus wrecking the home' and leaving it to abandonment and ruin. Such behaviour led straight to adultery – recorded many times – and its consequences, with accompanying problems and tragedies: a divinatory oracle mentions a 'woman, made pregnant by a third party, who ceaselessly implores the goddess of love, Ishtar, repeating: "Please let the child look like my husband" '!

It sometimes happened that the 'runaway' was caught, in flagrante, in her lover's arms; they certainly incurred capital punishment, as mentioned earlier, but here again the code of Hammurabi (§ 139) inserts a touching clause that throws light on either the weakness of the deceived husband and his 'masochism', as we would call it, or his love-in-spite-of-everything, bearing in mind his legal relationship of absolute superiority *vis-à-vis* his wife: 'If, however, the owner (*bêlu*) of the wife wishes to keep her alive [which he could evidently do by imploring the judge], the king will equally pardon his servant [the unfaithful wife's lover].'

Such leniency did not always bear fruit; we are told of women who left their home and husband to go gallivanting not just once, but two, three . . . as many as eight times, some returning later, crestfallen, or never coming back at all and taking up prostitution. Others acted on the sly, having recourse to indulgent women friends, or even to more or less professional go-betweens, in order to meet their heart's darling without their husband's knowledge. Some went even further, having their husband murdered 'because of another man', sometimes when they had already ruined him. We can see that, despite their physical, social and legal inferiority, women were well able to triumph in this rivalry with men, and lead them by the nose as they pleased – as is their unchallenged and immemorial privilege, in all places and at all times, if they are prepared to pay the price. A Sumerian 'proverb' simultaneously shows the extreme point of such a reversal in dominance, and all the obnoxiousness it suggests: 'My husband hoards money for me! My son works to keep me fed! If only my lover could skin the fish I eat! . . .' In truth, we have invented nothing!

In spite of the obstacles ranged in her path, if she had character, determination and intelligence – and provided that circumstances were favourable – a woman could none the less cope perfectly well on the economic level. It is true – and here we touch on a new point, almost unknown to the cultures represented by the Bible and Koran – that on this plane the law itself, reflecting commonly held views, admitted that a woman in Mesopotamia had real independence and a genuine personality. She was no longer, as in family and social life, a sort of object, but a subject.

When she arrived in her husband's house, she brought with her a dowry, its value depending on the financial state of her family; clothing and jewels, toilet articles, kitchen and household utensils but also, possibly, money, servants and land. In addition to these possessions – which remained her own property during her lifetime, reverting to her new family only upon her death if she still belonged with them – she often had a sort of dower, formed for her by her husband at the time of their wedding, and jewels which traditionally he gave her then or on later occasions. She was free to top up this nest-egg in a variety of ways, starting with the 'secret funds' she managed to put aside from day to day during her married life.

The most significant case under this heading is that of the women called *nadîtu*, who are best known in the middle decades of the second millennium. This Akkadian name, meaning 'left fallow' – like an uncultivated field, a transparent metaphor – applied to the daughters of great families who, perhaps to avoid the splitting up of inheritances – for their possessions returned to their family after their death – were pledged to a god. Especially devout, as we gather from the phrases, tone and content of their letters, they lived together in a sort of convent called *gagû*, adjoining the temple or in its grounds, under the leadership of a 'mother', surrounded and assisted by both male and female staff.

Normally, they were not married, but chiefly they were forbidden to have children. They led a secluded and fairly edifying life – threatened with being burnt alive if they showed themselves in some place of ill fame. Wealthy and free, they appear to have organised an industrious existence for themselves in their retreat, each following her tastes and capabilities. Some, for instance, spun and wove to earn money; but the majority seem to have been devoted to business. They sold and bought landed property and houses, or they rented them out; they lent at rates of interest: money or grain; they invested and formed associations with itinerant business agents to organise a whole export trade in native products, and the import of foreign goods; they bought and sold slaves; they kept an eye on the working of their lands, engaged tenant farmers, growers, day-labourers and specialists in the cultivation of date-palms, giving orders to some, reprimanding others, demanding reports on the state of works in progress – in short, in the tranquillity of their 'convent', leading the true life of 'business women', adventurous and hectic. The code of Hammurabi (§ 40) mentions them alongside the *tamkaru*, business agents, who were responsible for virtually all the main commercial activity in the country, and thus suggests that they formed the female counterpart. Quite an astonishing success in such a 'masculinised' and male-centred cultural context!

We must now recognise that, to achieve such results, the true feminine condition in this country, at least in some ways, was not in strictly logical agreement with the premise set out earlier: the absolute primacy of the masculine element; and that unlike in other Semitic cultures women had been granted a few advantages and freedoms not enjoyed by their sisters from a biblical or Koranic culture.

As we have seen, the Mesopotamian woman – married or not – could freely possess her own property of any kind, jewels, money, slaves, and dispose of them as she wished; she could sell them, have them brought back, give them away as presents in her lifetime or leave them to whomever she wished after her death – because she was completely free to make a will.

It is self-evident in such conditions that she could buy what she wanted, borrow funds, lease or rent land or premises. She could adopt children or adults – for in this country adoption was not confined to the young; anyone, even fully adult, was enabled by means of such a 'contractual filiation' to enter a family, if he did not have one, or change it, if he did. Most often the whole affair was a simple legal fiction intended to legitimise and cover more than one operation relating, for example, to landed property, which must not leave the family's hands and could therefore be granted to a stranger after carefully arranging to have him artificially included among the family members.

A woman similarly had the right to act as witness to a transaction, and legally guarantee its authenticity, by affixing her signature-seal on the relevant deed – for she possessed her own personal seal, the indubitable mark of her legal independence. She could institute proceedings, bring a legal action, not only without her husband and doing without his authorisation, but also – and there are examples – even against him. She could be summoned to court as a witness, and her testimony was just as valid as that of any adult male.

Consequently, a woman could equally furnish the legal proof of an event, either by swearing an oath before a god or by submitting to the 'ordeal' process, a kind of 'judgement of God' – then practised preferably by submersion in the river, which was regarded as a supernatural being, supposed to drag to the bottom and drown those who were guilty, and allow the innocent to swim to the surface (see p. 199). In short, and unlike her younger sisters of the Bible and the Koran, the Mesopotamian woman had a complete and independent juridical personality.

She seems also to have been superior to her 'sisters', though less openly, on a political level. Certainly, it was a constant feature in Mesopotamia that in matters of public authority and sovereign power the foreground was occupied exclusively by representatives of the male sex. The female side just supplied the trump cards: for example, the kings' daughters, whom their fathers married off to foreign heirs apparent to set the seal on sounder alliances with their dynasty; or extra help: many queens – from those of Mari around 1780 BC up to the wives of the last kings of Assyria a thousand years later – evidently played an important role in the shadow of the ruler, influencing their august husbands in bed or manœuvring, for instance, so that the succession went to this prince rather than that one. But in that era of history, the hypothesis of a woman's accession to supreme power was put forward in only the tiniest number of divinatory oracles. They probably referred principally to a venerable tradition, according to which, around 2500 BC, the town of Kish was ruled not by a king but by an energetic queen called Ku-baba, a former 'tavern-keeper', about whom we know nothing else.

The Eclipse of the Goddesses

This recalls a few scattered mentions which, although not strictly speaking part of historical tradition, appear in mythology – and everyone knows how likely that is to have been transposed from reality and therefore to bear indirect witness to the latter. Sovereignty of the Underworld – that hemisphere symmetrical with the sky, beneath our feet, where all the numbed, dismal, misty 'phantoms' of men went after death – was at first attributed to the goddess Ereshkigal (an obvious Sumerian name meaning 'Sovereign of the Great Netherworld'). It was not until later that this supernatural queen was to share her power with the god Nergal, who had become her husband at the end of adventures recounted in a myth. To judge by her name, Ereshkigal was of Sumerian origin. In the oldest local pantheon, in the formation of which the Sumerians must have played a large part, there were a good many goddesses, whose number dwindled sharply when with the disappearance of the Sumerians only the Semites remained. Would this not be some sort of indication that the first, much more than the second, accorded women and 'woman' a less depreciated status, greater consideration and increased equality with men?

And more than one ancient myth, composed in Sumerian and dating back at the latest to the end of the third millennium, concerning the matrimonial or simply amorous relations between gods and goddesses, ascribes to the latter initiatives and prerogatives which do not fit well with what we know of the ritual accepted in this matter by current practice and law. This is another possible sign of a more liberal and 'egalitarian' outlook towards women, and one which it is difficult to attribute to the Semites, given its diametrical contrast with the representations and customary law of all known Semites since time immemorial. We are thus led back, at least by reasonable conjecture, to the other original source of the country's civilisation – the Sumerians.

These data are meagrely measured out to us, and are fragile: lost in a venerable tradition of which, above all in the earliest period, only fragments remain and these are not always clearly discernible and usable. But they are convergent, which considerably strengthens their value. They enable us to conclude – by virtue of what we already have and subject to new discoveries which might give quite another meaning to our documentation – that if women in ancient Mesopotamia, even though regarded at all levels as inferior to men and treated as such, nevertheless seem to have enjoyed also consideration, rights and freedoms, it is perhaps one of the distant results and vestiges of the old and mysterious Sumerian culture. In the matter of feminism, this culture did not have the same outlook and hierarchy of values as those terrible Semites.

CHAPTER 8

The Women of the Palace at Mari

Bertrand Lafont

Historians hardly ever write anything but the history of man; and the ambiguity of a word which simultaneously applies to the human species (*anthrôpos*) and an individual of the masculine sex (*anêr, andros*) is perhaps very convenient for them because sometimes it allows them not to confess their ignorance on the history of half of humankind – that half represented by women (see p. 90ff.).

In this respect, the written documentation available to the historian on the ancient Near East is typical; of the 3000 years of history which characterise Mesopotamian civilisation, from the Sumerian period up to the Hellenistic era (305 BC), there are innumerable documents showing the individual in his role as father, son, brother and husband. But almost never is there any mention of mothers, daughters, sisters and wives. Specialised works evoke only a few figures of priestesses and queens – sometimes legendary – or the enclosed and very special worlds of some cloisters in Babylonia; there are the archives of a few 'business women', or certain legal arrangements relating to women in what are generally known as the 'codes of laws', such as that of king Hammurabi.

During the summer of 1986 a symposium was held in Paris on the subject of 'Women in the Ancient Near East'. What prompted such an enterprise was the accumulation of new data over the past decade, encouraging certain questions to be raised again regarding the role and status of women in the old societies of the Near East. It was notably the use of documents found at Tell Hariri, the ancient Mari on the banks of the Euphrates, that led to a real revival in our knowledge about this subject.

The archives from Tell Hariri form a considerable mass of documents: almost 20,000 cuneiform tablets written in Akkadian (a Semitic language akin to Hebrew and Arabic). They are around 4000 years old and for the most part relate to the last of the kings of Mari, named Zimri-Lim. He reigned for some fifteen years (1775–1760 BC), after recapturing the throne which his father had had to yield to the great rival kingdom of Ekallâtum, a capital town situated on the Tigris, not far from the present-day town of Mosul (Iraq) and at the heart of what would later become the great kingdom of Assyria. Roughly speaking, these archives are divisible into two parts: on the one hand, a very ample correspondence which the king of Mari maintained with his neighbours, governors, officials or nearest and dearest; on the other, important files of administrative or accounting material illustrating daily life in the palace.

This evidence discovered at Tell Hariri presents an interesting special feature; unlike the rest, it contains a number of texts relating to the female population of the kingdom, notably many letters from women who, because of their birth or duties, sometimes played an important role at the court of Mari or in affairs of state. These letters have been assembled under the title 'female correspondence',[1] and

[1] This correspondence was for the most part published in 1967 and 1968, in volume X of the collection *Archives royales de Mari* (abbr. *ARM* X). Since then it has been the subject of numerous studies, notably *cont'd over/*

among them we find missives exchanged between the king Zimri-Lim and the queen – named Shiptu – when the sovereign was away, but also letters from the secondary wives, the king's daughters, priestesses and other high-ranking women. We have a whole dossier made up of exceptional documents that throw a vivid light on the situation of women in the kingdom, especially the great ladies of the palace.

It is now known that the queen Shiptu – daughter of one of the period's most powerful dynasties, king Yarim-Lim of Aleppo – came to the throne of Mari during the fourth year of Zimri-Lim's reign. It is interesting to note that she took some time to establish her place as first wife and queen among a harem that was already in existence on her arrival. It seems that she had to await the death of the queen mother, Adad-dûri who died in the sixth year of her son's reign, before she could really become the palace's first lady. From her letters, one receives the impression – unless it is no more than an official manner of conducting and expressing herself – that she was entirely devoted to her royal spouse, and full of concern for him.

Royal Correspondence

Thus, while the king was away waging war, which he did frequently in the north of his kingdom, she wrote to him:

> To my lord, a letter from Shiptu, your servant. All is well at the palace. All is well, too, with the temples of the gods and

cont'd J.-M. Durand's – the epigraphist of the archaeological mission of Mari – in volumes 3 and 4 of the specialist review *Mari: Annales de recherches interdisciplinaires* (abbr. *MARI*), in 1984 and 1985. It must also be noted that the interpretation of the documents is today made easier by the progress that has been made in the chronological classification of the texts, which are gradually being reclassified in the framework of a fairly certain and precise development of factual history.

the workshops. I have had omens read for the health of my lord. These omens are good until the end of the month; but my lord must take good care of himself when he is in the full sun! (*ARM* X, 11)

Or this letter, probably sent with some garments as a present: 'To my lord, a letter from Shiptu your servant. May my lord conquer his enemies and return to Mari in peace and with a joyful heart! For now, may it please my lord to wear the robe and cloak that I have made [for him]' (*ARM* X, 17).

In another letter, Shiptu is worried: 'My heart has been greatly alarmed [. . .] May a tablet come from my lord [so that] my heart may be calmed' (*ARM* X, 24).

And here is one of the replies that Zimri-Lim might have sent her: 'To Shiptu, a letter from your lord. I fear that your heart may have been perturbed by some piece of news that you have learnt. [In reality], the enemy has in no way threatened me with weapons. All is well. Let your heart no longer be afflicted' (*ARM* X, 123).

But it is not about the personality of Shiptu, the apparently docile and loving wife, that our texts give us most information; the largest number of testimonies concern her role as queen. We saw earlier (*ARM* X, 11) – and the same is to be found on several occasions – that in her correspondence with the absent king she begins by writing, 'All goes well with the palace, the temples and the workshops'. She sometimes adds 'the city of Mari' to this list, and this is what enables us to define what may have been the queenly prerogatives: in the king's absence, it was she who ruled over the palace. Moreover, we see Zimri-Lim send her instructions and keep her informed about certain political matters, which must have enabled her partly to supervise the officials, governors of provinces and so on, as she seems to have been responsible, at those times, for the interests of the king and the kingdom. Otherwise, in ordinary times, Shiptu seems to have had two chosen areas: organising the worship rendered to the country's various deities, and the 'running' of the plentiful workforce, notably female, employed by the palace.

About the situation and role of high-ranking women, we similarly possess the evidence of Zimri-Lim's numerous daughters (we know of ten or so who, at the start of his reign, were married or of marriageable age). Indeed, the king resorted widely to a policy of matrimonial alliances affecting them; he married the majority to neighbouring kings, especially to certain of his vassals in Upper Mesopotamia (the region of the present-day frontier between Syria and Turkey), doubtless in the hope of strengthening his hold over these petty kings, whose internal wranglings and ambitions marred his policies throughout his reign. However, life in the palace of Mari must have been more pleasant than in the courts of those minor kings 'of the north'. At all events, this is what we may conclude from the complaints and recriminations that abound in the letters addressed by the daughters to their father, lamentations to which, incidentally, Zimri-Lim appears to have paid little attention.

One particular instance, however, concerns the alliance contracted by the king of Mari with the ruler of one of those northern towns, Hâya-Sûmû, king of Ilânsurâ (a city close to the present Syro-Turkish border, between the towns of Mardin (Turkey) and Haseke (Syria). In the space of under three years, Zimri-Lim gave him two of his daughters to be his wives: Shîmatum and Kirûm. We still have the texts relating to the marriage and arrival in Ilânsurâ of the older of the two daughters, Shîmatum, as well as an exact catalogue of her dowry; many sumptuous jewels, luxurious clothing and materials, costly furniture and some ten maidservants.

However, after three years of marriage, Kirûm came on the scene. We have good reason to believe that this second alliance was contracted because Shîmatum had not managed to present Hâya-Sûmû with a child. Kirûm had scarcely arrived when she began to conduct herself openly as queen. Moreover, she seems to have had a clearly more decisive nature than her sister; we therefore see her, in her first letters to her father, talking about important political matters. Truth to tell, from then on a considerable rivalry set the two sisters at loggerheads; it was a matter of establishing who was to be the principal wife, Babylonian law of that period relegating second wives to the level of servants of the first. In the correspondence of each sister, we can see very clearly that during an entire period they were both trying to obtain their father's support to strengthen their own situation at Ilânsurâ.

But this competition came to an abrupt end when, after some time, Shîmatum was able to send her father a brief note as follows: 'To my lord, a letter from Shîmatum your servant. I have just given birth to twins, a boy and a girl; may my lord rejoice!' (*ARM* X, 26).

Kirûm had lost. There then began for her a period of difficulties that were all the greater because Shîmatum, having in all likelihood regained her supremacy, seems not to have lost an opportunity to make Kirûm pay dearly for all the wretched times she (Shîmatum) had endured. So we see Kirûm complain about the many snubs she had been forced to suffer: some of her servants had been withdrawn from her; 'no one ever asked for her opinion any more' – she who had been in the thick of things; and following doubtless ill-timed complaints on her part, she had been severely reprimanded by her husband and threatened by her sister.

Anyway, that is what she reports here to her father whom, as do several of her sisters, she sometimes calls 'my Star':

> To my Star, father and lord, a letter from Kirûm your daughter [. . .] Hâya-Sûmû rose up against me and said, 'Do you act as prefect here? When I have done with you, let your Star come and take you away!' Then he took away [from me] my very last maidservants. May my father send me a single soldier, a single reliable man among his servants, so that I may be brought home quickly. Shîmatum too opposed me and declared, 'My Star may do all he pleases with me, but as for me, everything I want to do, I shall do it to thee!' If my lord does not write to me and does not bring me home, I shall surely die; I can no longer go on living! (*ARM* X, 32 and *MARI* III, 169)

This passionate, not to say dramatic, tone reappears in another letter from Kirûm, which she had conveyed to her father by one Yarîm-Dagan and which probably came hard on the heels of the preceding letter. In this letter one understands what Hâya-Sûmû meant when he told Kirûm that he would 'have done with' her:

> To my Star and lord, a letter from Kirûm your daughter. I have had enough of life, through listening to what Shîmatum has to say! If my lord does not bring me back to Mari, I shall cast myself from the highest rooftop. Let Yarîm-Dagan relate the whole matter to my lord! As for me, I went to Hâya-Sûmû and said: 'You are a king . . .; and what am I, then? A poor man's maidservant? Because of . . . an affair like this, I have had enough of life! May my father write so that I may be taken back to Mari. There I will not demand a top situation. Meanwhile, I wish you much pleasure!' Then in the presence of the kings he broke my cord, saying: 'Be off to your father's house! I have turned my eyes far away from my wife's face.' Another thing – he has taken from me the woman of whom I spoke to my lord, and has given her to Shîmatum. (*ARM* X, 33 and *MARI* III, 170)

'Cutting the cord' was a symbolic gesture, fundamental and well known, pertaining to the Babylonian divorce ritual. We must therefore understand that this is the final episode which is being recounted by the insolent Kirûm; her exasperated husband has decided to make the break and, solemnly and in public, has performed all the necessary actions, the kings mentioned probably being representatives of the local powers and the chiefs of the nomadic tribes dependent upon Hâya-Sûmû. Furthermore, it is interesting to pick out the speech of the king of Ilânsurâ: by 'turning his eyes away from his wife's face', he has used a phrase in exact contrast to the biblical expression 'to cast one's eyes upon a woman' to mean that one has chosen her.

So that is how the disgrace into which Kirûm had gradually fallen and which was driving her to despair reached its conclusion; a harsh one certainly, but which in the end she seems to have brought upon herself. We do not know exactly when the divorce took place, but it happened probably seven years after Kirûm's arrival at Ilânsurâ, because we know that at the time of a great journey which Zimri-Lim made in the north and then the west of Syria during the eleventh year of his reign, he went by way of Hâya-Sûmû; and we are told that he took advantage of it to 'liberate the palace of Ilânsurâ', a discreet turn of phrase to indicate that he had probably taken back his daughter.

The Harem

Using texts as a starting point just as much as traces on the archaeological site, research has enabled us to gain a better knowledge of the female population of the palace of Mari, notably the harem, whose very existence has at times been disputed. Of principal use was a precious collection of accountancy items which had recorded, month by month, the oil rations distributed to each of the ladies of the palace for their *toilette* and for lighting. These documents are datable to the reign of Yasmah-Addu, son of the king of Ekallâtum and the unfortunate rival of Zimri-Lim, who had finally managed to drive him from the throne of Mari. Each bears the names of some forty women, recorded in strict order and with a note of the larger or smaller rations allocated to them. Moreover, all the texts invariably end with the names of three men, whom one may suppose to have been the 'doorkeepers' of the harem. By all the evidence, this meticulous payment order reveals that a real hierarchy existed among these forty women.

For the period following, in the reign of Zimri-Lim, unfortunately we possess only a few texts, often in poor condition, that might give us similar information. On one of these documents – of fundamental importance, but fragmentary – it is noticeable that the number of women is much larger (almost 250 instead of 40) and that they are separated into categories, allowing us a glimpse of the very structure of the harem. So, by combining the information contained in the whole of the 'oil office' texts, we gather that this female population was made up of:

royal personages (the sovereign's mother, his first wife, his sisters and daughters), who received the maximum allowance of oil;

the royal concubines (or secondary wives);

the group of 'singers' (*nârtum*), which must be understood as, in fact, another category of concubines (see the letter in *ARM* X, 126, quoted below), and who were themselves divided between 'major' and 'minor' singers; moreover, they were under the supervision of 'governesses' (*mushâhizâtum*);

the group of the 'cloistered' (*sekertum*), who must have

been in charge of the good internal running and management of the harem, as it can be seen that some of them explicitly received the allocations of 'cook', 'cupbearer' and so on. Another category was that of the *kezrêtum*; domestic staff and doorkeepers.

It is clear, therefore, that not all the women in the harem were the sovereign's wives. Thanks to letters, we can get a vivid picture of how this female population within the palace was organised, and the relationships the women could have with one another (for example, we have accounts of disputes, notably on the subject of jewellery) as well as with the king or other important personages in the kingdom. Some gradually ascended the ladder of the 'hierarchy', sometimes passing from the level of simple 'singer' to that of 'concubine'; others, on the contrary, sank until they disappeared into anonymity.

We must, however, take care not to yield to the temptation provided by these few pieces of information to form visions of an oriental *Thousand and one Nights* harem with its eunuchs and odalisques, as it often exists in our Western imagination.

Indeed, we are forced to accept that there is no specific term in the vocabulary of the Mari texts to designate the harem. Besides, in the vestiges of the royal palace, the part that it has been possible to show as having been reserved for the women was certainly not a completely enclosed area, far less a prison. To be convinced of this, one has only to see the large number of documents that allude to the movements of ladies or wives of the king. Only the women belonging to the 'cloistered' category were most probably obliged to stay in the palace, as they were particularly involved in its good management.

The deciphering of the 'oil office' tablets also disclosed another big surprise. We discovered that several of the ladies in Zimri-Lim's harem had already been in Yasmah-Addu's. Better still: we have succeeded in finding in Yasmah-Addu's harem some ladies from that of his predecessor Yahdun-Lim, the father of Zimri-Lim. Yahdun-Lim's ladies had doubtless been 'captured' when the Ekallateans seized Mari. And when Zimri-Lim, in his turn, had driven out Yasmah-Addu, some twenty years later, he similarly took over the latter's harem. Taking possession of the enemy leader's women thus appears to have been a basic requirement of royal conduct in that period. And that way of showing power receives final confirmation when we note that Zimri-Lim himself continued to increase his own harem with those of the conquered kings of northern Syria, whom he had been fighting for so long (hence the larger number mentioned earlier). It is also interesting to find an echo of this practice in the passage in the Bible recounting how Absalom, rebelling against his father David, was advised to perform the symbolic act that would definitively show his rebellion and affirm his power: to seize his father's harem (2 Sam. 16: 21).

On the way in which Zimri-Lim augmented his own harem, following the victories he won in the north of his kingdom, we have the testimony of letters he wrote to the queen, who had remained at Mari. For instance:

> To Shiptu, a letter from your lord. With regard to the choice of the female musicians among the booty that I have had sent [to you] and about which I have already written [to you], in the end [I prefer] that no musician should be chosen from this booty. These girls are to be accepted only as weavers. Booty has reached me: I myself will choose musicians from among them. I will then have [them] brought [to you]. (*ARM* X, 125)

In another letter, the instructions given are different:

> To Shiptu, a letter from your lord. Now I am having weavers sent to you [. . .] Choose some thirty of them, more or less, as you need, who are perfect and flawless, from their toenails to the hair of their head. Then entrust [them] to Waradilishu so that he may teach them Subarean music; let their status then be altered. Give [also] instructions concerning their food, so that their appearance may not be displeasing. (*ARM* X, 126)

This last missive clearly shows that the king's aesthetic concerns and intentions prompted him unhesitatingly to favour the physical attributes of his 'singers' rather than their artistic or musical talents. As for the 'change of status' he desires, this doubtless involved passing from the category of 'weavers' (regarded as the basic female qualification) to the superior one of 'singers'.

But, in the wake of these various deportations, the number of humans concentrated in the palace probably reached a high degree, which brought about serious inconvenience, notably when epidemics erupted. Two letters, among others, pass on an echo of such vicissitudes:

> To Shiptu, a letter from your lord. I have heard that Nanna is sick with the *simmum*, and yet [in spite of that] she has remained in complete contact with the palace maidservants and by that contact alone has contaminated many women. For the present, give strict orders that no one is to drink from the cup from which she drinks, or sit on the seat where she sits, or lie on the bed where she lies, so that she does not infect many women by her contact alone. This *simmum* is easily caught! (*ARM* X, 129 and *MARI* III, 144)

The *simmum* was an illness that showed itself in red patches and outbreaks of spots; it was contagious and could be fatal. The measures taken were therefore purely prophylactic; there is no evidence of any doctors being summoned, although they are to be found elsewhere in the Mari documents. But sometimes the solutions envisaged to avoid the risks of contagion and wipe out the disease were markedly more brutal, as is shown by a passage from Zimri-Lim's other letter to his wife:

> [Regarding Summudum] about whom you have spoken to me: concerning the illness of this woman, many [other] women will catch this *simmum* sickness. Let this woman [therefore] live in a room apart. Let no one visit her. And if, as I fear, there is no separate room, as soon as the omens concerning Summudum are not favourable, if this woman is cared for, whether she lives or dies, [other] women will suffer from this illness. So let this woman die, she alone, and that will cause the illness to abate. (*ARM* X, 130 and *MARI* III, 144)

Thus the advice consisted purely and simply of letting the sick woman die, as bad omens had condemned her. History does not tell us how efficacious this radical measure proved!

Throughout its history, Mesopotamian society remained based on a strict patriarchal concept of the family, this aspect being strengthened, as far as Mari is concerned, by the presence of a large nomadic element. It is in this context that the documents discovered at Tell Hariri come to illustrate partly what the role and situation of women may have been almost 4000 years ago. Of course, these texts throw light mainly on a tiny minority of them: those who moved in the immediate entourage of the sovereign. But we can see how important a place these people occupied in the life of the kingdom, both in the socio-economic field and in that of politics or religion. Some have ascribed this phenomenon to the fact that the patriarchal monarchy of Mari had been marked by its nomadic origins, the monarch's private domain being barely distinct from the domain of the state. Women were thus associated with the affairs of the palace, and therefore of the kingdom, in the same way that they were with domestic matters.

The reader will also have observed the parallels that are sometimes evident between the content of the tablets of Mari and biblical sources. There are many others (institutions, developments in language, the existence of prophetism and so on). But it must be borne in mind that nearly eight centuries separated the reign of Zimri-Lim from that of king David; and that these parallels cannot ignore the various sociohistoric contexts and specific features of the many cultural areas of the ancient Semitic world.

CHAPTER 9

Semiramis: The Builder of Babylon

Georges Roux

Four soft but titillating syllables, sweet to the memory; a name that is quite well known, and one which for most evokes an eastern queen, legendary and lascivious, vaguely connected with Babylon and its 'hanging gardens'. But how many of our contemporaries know this legend of Semiramis? And how many remember the extraordinary renown she enjoyed throughout Graeco-Roman antiquity; then, manipulated and unrecognisable, from the Renaissance to the mid-nineteenth century? Glück and Rossini turned this queen into an operatic heroine, and Crèbillon, soon imitated by Voltaire, into a heroine of tragedy; in the wake of Vivaldi, some dozen Italian composers gave her name to several of their works, and in their turn, many painters chose her for their subject. Degas himself, the great Degas, devoted the last of his academic pictures to her, in 1861. Most curious of all, while playing with a legend, those ancient and modern artists and authors believed in the reality of Semiramis, simply because this queen and her husband Ninus – to whom must be added Nimrod and the famous Sardanapalus – represented almost all they knew of a long-vanished Assyria.

At the end of the nineteenth century, the texts originating

from the Mesopotamian excavations taught us the real history of that country, and it was then that Assyriologists and historians began to ask themselves questions. What did the legend conceal? Had Semiramis existed and, if so, how and why had a woman, even if a queen, acquired such importance in the minds of the ancients that she ended by personifying, on her own, all the power and glory of an empire built by a long line of male and virile kings?

No one can approach this question without first poring over the legend of Semiramis as it is found in the second book of the *Bibliotheca historica* of Diodorus of Sicily, a Greek writer of the first century BC, to whom we are indebted for the most complete and detailed history of the woman he presented as 'the most famous of all known women'.

The Legend

Semiramis was born at Ascalon, a town founded by the Philistines on the Mediterranean coast of the country to which they gave their name: Palestine. She was the fruit of the guilty love of the goddess Derceto, the patroness of Ascalon, and a handsome anonymous young man 'who was going to offer her a sacrifice'. Overcome with shame when she gave birth, Derceto killed her lover, abandoned her child 'in a deserted and rocky place', then threw herself into the lake near her temple, where she immediately changed into a fish. By great good fortune, doves nesting nearby watched over the baby, some warming her with their wings, others feeding her with beakfuls of milk, then cheese, stolen from the herdsmen's huts. After a while, the herdsmen discovered this little girl 'of remarkable beauty' and entrusted her to the head of the royal sheepfolds, a man called Simma, who brought her up with great care and gave her the name Semiramis – a name which, according to Diodorus, is a slight variation on the word dove 'in the language of the Syrians'.[1]

The years went by. Semiramis was now nubile and 'surpassed all her companions in beauty'. One day, Onnes, the Assyrian governor of the whole of Syria, visited the sheepfolds and, in keeping with oriental custom, was the guest of Simma. He noticed the young maiden, fell in love with her at once, asked for her hand, married her and took her away to Nineveh, where she bore him two children, Hyapatus and Hydaspus. But he had to rejoin the army of his sovereign Ninus, the founder of Nineveh and 'the first king of Assyria mentioned in history'. Ninus, who had already conquered virtually all the Near East, including Egypt, had set his heart on subjecting Bactriana, a region broadly corresponding to the north of Afghanistan. After seizing several towns, he was impatiently champing at the bit outside the capital Bactra, a powerfully fortified and bitterly defended city. Onnes, fretting in the Assyrian camp, sent for his wife, Semiramis, not merely for his pleasure but also because she was supremely intelligent and an excellent adviser. Semiramis arrived in a garment 'which did not enable anyone to see whether it was worn by a man or a woman' and soon noticed that, each time the Assyrians attacked, the defenders of Bactra left their citadel perched on the heights to go and lend a hand to those who were fighting on the ramparts of the lower town. During one of those attacks, together with a few soldiers she climbed the difficult path leading to the citadel and managed to penetrate it. Demoralised, the Bactrians surrendered; the capital was finally captured and duly pillaged. Ninus admired the woman's courage, heaped gifts upon her and, of course, fell

[1] For a long time classical authors confused Syria proper and Assyria under the name Syria. The word 'dove' to which Diodorus alludes is probably the Assyrian *summatu*, but in no way can 'Semiramis' be derived from it.

in love with her. He asked Onnes to hand her over to him, promising his own daughter in exchange. Then, faced with refusal, he threatened to have his eyes put out. Panic-stricken, the unfortunate man hanged himself, and Ninus then married Semiramis, who became queen of Assyria and later had a son by him, named Ninyas.

Soon, however, Ninus died at Nineveh, after entrusting the empire to his wife; now sole sovereign, she reigned for forty-two years. Her first act was to have her husband buried 'in the palace of the kings' and to order that a gigantic terrace be raised on his tomb. Then, 'eager to surpass her predecessor in glory', she decided to found in Mesopotamia a town worthy of her ambition, which would be Babylon. She had architects brought from all over the world, and assembled two million labourers who built successively an enclosing wall, 360 stadia long (around 70 kilometres!), equipped with 250 towers and so broad that more than two chariots could go along it side by side; 30 kilometres of quays; a big stone bridge over the Euphrates, and two magnificently decorated circular palaces, facing each other from either side of the bridge (these palaces were connected by a subterranean way, for the construction of which the course of the river had to be diverted into an immense reservoir excavated for this purpose). She completed her work by raising a temple to Zeus ('whom the Babylonians called Belus'), adorning it with gold statues; and, in the town centre, erecting a colossal monolith hewn from the mountains of Armenia. As for the hanging gardens, which popular rumour and guides to Babylon attributed to Semiramis, Diodorus describes them at length but states that they were the work of a 'Syrian' king who came after this queen. According to Berosus – a Babylonian priest who, in the early third century BC, wrote a history of his country in Greek – they were built by Nebuchadnezzar to please his wife Amytis, originally a Mede, thus reminding her of her mountainous country.

When Babylon had been built, Semiramis set off to visit her empire, leaving remarkable works everywhere along the way that would forever bear her name. She began with Media, the western and mountainous part of Iran. In Bagistan she founded a park (in Greek *paradeisos*, from which we have derived the word 'paradise') and had an inscription carved 'in Syrian characters' at the very top of the immense vertical rock that dominated the town. At Khaun, it was another park, around a pleasure palace where she stayed for a long time, leading the dissolute life that Diodorus sums up in a few words: 'She never wanted to remarry legally, fearing that she would be deprived of her sovereignty; but she chose the handsomest men in her army and, having granted them her favours, caused them to disappear.'

Continuing her route towards Ecbatana, she reached the foot of a great mountain, the Zagros (Zarkaios), 'full of gulfs and precipices', which necessitated a long detour. In haste to arrive, she had the rocks levelled and the precipices filled in to form a fine direct road. At Ecbatan a itself, she created a royal residence and made a water supply to the town by having a canal pierced under Mount Orontes (Alvand) which separated it from a great lake.

From Media the queen went on to Persia and 'travelled through all the other lands she possessed in Asia', opening mountain roads everywhere, setting up her camps on artificial knolls and dotting the plains with hills which are either the vestiges of towns she founded or the tombs of her dead generals. Then she made an about-turn and went westward. There she was in Egypt, visiting Amun's temple in the oasis of Siwah 'to question the oracle about when she was to die'. She subjected almost all Libya and pushed on as far as Ethiopia 'to examine its curiosities'.

We then find her at Bactra, the point of departure for the great campaign which she planned for India, a country that no one had yet conquered. She knew it would be a hard struggle, that she would have to cross the Indus and confront innumerable troops and the terrible elephants of her foe, Stabrobates, king of the Indians. So she took three years to make ready for the expedition with the utmost care, gathering three million footsoldiers, 500,000 cavalry, 100,000 chariots and the same number of camel drivers, having Phoenicians, Syrians and Cypriots brought to build a fleet of boats that could be dismantled. Better still, she would have false elephants secretly constructed, made of 300,000 black oxhides stuffed with straw and concealing the camels that would move them. When all was ready, she unleashed her offensive. Beaten in a naval battle, the Indians withdrew to the eastern bank of the Indus, pursued by the Assyrians, then they counter-attacked, using real pachyderms. During an atrocious free-for-all, Semiramis's troops were decimated. Wounded by Stabrobates with an arrow in the arm and a light javelin wound in the back, she took flight and returned to Nineveh.

That was the end of the 'sovereign of all Asia, except India'. Some time after this defeat, her son Ninyas plotted against her, as Amun's oracle at Siwah had predicted he would. All the more tired of fighting because she was now aged sixty-two, Semiramis yielded the sceptre to him and disappeared mysteriously. 'Some mythologists', adds Diodorus, without lending it too much credence, 'recount that she was changed into a dove and flew off with several of those birds which had settled on her home.'

As for Ninyas, he reigned in peace in the heart of his harem, 'in idleness and the never-ending enjoyment of the voluptuous pleasures of life'. His successors would do likewise for 'thirty generations' until the reign of Sardanapalus, the 'king under whom the Assyrian empire fell into the hands of the Medes, after enduring for over 1360 years'.

Anatomy of a Legend

Diodorus did not invent the story above; for a very large part of it he drew on Ctesias, whom he quotes on several occasions. This Ctesias was a Greek doctor, a native of Cnidus in Caria (south-west Asia Minor), who emigrated to Persia around 415 BC and practised his profession at the court of Artaxerxes II. In 397 BC, he returned to his native town and composed several works, including a history of India (*Indica*) and one of Persia (*Persica*). The latter dwelt at length on Assyria and enjoyed such success that it was used as a framework for many Greek and Latin authors until the second century AD. Unfortunately, the writings of Ctesias are lost; we know them only through quotations and the condensed version of them given in the ninth century by Photius, patriarch of Byzantium, in the great work *Bibliotheca*.

In the view of the ancients, Ctesias had two qualities: a style judged by Photius to be 'full of charm' and an overflowing imagination which made him prefer 'stories' to history. Although he claimed to have used the royal archives of the Achemenid dynasty to write his *Persica*, he seems to have delved chiefly into oriental popular tradition, from which he probably drew the story of Semiramis. In any case, several versions of this legend existed. One, taken up by Diodorus in an appendix to his account, made Semiramis a beautiful courtesan whose charms enabled her to wed 'a king of the Assyrians'. On a whim, she asked him to hand over the throne to her for five days, and the unfortunate man agreed. The first day was spent in festivities but on the following day she had him thrown into prison, seized the empire and 'reigning until her old age, accomplished many great things'.

Thus reduced to its broad outlines, the legend of Semiramis, gathered by Ctesias and passed on by Diodorus, is rather disappointing. It contains no 'suspense', no deep ideas, no moral lessons, no spicy details, and cuts a poor figure beside the epic of Gilgamesh or the adventures of Ulysses. Anything wonderful or irrational is encountered only at the start or the finish, and belongs to the old fund of legends common to the Orient and Greece. The daughter of a goddess, our heroine is semi-divine, but how many monarchs, from the ancient Egyptian or Sumerian kings to the Roman emperors, claimed to be descended from gods or were proclaimed divine! No less commonplace is the theme of the abandoned child who becomes a king or a hero, which applied to Sargon of Akkad, Moses, Cyrus, Oedipus, Perseus, Romulus and several other famous personages. As for her final disappearance, whether or not accompanied by a flight to heaven or a metamorphosis, it abounds in all mythologies.

In fact, the exploits of Semiramis, which form the main body of the tale – wars, conquests, the founding of towns, palaces, parks and hydraulic operations – remain on the human plane; to various degrees they are the royal work of all times and all countries, and it is known that the Assyrians were particularly outstanding in both military activities and engineering. Moreover, these exploits have very real locations as their backdrop, towns that still exist, such as Ecbatana (Hamadan); or dead but explored, such as Bactra (today Balkh), Nineveh and Babylon. Here the fantastic element lies in the number of soldiers or workmen, the boldness or originality of the works undertaken and, still more, in the size of the monuments and *objets d'art*. So the 'terrace' raised by Semiramis on Ninus's tomb was probably the *ziggurat* (storeyed tower) of Assur, the old capital where the majority of the kings of Assyria were buried; its imposing mass towered over the city, which itself was built on a cliff, and could be seen from a great distance, but obviously could not reach the nine stadia (1700 metres) attributed to it by Ctesias.

Similarly, Bagistan is the old name for Behistun; its rock which, in the legend, bears an inscription by the queen and dominates the plain from its seventeen stadia (2850 metres) certainly exists, but is only 166 metres high, and the inscription is by the Persian king Darius. Although an enclosing wall of 17 (and not 70) kilometres was found at Babylon, as well as the remains of a bridge, quays and several palaces, not one of the latter was round and 12 kilometres in circumference. And the mind boggles at those 24–30 ton gold statues which adorned the temple of Belus (Marduk). The ancient Greeks seem to have had a taste for impressive numbers. For their 'historians', the distant East, both admired and feared, could not fail to be a land of wonders.

The author of these Herculean labours was an exceptional, but not superhuman, being. She was a very beautiful and desirable woman, sensual and cruel, since she sacrificed her one-night-stand lovers, but at the same time she was extremely intelligent, energetic, indefatigable and courageous, outstripping her royal spouse in ambition and abilities as a strategist. In short, a superwoman doubled with a superman, a person whose strongly androgynous aspect is emphasised by the garment she wore and the contrast between this virile queen and her son and successor, Ninyas, who was soft, sensual and cowardly. We shall return to these aspects of our heroine later.

Can we extract from the legend any information about the period when Semiramis is supposed to have lived? At first glance, two of the four sovereigns mentioned – her husband and son – are fictitious, for no king of Assyria exists whose name even remotely resembles Ninus or Ninyas, and it is most likely that the two names are derived from Ninua, the Assyrian name for Nineveh, and symbolise that town. Stabrobates has the appearance of an Indian name transcribed into Greek, but this king can be found in no other text. Moreover, Semiramis's campaign in India is too much like that of Alexander (327–325 BC) not to be a later addition of the Hellenistic era, intended to embellish a story already known to Herodotus (died c. 420 BC) and recounted by Ctesias in 370 BC. Besides, Megasthenes, a Greek ambassador to India shortly after the time of Alexander – quoted by the geographer Strabo and the historian Arrian – states that Semiramis died before attempting the conquest of India. There remains Sardanapalus, otherwise known as Assurbanipal (668–627 BC), who was a real person; but the thirty generations (or about 1000 years) which in the legend separate this king from Ninyas are not reconcilable with two historical highlights: Assyria's domination over Egypt, which began under Asarhaddon (680–669 BC) and ended with Assurbanipal, and its seizure of Ascalon, dated 734. Finally, let me point out the flagrant anachronism of the foundation by an Assyrian queen of a Babylon which, by the evidence, was the one constructed by Nabopolassar but especially by Nebuchadnezzar after the collapse of the Assyrian empire between 612 and 609 BC.

It is evident that these calculations reach no precise conclusion, but the general context suggests that Semiramis should be placed in the period known as 'neo-Assyrian', namely, between the beginning of the ninth and the end of the seventh century BC. During those three centuries did Assyria have a queen who could have served as a model for this legendary woman? That was how the question was put when, in 1843, archaeological excavations began in Assyria. Would the inscriptions of the Assyrians themselves provide the elements of a solution?

Sammuramat, the Lady of the Palace

In 1853, Hormuzd Rassam, assistant to Henry Layard who was leading the British excavations of Nimrud (the former Kalhu), brought to light two statues of minor gods situated at the entrance of the Ezida, the temple of the great god Nabû. One of these statues bore an inscription saying that a certain Bêl-tarsi-iluma, governor of Kalhu, was dedicating it to Nabû 'for the life of Adad-nirâri, king of Assyria, his master, and for the life of Sammuramat, the lady of the palace, his mistress', as well as for his own life. The statues were sent to the British Museum and a copy of the inscription was published in 1860.

Though the name Adad-nirâri was already known from other inscriptions, Sammuramat was new and curiously brought Semiramis to mind. The title 'lady of the palace', encountered for the first time, greatly intrigued the Assyriologists, but in the end they admitted that it was the equivalent of 'royal spouse' or 'queen'. Thus, after so many centuries, Semiramis, queen of Assyria, had finally been rediscovered under her true name! This sensational news item revived interest in an ancient legend that was beginning to go out of fashion. A French scholar, François Lenormant, devoted a book to her, which was published in 1873.

We have to believe that the Assyrio-Babylonian god Nabû, protector of literature and sciences, must have had a finger in the pie, since Sammuramat emerged again, almost miraculously, some fifty years later. In 1909, the German Walter Andrae, excavating at the ancient city of Assur, discovered – on a narrow esplanade separating the two enclosing walls of the town – two rows of stelae inscribed and planted in the soil; some bore the names of high-ranking dignitaries, others those of several kings of

Assyria and two queens – Ashur-sharrat, 'lady of the palace' of Assurbanipal, and . . . Sammuramat. This time it was 'Semiramis' herself speaking and setting out her identity: 'Stele of Sammuramat, lady of the palace of Shamshi-Adad, king of the Universe, king of Assyria, mother of Adad-nirâri, king of the Universe, king of Assyria, daughter-in-law of Salmanasar, king of the Four Regions [of the World].'

Sammuramat had therefore been finally 'pinned down' in the time scale: she was the wife of Shamshi-Adad V (823–811 BC), son of Salmanasar III (858–824 BC), and the mother (not the wife, as the first inscription had suggested) of Adad-nirâri III, who reigned from 810 to 783 BC. The presence of her stele (funerary? commemorative?) in this place, and the relative length of the inscription put Sammuramat on the same level, if not higher, as the wife of Assurbanipal, the supreme master of the great Assyrian empire in the seventh century BC. One difficulty remained, however; Semiramis had reigned alone for a long time, whereas there was no chronological hiatus between the reign of Sammuramat's husband and that of her son.

The Assur stelae were published in 1919, but as early as 1916 another text had appeared, coming from a place called Sabaa, in the desert, west of Mosul. It was again a stele, but isolated and of classical type; one of those royal inscriptions like so many that Assyria has yielded, in which kings describe their wars or their building works. The stele of Sabaa, dedicated by Adad-nirâri III to the god Adad, recounted a campaign in Syria. Now, after the customary introduction (the sovereign's genealogy and self-praise), the account of the campaign began like this: 'In the fifth year of my reign, when I was seated on the royal throne in all my grandeur, I mobilised [the troops of] my country'.

Given that the kings of Assyria used the phrase 'when I was seated on the royal throne' only for a campaign in the first year of their reign and omitted it for those of following years, it was deduced that although Adad-nirâri had succeeded his father officially in 810 BC, he had not reigned in fact until five years later, probably because he had still been too young when Shamshi-Adad died. During the first four years, Sammuramat would have been regent and had the power in her hands, just like Semiramis. This would be the only known instance of a queen of Assyria who had, for some time, become the absolute mistress of the kingdom, an example so striking that it had been written into Mesopotamian annals. Indeed, in his *Babyloniaca*, written in Greek but based on genuine local archives, the Babylonian priest Berosus interrupts the list of the kings of Babylon to cite 'the government of Semiramis in Assyria'. Better still, he places this queen after the ninth king of the twelfth Babylonian dynasty, and as the reign of that obscure king began in 812 BC and was very short, this perfectly matches the regency of Sammuramat (810–807 BC).

Although certain modern Assyriologists have expressed doubts about that regency, the theory is still seductive. If we reject it, we know nothing about Sammuramat except that she lived during at least part of the seven years of civil war that preceded and followed the death of Salmanasar III and drenched Assyria in blood. On the other hand, if we accept it and refer to the 'Canon of Eponyms'[2] for the first four years of the reign of Adad-nirâri III, it appears that the regent ordered – if not led – four military expeditions, including one against the Medes, which, as we shall see, is not without interest.

[2] As a method of dating, the Assyrians gave each year of each reign the name of an important person: first the king, then the top dignitaries of the kingdom. This was the system of eponyms; the whole of the lists established on this basis is called the 'Canon of Eponyms' or the limmus lists (*limmus* was the Assyrian word for this honorific office). In the neo-Assyrian period, these lists also indicated the most outstanding event of the year, usually a military campaign against another country.

As for the origins of Sammuramat, they remain unknown. Using onomastics and toponymy as a basis, the German philologist Wilhelm Eilers thought she might be a native of the mountainous regions that border Assyria on the north and east, more precisely, Armenia, then called Urartu. It is possible, but more direct proof would be preferable.

Naqîa–Zakûtu, the Pure

Almost universally accepted today, the equation Semiramis = Sammuramat is not altogether satisfactory, for it leaves certain aspects of the legend unexplained, notably Ninus, Ninyas and the claimed foundation of Babylon. Having founded Nineveh, Ninus must have resided there, and Diodorus describes him as a very powerful ruler, master of all the Near East, including Babylonia and Egypt. It has been established that Shamshi-Adad V lived at Kalhu (Nimrud), that he had a difficult reign, troubled by civil war, that he governed a kingdom of modest size and made no major conquests. Quite the opposite of Ninyas, Adad-nirâri III was an energetic and daring king who made war victoriously in Syria, Babylonia and Media, and there is nothing to suggest that he conspired against his mother. Egypt in that period was divided but independent. As for Babylon, it is not very likely that Sammuramat ever set foot there, and neither she nor her husband or son had the slightest work carried out there. Did that part of the legend come from the imagination of Ctesias or other Greek authors, or does it rest on events that were real but belonged to another period of Assyrian history?

In an article published in 1952, the American Assyriologist Hildegarde Lewy tried to answer the question by taking Herodotus, instead of Diodorus, as her point of departure. Describing Babylonia and Assyria, the 'father of history' speaks of two great queens: Semiramis and, five generations later, Nitocris. Of the first, he says only that she had immense earth levees built near Babylon against floods, and gave her name to one of the town gates. In contrast, he devotes a long passage to Nitocris, ascribing to her huge works intended, on the one hand, to dry out the region of Babylon by creating an immense basin, on the other, to divert the Euphrates while a bridge was built to link the two halves of the town.

Most historians regarded 'Nitocris' as a deformation of 'Nebuchadnezzar', but Hildegarde Lewy saw no reason to turn that queen into a man, and preferred to see Nitocris as the queen Zakûtu, wife of Sennacherib, king of Assyria (704–681 BC), and mother of Asarhaddon (680–669 BC), on the basis of a series of arguments:

1. Zakûtu's real name was Naqîa, a west-Semitic epithet meaning 'the Pure' and corresponding to the Assyrian Zakûtu. Naqîa–Zakûtu thus probably originated from the western, Mediterranean, part of the Near East, just like Semiramis.
2. At the time when Sennacherib – son of the great Sargon – reigned, Assyria was in the throes of expansion. Babylonia came into its sphere of influence and he ruled it himself for a short while. He undertook the invasion of Egypt, but an epidemic decimated his army and he had to backtrack. It was his son who conquered that country.
3. In the same way that his father, Sargon, had founded a new town (Dûr-Sharrukîn, present-day Khorsabad) in order to reside there, Sennacherib turned Nineveh, hitherto a secondary town, into the capital of Assyria, enlarging and embellishing it to the point where he could have been considered its 'founder'.
4. In 689 BC, exasperated by the incessant rebellions of the Babylonians, Sennacherib seized Babylon, and had it

razed and flooded. Eight years later, he was assassinated by one of his sons, born of a first wife, who was furious that he had chosen as his heir Asarhaddon, his youngest son, born of Naqîa-Zakûtu, whom he loved dearly. Asarhaddon had Babylon rebuilt. Certain texts suggest that he gave his mother the task of overseeing all these works, and it would seem that she exercised a kind of regency over the Mesopotamian south. In some way, she 'founded' Babylon again.

5. A capable woman, Naqîa–Zakûtu had a very great influence on her son, and took part indirectly in the government of the Assyrian empire. When Asarhaddon divided the patrimony between his two sons – Assyria for Assurbanipal, and Babylonia for Shamash-shuma-ukîn, the former having precedence over the latter – she intervened personally and made the Assyrians swear an oath of loyalty to Assurbanipal. Soon, however, Shamash-shuma-ukîn plotted against his brother, then openly rebelled, thus being a traitor to his mother, whether she was alive or dead at that time.[3]
6. Lastly, between Shamshi-Adad V and Sennacherib we find the five generations which, according to Herodotus, separated Semiramis from Nitocris.

From her studies, Hildegarde Lewy concluded that the legend of Semiramis is an amalgam of traditions concerning two historic queens: Sammuramat–Semiramis, the warrior queen, and Naqîa-Zakûtu *alias* Nitocris, the foundress of Babylon. On the whole, the arguments she presents are impressive and seem to be convincing.

Another interpretation of the legend exists, which is in no way incompatible with the first two, but which imparts quite a different dimension. Although behaving like a

[3] To the objection that Shamash-shuma-ukîn was the grandson and not the son of Naqîa–Zakûtu, the answer is that Diodorus translated as 'son' a Semitic word that may mean either (H. Lewy).

human being, Semiramis may be the personification of the greatest female deity in the Assyrian pantheon: Ishtar of Nineveh.

Ishtar was fundamentally the goddess of love, especially carnal love. Linked, of course, with reproduction in her role of inspirer and partner of man in the sexual act, she was clearly distinct from the mother-goddess, the progenitress, whom she would eventually supplant. She was the supreme Woman, beautiful, desirable, 'with a fondness for sensual pleasures and delights, full of seduction, charm and voluptuousness', as a lovely hymn says, but also changeable, treacherous and subject to violent rages. She had no real husband, but lovers; demi-gods like Dumuzi-Tammuz, or mere mortals, whom she soon scorned and rejected, sending them to the Netherworld or changing them into repulsive animals. Pictured naked, supporting her breasts with her hands, she was surrounded by hierodules (sacred prostitutes) who bore her name (*ishtarîtu*). The vicinity of her temples, where licentious rites were performed, was the haunt of courtesans.

Semiramis, Median Legend?

But Ishtar had another aspect, apparently in radical opposition: she was the goddess of war, 'the valiant one', 'the lady of battle and combat', who marched at the head of armies, flew 'like a swallow' over the mêlée, led the king who had been able to gain her favour in the attack and protected him. Noticeable in the land of Sumer as early as the third millennium, this eminently masculine aspect of the goddess was chiefly developed by the Semites of the Mesopotamian north, notably the Assyrians, doubtless because they were themselves great warriors. This battling Ishtar was nicknamed 'the Assyrian woman' (*ashshurîtu*), and was generally portrayed standing upright on a lion or lioness, holding a bow in her hand or brandishing the curved-bladed dagger, the 'harpè', the weapon of kings. Two very famous sanctuaries of Ishtar existed in Assyria: at Arbela and Nineveh.

The resemblance between this goddess and our androgynous Semiramis springs immediately to mind, but other arguments come to the support of the theory that Semiramis also represented a goddess. Thus, by marrying Semiramis, Ninus closely connected Ishtar with Nineveh; while the 'gate of Semiramis' at Babylon, which Herodotus mentions, can only be the famous gate of Ishtar – with its friezes of enamelled bricks with alternating dragons (the attributes of Marduk, the great god of the Babylonians) and bulls (attributes of Adad, god of the storm and also of war) – which is preceded by the processional route with friezes of lions, attributes of the goddess. Describing one of the town's two palaces, Diodorus speaks of a hunting scene where Semiramis is pictured on horseback, hurling a javelin at a leopard, beside Ninus spearing a lion; unknown in Babylon, hunting scenes were typically Assyrian, but never show a queen, and an Ishtar of Nineveh would be more probable in this context. We must not forget that the goddess of Ascalon, Derceto, the mother of Semiramis, is only a local variant of Atargatis or Astarte – names by which in the Graeco-Roman period, in Phoenicia as in Syria-Palestine, Ishtar was worshipped, or west-Semitic goddesses very close to her, such as Athar or Anat.

For Wilhelm Eilers, who saw the warrior Ishtar as a divinity of the mountains (Taurus and Zagros), Semiramis was situated at the confluence of two currents of mythical tradition, one secular (heroes and heroines, in this instance Sammuramat), the other religious (gods and goddesses, in this instance Ishtar). She represented an archetype joined, in race memory, by those celebrated and historic women –

such as the queen of Sheba, Judith and Salome, Cleopatra and Zenobia, queen of Palmyra – to be found later, notably in Iran, in the story of Khosroes and Shirin[4] and the Scheherazade of the *Thousand and One Nights*, and also in Armenia, where a legendary sovereign was actually called Samira or Samiran, not to mention the numerous ancient sites and ruins which, to this day, have names which are very like 'Semiramis'.

However satisfying it may be to liken Semiramis to Sammuramat, Naqîa–Zakûtu and Ishtar, many questions still remain open. Some will probably never find an answer, since the account of Ctesias itself is lost, and other slightly differing versions are known only from scraps scattered throughout Graeco-Latin literature. Others, in contrast, can give rise to theories that I shall mention briefly.

Where and when was the legend of Semiramis born? Like Wilhelm Eilers, but for other reasons, I think that Ctesias drew it from Iranian, and not Babylonian, tradition. First of all, this author lived for seventeen years in Persia, and stayed only a few weeks in Babylon. Secondly, it is noteworthy that the majority of Semiramis's constructions were situated not in Assyria but in Iran and that, outside Babylon, the only towns she founded on the banks of the Tigris and Euphrates were used as depots for 'goods coming from Media, Paretacenia and neighbouring countries'. Lastly, the most striking event of Sammuramat's regency was her campaign against the Medes, which is well attested by the Canon of Eponyms.

In the late ninth century BC the Medes and their 'cousins' the Persians had not long been settled in the north-west of Iran – south of Lake Urmiah, at Assyria's gates – and were

[4] This was a romantic epic written by the Persian poet Nizâmi (twelfth century), recounting the loves of the Sassanid king Khosroes II Parviz (590–628) and the Christian woman Shirin ('the Gentle') whom he married. She exerted a great influence in Persia, and her name, like that of Semiramis, is still connected with many castles and works of art.

beginning to cause the Assyrians grave concern. Towards the end of his reign, Salmanasar III had crossed this region twice and received tribute from the 'kings of the Persians' (Parsua), but the first military expedition against the Medes took place in 810, the same year in which Sammuramat became regent, starting a fight which Adad-nirâri pursued vigorously, since he led no fewer than seven campaigns against this people. The first Mesopotamian adversary of the Medes (and, indirectly, of the Persians, their heirs) was therefore a woman, which cannot have failed to surprise and impress them. Whether or not she was at the head of her troops, how tempting it is to liken Sammuramat to a warring Ishtar, of Arbela or Nineveh!

The embryo of the legend had been formed, but probably did not develop until later. If I had to give an approximate date, I would say under the first Achemenids, for the empire of Ninus – as described by Diodorus, following Ctesias – is in reality that of Darius. The Assyrians never conquered Asia Minor as far as the Aegean; they never thrust as far as Afghanistan, and they only partly conquered Egypt and for a short time. Now, in the time of Darius, Assyria no longer existed, whereas Babylon was the second city in the Persian empire, but there was a vague memory that a couple of centuries earlier, a queen of Assyrian origin had ruled Babylon for some years and reconstructed that great city. It is therefore not surprising that a Persian storyteller merged the two women, Sammuramat and Naqîa–Zakûtu.

That She-Devil

Why did Ctesias expand the story of Semiramis while the rest of his *Persica* – if we are to judge by the condensed version of Photius – seems to have been much more matter-of-fact? There are several possible explanations, but I was struck by the fact that this author was staying in Persia at the time when that country was shaken by a violent dynastic crisis: the rebellion of Cyrus the Younger against his brother Artaxerxes II. The Achemenid court, frequented daily by Ctesias, then seemed like a nest of vipers and he must have had a close view of the woman at the centre of it – the queen Parysatis, the real mistress of the kingdom and the instigator of many murders accompanied by torture. He must also have known Roxane, the half-sister and mistress of another brother of Artaxerxes, depicted as 'semi-masculine' and whom Parysatis had killed. In those conditions, it can hardly be wondered at if he was especially interested in a queen of Assyria, of whom a distressing example and coarse and bloody caricature was before his very eyes.

One may equally wonder about the reasons why this legend enjoyed such success in the Graeco-Oriental, and then Roman, world. The talent of Ctesias and the fact that his work appeared at the beginning of the fourth century BC – an era when an extraordinary renewal of interest in women in general manifested itself in Greece, when they had hitherto been confined to the gynacaeum in Athens and treated as breeders of warriors in Sparta – probably had a lot to do with it, but here the Hellenists have the floor. This story has already taken us a long way, perhaps too far, into the realms of imagination. My only excuse is that the more one pores over this she-devil of a Semiramis, the more fascinating she becomes.

CHAPTER 10

Magic and Medicine

Jean Bottéro

Every civilisation and every era has its share of the rational and irrational. If there is an area where this choice is most apparent it is probably in the struggle against evil; because evil is not only vexing, but absurd, and 'Euclid's geometry' has never succeeded in explaining it or logic managed to dispel it. Ancient Mesopotamia has left us an astonishing example of this paradox in the form of its medicine – its organised battle against physical evil, illness.

Virtually unknown to non-Assyriologists, we have been left a considerable dossier, from the early third millennium right up to the disappearance of that ancient culture, shortly before the Christian era began; it consists of several thousand quite copious technical documents, fairly well spared by the ravages of time, and an impressive accumulation of allusive data, drawn from all sections of literature. But we shall understand almost nothing about it unless we realise that these people had, in fact, constructed two techniques, vastly different in both inspiration and application, but with the same therapeutic intent – a medicine for doctors and a medicine for 'magi'.

In every culture people very soon learned to fight physical ills with the means to hand; this was empirical medicine, and was known in Mesopotamia as early as the first half of the third millennium, shortly after the beginnings of writing, and first of all by its specialist, its technician – the doctor, in Akkadian *asû*, a word whose root meaning we do not know.

Coughs, Fevers and Headaches

Trained either by a master, himself a practitioner, or in some famous school, such as 'the Faculty of the town of Isin', doctors are to be found nearly everywhere in the texts. If we are to believe a rather satirical tale, the 'classiest' ones adopted a special appearance: shaven heads, pompous, stiff and starchy, 'showing off their instrument case', and gawping onlookers would say 'He's very powerful!' Sometimes they specialised; an 'eye doctor' is known, and there is even evidence of a few rare 'women doctors'.

The *asû* made use first and foremost of 'remedies' (*bultu*: lit., 'which-restore-life'), drawn from all natural sources, but mostly plants, hence their generic title of 'simples' (*shammû*). These were used fresh or dried, whole or powdered, most frequently mixed to increase their effects. This was also the case with various mineral products, salts and stones, and animals – blood, flesh, bones, excreta . . . Interminable catalogues of these drugs were drawn up, sometimes accompanied by useful data for identifying them, together with a mention of their specific use. Doctors administered them after dealing with the preparation themselves – there were no apothecaries – in a variety of forms: after soaking or decoction in various liquids, in potions, lotions, ointments, poultices, packs, pills, suppositories, enemas and tampons or swabs. They had also perfected gestures and manipulations – with their bare hands or with the help of various instruments – suitable for direct application to the afflicted parts: fumigations, bandages, massages, palpations and various operations. In the code of Hammurabi, the doctor is seen reducing fractures and using a 'lancet' to make incisions even in the vicinity of the eyes.

In keeping with the spirit of a country that had long been bound by written tradition, these methods, prescriptions and treatments were recorded in veritable 'treatises' that were fairly extensive and quite specialised: against 'the cough', 'the fever', 'headaches', 'afflictions of the eyes' or 'of the teeth', internal ailments and so on. In these the various ills studied were named and described, with formulas allocated to each; they were sometimes numerous, and it was up to the practitioner to make his own choice.

To give a better picture of this medical practice, here is a letter written in 670 BC to the Assyrian king Asarhaddon (680–669) by a doctor whom he often consulted, named Urad-Nanâ:

> Good health! May my lord the King enjoy excellent health! And may the healing gods Ninurta and Gula grant him wellbeing in his heart and body! My lord the King continually asks me why I have neither made a diagnosis of the illness from which he suffers, nor yet prepared the appropriate remedies. (Let it be said in passing that Asarhaddon seems to have been a very sick man. After analysing his copious pathologial file, an Assyriologist has even advanced the theory, perhaps with a certain medical naivety, that he must have suffered – and died – from disseminated erythematous lupus. . . .) It is true that, speaking earlier to the King's person, I had admitted that I was unable to identify the nature of his illness. But now I send the King this sealed letter, so that by reading it he may be informed. And if it please my lord the King, he may even have recourse to the Haruspex [for confirmation]. The king must therefore use the enclosed lotion; after which the fever from which he is

> now suffering will leave him. I had already prepared this remedy two or three times, with an oil base; the King will doubtless recognise it. Its application may be postponed until tomorrow if such is the King's wish. It is bound to get rid of the illness. On the other hand, when the King is presented with the said lotion with *sillibânu* [dried liquorice root?], it may be applied, as it has been once or twice already, in a closed room [?]. The King must then sweat, which is why I have added, in a separate package, these little amulet-pouches; the King will keep them hung around his neck. I also enclose the ointment with which the King may rub himself, in case of an attack.

It is plain that the doctor was acting by himself and directly on the patient, using drugs which he had chosen, prepared and mixed, all this after trying to 'identify the nature of the illness', in other words, to diagnose it by examining its symptoms – here, among others, the fever and whatever the king might have revealed about his feelings of malaise. It is true that the professional man may hesitate, even declare himself inexpert; but when he has made his decision, he is so sure of himself that, as a counter-check, he spontaneously proposes an oracular consultation by examination of the entrails of a sacrificial victim – a technique of 'deductive divination' then in common use and held to be 'scientific' and infallible. For some obscure reason, Urad-Nanâ does not think it necessary to specify the name of the illness or explain its nature to his august patient. He is content with the essentials: 'the prescription', we would say, after he himself had prepared the specific. It has an oil base, but also other 'simples', in particular *sillibânu*. More precisely, it is a lotion to be applied as soon as received or, if the king prefers, the next day. It should act immediately, following a natural process, releasing a heavy sweat that will cause his temperature to drop. In addition, Urad-

Nanâ sends some 'amulet-pouches' (more about this later), and an ointment he has made up in case there is an acute attack of the ailment. Here we have 'professional' language and behaviour – the rudiments of our own medicine.

The Exorcist

The other form of treatment, that of the 'magi', was deeply rooted in a system of thinking that is far removed from our own, so a few introductory explanations may be useful.

In the view of Mesopotamians, physical ills and maladies were only one of the manifestations of that omnipresent parasite on our existence that we would call 'suffering'; everything that thwarts our legitimate desire for happiness. How can we give it a reason, in order to be able to cope with it more successfully? Where do these ailments of the body, and also of the mind and heart, come from, with their pains, sorrows, hardships and misfortunes, cutting across our life, casting a shadow over it or rudely interrupting it 'before time'? To these questions, which are as old as man himself, every culture has worked out replies, adjusted to its own parameters.

In their search for causes, even if neither immediate nor obvious, Sumerians and Babylonians did not have our conceptual logic, with the entire arsenal of strict analysis and deduction of ideas that we can call upon. To start with, they had hardly any other expedient than to resort to invention, but a 'directed', 'calculated' invention: the construction, in their fancy, of imaginary persons or events – linked, however, both to the agents invoked and the disposition of the happenings to be explained – which were presented as their effects or results. That is what we call myth.

To make sense of both the world and their own existence, they had therefore postulated a supernatural society of 'gods', conceived in their own image but to a superlative degree; infinitely stronger, wiser and endowed with endless life. These beings, leading a happy-go-lucky, idle and carefree life, yet wanting to obtain an abundance of all that was useful and agreeable, had created men to work for them as labourers, producers and servants, and had control over them as long as they lived. It would have been unreasonable to impute to these 'boss'-gods the ills that assailed their servants, repressing both their zeal and their capacity for productivity. To explain 'suffering', another set of beings had been concocted, inferior, it is true, to the creators and sovereigns of the Universe, but superior to their victims, and freely able to provoke the misfortunes likely to poison the latter's existence. They were what we would call 'demons'.

In the early days, it would appear that their attacks were regarded as spontaneous and motiveless, rather like those of aggressive little lap-dogs which suddenly leap at you and bite you. As their assaults were incessant and spared no one, it had been necessary to perfect a real technique to counter them, in other words, a collection of traditional procedures considered to be effective against the distress they caused; illnesses as much as other misfortunes. The procedures in question were taken from the two great areas of man's ability to act on other beings: manipulation and words. It was enough to know how to command in order to be obeyed; and elements, instruments and forces could be found everywhere that could be used to transform things; water to clean or drown them, fire to purify or annihilate them; and many other products to keep them at a distance, alter them, dissolve them. Besides, there were constants, 'laws' to which they could be subjected: the law by which like attracted like, or opposites repelled, or 'contact' which allowed the same phenomenon to pass from one subject to another . . .

Supernatural Forces

Just as much as in the various areas of technique, including empirical medicine, a number of 'recipes' were worked out that were suitable – or so it was imagined – to drive out the 'demons' and defend oneself against their attacks, and to ward off the ills with which they had inoculated their whipping-boys. It is for this level of the battle against evil, in which the capricious activity of 'supernatural forces' was directly countered by the effective actions or words of their victims, that 'magic' should be reserved, for it is a word which, like so many other terms, is too often used quite wildly.

There is scarcely any evidence of magic *per se*, however, in our enormous dossier: at a time which we do not possess the means to determine – at the latest, it would seem, early in the third millennium – it had been overtaken by another attitude, firmly religious and 'theocentric'. On the one hand, and perhaps in keeping with the movement of devoutness that produced an initial systemisation of the pantheon in the country, the empire of the gods was extended over the entire Universe; and at once, losing their first freedom of movement, the 'demons' came under their thumb. On the other hand, by analogy with the sovereigns of this world, those in the heavens were credited with responsibility for all the obligations and prohibitions that constrain mankind: religious, social, administrative, juridical and political. Every breach of whatever norm – immemorial 'bans'; customary imperatives; implicit instructions of the law, or explicit instructions of the authorities – became *ipso facto* an offence against the rule of the gods, a 'misdeed' against them, a 'sin'. And as sovereigns punish anything that defies their authority, it was now up to the gods to suppress such unruliness with suitable punishments. These punishments were the ills and misfortunes of life, no longer inflicted by 'demons', on a whim, as in the 'magical' view of things, but henceforward on the orders of the gods. Thus 'suffering' in general and illness in particular, incorporated in the religious system of the Universe, had found their justification, explanation and ultimate *raison d'être* – but also their antidote. For the technique against 'evil forces' had been preserved, materially unchanged, from the earlier magic; still composed of the same words and gestures – oral and manual rites, formerly supposed to act immediately on those hostile 'demons', but now incorporated into sacred worship, of which they formed the 'sacramental' part, let us say. By means of ceremonies – sometimes attaining the dimension of solemn liturgies and of which a surprising number of rituals remain – the sovereigns of the world were implored to command the 'demons' and maleficent forces not to come near the supplicants, or to retreat, taking away the ills with which they had overwhelmed them. That was properly called exorcism.

Thus there were other means of combating illnesses; another medicine, not more specific but, so to speak, 'universal', because its aim was to get rid of the 'evil of suffering' as such. It was no longer based on empiricism, but on a true system of thinking that was mythological and in short 'theological', of reliance on the gods and recourse to their powers. Its specialist was no longer the *asû*, but quite a different person, a 'cleric' – the exorcist. In Akkadian he was called *âshipu*, rather like a 'conjurer' (of evils), or 'purifier' (of the misdeeds or blemishes deemed to have provoked the said evils).

If we want to watch the exorcist at work and in doing so perceive to what extent his behaviour towards an illness differed from that of the *asû*–doctor, here are extracts from an *ad hoc* guide, the instructions given to him for proceeding ritually to drive out a 'malady' – whose name (*dimîtu*) tells us nothing and which, besides, in the obscure classification of illnesses obtaining at that time, may well have represented a whole family of ailments rather than a single affliction.

1. Presentation of the illness and recall of its origins: 'the *dimîtu* came from Hell [. . .] and the demons that brought it, falling on the patient abandoned by his protector-god, whom he had offended, enveloped him in it as if in a cloak!'
2. Description of the wretched state in which the sick man finds himself, with the intent of making the gods take pity. 'His body is infected with it; his arms and legs are paralysed [. . .]; his chest is worn out with coughing; his mouth is full of phlegm; behold him, dumb, cast down and prostrate!'
3. The supernatural origin of the remedy: emphasised both to guarantee its efficacy and to suggest that, in its application, the officiant will act only in the name of the great divine masters of exorcism – Ea and Marduk. 'When Marduk had seen him in this state, he sought out his father Ea, described the invalid's condition and said to him, "I do not know what this man has done to be thus afflicted and I do not know how to heal him!" But Ea answered his son, "You know all! What could I teach you since you know as much as I do?" '
4. The treatment, in the form of instructions from Ea to Marduk, whose role the exorcist will play here. 'This is what you must do to cure him: "You must take seven small loaves made of coarse flour [?], and join them by means of a bronze fastener [?]. Then you must rub the man with them, and make him spit on the remains that fall from them, uttering over him a 'Formula from Eridu' [special prayer or conjuration, reputed for its effectiveness], [all] after taking him to the steppe, in an isolated place, at the foot of a wild acacia. Then you will pass on the malady that struck him [through the mass of bread

used to rub him and the crumbs that fell as a result] to Ninedinne [the patron-goddess of the steppe], so that Ninkilim, the patron-god of small wild rodents [which inhabit the same steppe], may cause these animals to take on his illness" [by giving them the edible remains of the bread to nibble].'

5. The oral rite, in the form of a final invocation: 'May the divine healer Gula, who is able to restore the dying to life, make him whole again by the touch of her hand! And you, compassionate Marduk, utter the formula that will free him from his trouble, so that he is completely out of danger!'

It was therefore not a matter of an approach left to the initiative of the operator, as in the case of Asarhaddon's doctor, but a veritable ritual, laid down beforehand and *ne varietur*, in which the exorcist has only to carry out the automatically effective ceremonial. Moreover, the *âshipu* effaces himself completely before the gods he represents. As we can see from the final address (5), they are the true healers! The sickness here is regarded as a material reality, brought from outside ('Hell') by 'demons', and deposited in the body of the sick man, who has found himself exposed and defenceless against such a danger by his god, whom he had offended and who had handed him over to the executors of his vengeance (1). To drive out this intrusive illness, the treatment (4–5) – the recipe for which is attributed to the supreme master of exorcism, Ea, the inventor of all techniques – must be applied, in the person of the exorcist, by Ea's son, the great Marduk (3). It is based on the 'law' of contact and transference; small loaves (which the little rodents of the steppe will unfailingly gobble up), in the 'sacred' number of seven and joined into a mass, are rubbed on the patient's body to 'absorb' his illness by means of this close contact. In keeping with another 'law' – just as fundamental in exorcism and according to which the repetition of words and actions strengthened their effectiveness – the sick man, by 'spitting' on the crumbs that fall during the rubbing and are carefully gathered up, also passes on to them the illness from which he is suffering. The operation is to be carried out away from inhabited areas, out in the steppe, so that the illness may be more surely isolated, not only from the patient but also from other people. It takes place near a shrub which grows only in the desert and to which – we do not know why – a 'purificatory' virtue is ascribed. There the bread (from then on the carrier of the sickness) is left and the small wild animals that will come to devour it, urged on by local deities, will thus make it pass into their own bodies, carrying away with them the 'illness' 'taken' from the patient. By this device the gods invoked at the end (5) are to 'heal' him.

We have a prodigious number of 'exorcisms' against all the ills and misfortunes that may befall human beings, in their situation, their heart, mind and body. It is the last two categories that are concerned with exorcistic therapy, but their immediate aim alone distinguishes them from the rest. All the procedures are built up on the same essential scheme; the only things that vary, adapted *toties quoties* to their particular goal and circumstances, are the manual rites and the content of the accompanying 'prayers', recourse to differing 'laws', and the 'drugs' used. As in medicine, they are borrowed from various natural orders, but far less diversified, because of the reduced number of their exploitable 'powers' (purification, expulsion, evacuation . . .). Unlike the medical 'remedies', they have only a 'mystical' and imaginary relationship with the evils they are supposed to drive out – for example, the wild acacia quoted above! For they are not by any means held to be specifics, intended to combat illnesses by virtue of their own properties, but only as back-up and reinforcement for the prayers addressed to the gods in order to persuade them to act.

In exorcistic medicine, only the gods took action; the exorcist merely implored them by means of a ritual that was traditional and reputed to be capable of influencing them more surely. Composed of fictions, myths and uncontrollable 'forces', it was a truly irrational therapy. In empirical medicine, the operator was the doctor–*asû* in person, who examined the patient and decided *hic et nunc* on the treatment to be applied, which he prepared with his own hands, choosing manipulations and 'simples' for their natural properties and to help slow down or stop the action or progress of the ailment. Causes and effects were thus proportioned, and of the same kind; it was a rational therapy.

The origins of both methods are lost in the mists of prehistory, but as by their constitution and spirit they are irreducible to each other, it would be ill-judged to insist at all costs that the first emerged from the second, or *vice versa*, or that this represents progress or a retrograde movement. In fact, they survived in company with each other throughout the long history of the country; from start to finish, exorcists and doctors may be seen striving side by side, often at the bedside of the same patients.

Let us take the sickly Asarhaddon, for example; we saw him place himself in the hands of his doctor, Urad-Nanâ, but at the same time he resorted to exorcists. We still have some thirty replies from one of them, Marduk-shâkin-shumi, in response to consultations with the king. Here is one, contemporary with Urad-Nanâ's letter, and apparently related to the same attack. The difference in tone and viewpoint is noticeable.

> Good health to my lord the King! And may the gods Nabû and Marduk bless him! My lord has informed me that he finds himself without any strength in his arms and legs, and is even unable to open his eyes, so poorly and downcast is

> he. It is the result of the fever, which clings to his body. But there is nothing seriously wrong; the gods Assur, Shamash, Nabû and Marduk will see to his recovery . . . his illness will leave him and all will be well! In truth, there is nothing to do but wait; and the King, with his entourage, will be able to eat anything he wishes!

Beyond this fine optimism, it must be understood that Marduk-shâkin-shumi would meanwhile have done what was necessary – rituals and exorcisms – to obtain the favour of the gods regarding his royal patient, without the latter and his circle running the risk of alienating them by breaking some food prohibition. So both doctor and exorcist were simultaneously treating the same illness and the same patient, each in his own way and using his own methods.

Two Therapies

It could happen that, if the treatment of one proved unfruitful, the other would be consulted. Here is what a medical treatise on the 'fever' suggests:

> If the patient has a pain in his temples that does not cease during the day, it is due to the intervention of a phantom [that is the cause]. When the exorcist has carried out his office [without effect, obviously] you [doctor] will massage the sick man with an unguent made up as follows: . . .

Naturally, the doctor had his failures too, as another tablet reveals: 'Despite the intervention of the doctor, there was a relapse!' And prescriptions were even provided to cope with a succession of fiascos: 'If the patient, possessed by a phantom, has not been relieved by the operations of either the exorcist or the doctor, here is a remedy to apply . . .' Such failures in no way shook people's confidence in these two therapies and their practitioners; the *asû* was fallible, like anyone else; he might hesitate – as we saw earlier in Urad-Nanâ's letter – or even make mistakes. As for exorcisms, the gods were at liberty to turn a deaf ear to the prayers addressed to them, and we know of rituals resorted to 'in cases where the gods have refused' to intervene on demand. For the sufferers, neither the coexistence nor the failures of the two therapies was shocking; they complemented each other, and excellent reasons could always be found to explain their shortcomings. That is why, without appreciable fundamental revolution or progress, empirical and exorcistic medicines were able to maintain themselves as long as the country's civilisation lasted.

With the passing of time, they rather 'contaminated' each other, so that we find exorcistic irrationality in medicine and medical rationality in the practices of the *âshipu*.

For instance, when, in order to strengthen the sudorific properties of his lotion, or perhaps to attenuate its over-violent effects, Urad-Nanâ (the doctor) sends his royal client Asarhaddon 'amulet-pouches to wear round his neck', he is behaving rather like one of our own practitioners who, as steeped in piety as his patient, might advise him to wear a miraculous medallion. These little pouches, known as *melû*, were in fact the concern of exorcists alone, who prepared them with ritually treated skins and enclosed in them, as 'back-up' for 'prayers' and devout manipulations, talismans that were supposed to ward off 'evil forces'.

Certain illnesses were commonly defined, not by proper names (*dimîtu*, *di'u* . . .) or kinds of description (such as 'suppurating wound'), but by resorting to the names of deities, demons or other maleficent supernatural agents who might have unleashed them. One was 'intervention' or 'seizure' 'of the god Shamash', 'of the god Sîn', 'of the goddess Ishtar', 'of a demon–*râbisu*' or 'of a phantom'. The exorcists, who were the originators of such fictional explanations of the patient's condition, must have taken them literally and doubtless took them into account when choosing the supernatural treatment to apply. Here and there, the doctors borrowed these denominations – as will have been noticed in the 'intervention of a phantom' mentioned earlier – but it is likely that in their view these were no more than descriptions of fairly well-defined morbid states or syndromes that would have spoken eloquently to them whereas to us they say nothing. For example, the 'intervention of a phantom' seems to have been the common definition of a pathological condition more concerned with what we would call 'nerves' or the 'state of mind' than the body's organism properly speaking.

Something worth pausing over for a moment is infection. In a letter written around 1780 BC, while on a journey Zimri-Lim – the king of Mari – warns his wife, who had stayed at home, in these words:

> I have heard that the Lady Nanna, although afflicted with a purulent skin ailment [lit., 'wound with discharge'], frequents the Palace and is in contact with many women. Strictly forbid anyone to sit in her chair or sleep in her bed. She must no longer mingle with all those women; for her illness is contagious [lit., 'is taken'].

And in a second letter (of which only scraps remain), the king – apparently speaking of the same unfortunate woman – adds that 'as so many because of her risk catching the same purulent illness in question, she must be isolated in a room apart . . .'. Probably the oldest medical evidence regarding contagion, these documents show that in the opinion of the *doctors* – as suggested by text and context – an illness could, by even indirect contact with the carrier, pass from an already afflicted subject to another person. In a country that, as we know, had from the dawn of time often been ravaged by killer epidemics, learning that lesson did not require superhuman genius. Nevertheless, the same considerations reappear in undoubtedly exorcistic contexts. For instance, a large directory entitled 'Combustion' (Shurpu) contains a long passage examining how the 'bad luck' that has seized on the patient came upon him, producing ravages in his mind, heart or circumstances. Perhaps, suggests the text among other conjectures, the unfortunate victim had been 'caught' by direct contact with someone already under the thumb of the same maleficent agent, either from 'sleeping in his bed, sitting in his chair or drinking from his glass'. Here we have the 'contagion', originally and fundamentally empirical, being exploited by exorcism. Still under this heading, there had been very early 'contamination' of the latter by medicine.

A final, but no less significant, reflection of this copenetration of the two forms of therapy: among the works concerning illnesses, the most remarkable – a real masterpiece if one takes into account that it was composed at the very latest nearly thirty-five centuries ago – was entitled *Treatise on Medical Diagnoses and Prognoses*. Distributed over forty tablets, in its entirety it must have comprised some 5000 or 6000 lines of text, half of which remain. Constructed on the same model as the manuals of 'deductive divination', its aim was to assemble all the 'signs' and 'symptoms' of illnesses observed in order to draw conclusions about the nature of the ill they indicated and its development. I will return to tablets I and II. From the IIIrd to the XVth – the XVIth is lost – these symptoms were classified carefully in an order that reviewed all the parts of the body, from head to feet, successively taking account, for each, of all the medically significant presentations: colour, volume, aspect, temperature, sensitivity, presence of adventitious data, general attitudes of the sick person in conjunction with the signs and so on.

For instance, referring to the nose:

> If the patient's nose bleeds . . .; If the tip of the nose is moist . . .; If the tip of the nose is alternately hot and cold . . .; If the tip of the nose is yellow . . .; If the tip of the nose has a white eruption . . .; If the tip of the nose has a black eruption . . .

Tablet IX, for example, making a study of the face, lists seventy-nine observations of the same ilk! Each was followed by its diagnosis ('It is such and such an illness') and often with the prognosis – 'favourable' (literally lit., 'he'll live) or 'fatal' (lit., 'he'll die'), or 'he has so many days before being cured' or 'before dying'.

Tablets XVII–XXVI, on the same pattern, assemble not just 'signs' taken in isolation but semiological data that accompany various ailments at their commencement and as they develop. We have nothing left of tablets XXVII–XXXIV, but the last ones, XXXV–XL, are concerned with pregnancy and the pathology of pregnant women and infants.

What strikes the reader of this work is its predominantly empirical character; by all the evidence, it is based on hundreds of observations, 'cases', in describing which enough was known to set aside the fortuitous features and retain only what was medically significant. This kind of curiosity, coupled with the utmost discernment, analysis, collection and comparison of nosological data probably went back a long way in the history of the country. A short divinatory anthology of around the eighteenth century BC presents us with the diagnosis of a cranial trauma with loss of consciousness, formulated on the basis of an observation of lateral strabismus: 'If the patient's eyes both squint, it is because he has received a blow to the cranium; and his reason is in the same condition as his skull' (in other words, 'his mind is disturbed, unhinged'). Analyses and reflections of this kind provided our *Treatise* with the largest number of its medical propositions. For example: 'If, from head to foot, the patient is covered with red blisters, while his skin remains pallid, he is suffering from a venereal illness'; 'If his state is immediately so grave that he does not recognise even his nearest and dearest, the prognosis is fatal'; 'If he has a fixed stare and his whole torso is seized up, it is the result of an attack of paralysis; prognosis fatal'. Here is the description of a sudden onset of malaria (which seems to be attributed to – or compared with? – sunstroke):

> If, from the start, his malady comprises recurring attacks, during which the patient suffers alternate bouts of fever then shivering and sweating, after which he feels a sensation of heat in all his limbs, and then suffers a heavy fever again, followed by fresh shivering and sweating: this is a fever – *di'u* [the precise meaning of this word eludes us], due to sunstroke – it will take him seven days to recover.

An attack of epilepsy: 'If, while walking, the sick man suddenly falls forward, his eyes dilated, and is unable to return them to normal, and if besides he is unable to move arms or legs, it is the beginning of an epileptic fit . . .'.

Another feature of the same, medical, kind is the empirical caution and realism of the prognoses. These qualities stand out all the more if this *Treatise* is compared with others in a neighbouring domain: those of physiognomic 'deductive divination', which draws its predictions from the consultants' various 'readings' of face and body. Although based on a special 'logic', to our eyes most of the forecasts found in them are wildly extravagant compared with the symptoms from which they are drawn, and the future envisaged relates to distant points of one, two, three or even more years ahead: 'He will die within two years'. Conversely, in its prognoses our *Treatise* never ventures further than a month after the observation – a plausible medical time-span; and, generally speaking, what it foretells is directly and admissibly related to the symptoms. Let us take, for instance, the observation of a 'livid face'. The physiognomist concludes that 'the patient will die from the effects of water; or as the result of Perjury; or, according to another interpretation, he will have a long life'; whereas the doctors of the *Treatise* content themselves with announcing that the sick man 'will soon die'. Confronted with his bloodless countenance, is it not more reasonable, more 'logical', to predict a fatal decline from anaemia, internal haemorrhage or some similar cause, than a death brought about 'by water' (in any case an ambiguous phrase, doubtless deliberately so) or by the mysterious action of a violated oath, and still less a long life?

Why Me?

In both the diagnostic and prognostic fields, there is thus in the *Treatise* a concern for probability, positive and observable truth, the direct outcome of a rational and, let us say, medical effort, in the strict sense of the word, to analyse factual data and reflect on what may be discovered, with the aim of classifying illnesses. It is a medical work.

And yet, amid all this common sense, these sober judgements, this reliable competence, here and there absolutely irrational features emerge that have come straight from exorcism. I will not linger over the fairly frequent diagnoses of the type 'intervention of this or that god', 'this or that demon', 'such and such an evil force'. As I suggested earlier, if their literal meaning involves 'mythology', it is likely that they were understood as expressions of syndromes in the classification of illnesses. Conversely, we are in the thick of 'the theological system of evil' when we read: 'If the sick person has pains in the pelvis, it is an intervention of the god Shulak, because the patient has slept with his sister; he will linger for a while, then die'; 'If he has pains in his temples and his eyes are misted, it is because he has cursed his own god, or the god of his town'.

But it is mainly in the first two tablets that the *Treatise* appears to be well and truly steeped in the mythological and irrational universe of exorcism. In these tablets, the *âshipu*, and he alone, is invited to keep an eye out for the incidental 'signs' that might present themselves to him while he is *en route* to visit the patient to whom he has been summoned. Even before he has examined him, he will be able to deduce from such signs both the diagnosis and prognosis for the illness. 'If, along the way, the exorcist sees a pink pig, the patient he is going to visit has dropsy'; 'If he notices a black pig, the prognosis is fatal!'

For want of adequate documentation covering a long enough time-span, the probably age-old history of the compilation of such a complex *Treatise* – in which many people have had a hand and many centuries passed – eludes us. It would doubtless explain how a frankly medical work managed to include tablets so obviously conceived in an exorcistic spirit. Whatever the circumstances that brought about this addition, it is clear that it was intended to present users of the *Treatise* with a view of the two kinds of medicine allied to some extent.

Since, by all the evidence, such a juxtaposition in no way altered the essential characteristics of either, what could have been the use of placing them together? In my own view, there are two advantages. Of the first, we already have some idea: as far as treatment is concerned – which is, after all, of fundamental importance – the joint application of the two techniques was only to be encouraged, thus increasing the chances of success. In any case, as we have seen, that was the custom, and it was supported by arranging the *Treatise* in this manner.

But perhaps there is another, even more important, point

to consider: although empirical medicine provided remedies, care programmes, possibilities of cure, as well as the names and descriptions of illnesses and, after diagnosis, even calculations regarding their progress, it put forward only the immediate causes – 'He has sustained a blow'; 'He has picked up this illness by sleeping with a woman'; 'He has spent too long in the sun', and so on. But exorcistic medicine went much further: systemised and directly in accord with the theocentric perspective, the only one that was universally valid and illuminating in that country and at that time, it linked the illness, like every other 'evil of suffering', not only with its one direct cause but also with the explanation for the unleashing of that cause – the castigatory will of the gods. In this way, exorcistic medicine alone was able to provide the ultimate reason for the ill; it alone could completely reassure the mind. If I am in this condition, it is because of a blow, a dubious association, sunstroke: but *why has it happened to me?* Here we have the real ultimate question that tormented – and still does – the sick and unfortunate! Of course, the reply could not then – and still cannot – be other than *a priori* imaginary, irrational. But we have to believe that humans really need such replies, which in their view are definitive even if they cannot verify or demonstrate them.

Nowadays, witnessing on the one hand the persistence of religious feeling and belief in a supernatural world of whatever kind, and on the other – in a totally different direction – the popularity of deliberately irrational, not to say ludicrous and useless, curative methods, one may wonder whether things have changed all that much since the days of ancient Babylon.

CHAPTER 11

The Birth of Astrology

Jean Bottéro

Especially since we have been able to examine those enormous astral spheres 'on the spot', or not far from it, it has become really difficult to see them as anything other than formidable masses of rock, each one set on its relentless trajectory; and huge cracks have developed in the walls of astrology.

Paying regard to the wise Aristotle – in whose opinion things can be truly known and understood only if they can be observed being born and growing – we too might be able to go 'to the spot' and travel back through time by the hidden paths of history to see at close hand how in those distant ages such a power of interference in people's lives could be ascribed to those immense dead globes, planted like lamps in the celestial vault. They twinkle forever, endlessly radiating splendour, heat and light, but when examined cold-bloodedly have really nothing else to do up there but tirelessly measure out their melancholy eternal round.

When, upon opening my newspaper, I cast an eye on my 'horoscope' – which this rag carefully provides for me every day – and firmly expect what I am promised, good or bad, I implicitly admit three postulates (otherwise, my faith in astrology would be no more than a vague childish superstition). First, that over the Earth, and especially over mankind, the stars exert a combined action, related to their respective nature, power and position, and that bearing these data in mind we can therefore know things in advance. Next, that such action is so strong at the moment when we come into existence, that it fixes our path and destiny irrevocably. Over a century ago, Auguste Bouché-Leclerc summed up the doctrine of *Greek Astrology*. For, as everyone knows, our astrology came to us from the 'Greeks'; those of Hellenistic times, in the wake of the tremendous intermingling between Greece and the East brought about by Alexander the Great (c. 330 BC).

Those 'Greeks' themselves were conscious of having received it from elsewhere, more precisely from venerable Mesopotamia and ancient Babylon. Indeed, it was from there around 300 BC that Berosus, a 'Babylonian priest of Bel' – if it is really he – had set off 'to settle in the island and town of Cos and become the first to teach this discipline there'. Thus, for a long time to come, his successors, the astrologers, would be known as 'Chaldaeans' or 'Babylonians', as the two terms had become synonymous.

In 1899, when Bouché-Leclerc published his great book, Assyriology was still in its infancy and experts had barely begun to explore the documentary treasures that were emerging fresh from the ancient soil of Iraq in the wake of excavation campaigns. Persuaded that the system adopted by the Greeks had pre-existed among the Babylonians, the great historian rather manipulated here and there the actual words of the small number of cuneiform documents containing astrological material in order to cram them by hook or by crook into the traditional Hellenistic mould. He was wrong. Today, with a century's hindsight and in possession of a prodigious authentic dossier, not only have we penetrated much further into the labyrinth of that ancient and imposing civilisation, but we have also obtained a better understanding of some of its secrets, including astrology. It is as clear as daylight that this must have been deeply rooted and, as such, could have originated nowhere else.

Mesopotamian astrology is fairly far removed from what those Greeks did with it, with the aim of 'continually improving upon what they had first learnt from the Barbarians' (as they boasted, most often with justification). In this instance, they systematised astrology quite differently, imbuing it with the special meaning, value and use which are still familiar to us today.

The first known cuneiform texts that give us information about Mesopotamian astrology belong in the region of the eighteenth century BC. There it is revealed as already rooted in local religious representations and practices, which would never cease to sustain it. At the risk of seeming at first glance to beat about the bush, we must approach it from this angle if we are really to understand it.

The ancient Mesopotamians saw the universe as an immense hollow ball, in two linked hemispheres: the 'on-high', the sky, and the 'down-below', 'Hell', cut across its diameter by the vast layer of the sea, in the middle of which emerged the Earth. They could not accept that such an enormous and complicated machine could function perfectly all by itself, so they created an entire supernatural population to pull the strings and govern it properly. They imagined these deities as modelled upon themselves, but sublimated to the nth degree; far more powerful and intelligent, and endowed with eternal life.

Like humans, the gods were grouped in families that were co-ordinated in a single society, as monarchical as the one in our world, governed by one sovereign god who delegated to his various subjects the powers that each needed to look after his own area in the best possible way, whether in nature or culture. One supervised the mountainous region, another the desert and the steppe; another ruled the water-courses, and still another the maritime district. This one was in charge of the vast area of cereal farming, and another of what constituted the second 'lifeblood' of local economy – breeding small live-stock (sheep and goats). There was a patron god of wild animals, of fire, beer, war, and even a goddess of physical love, and so on. In the same way, each of the stars, haunting the sky, had its own guiding deity: the Sun, Moon, planets and fixed stars, no less than the equally 'aerial' meteors, together with winds, rains, storms and tempests. Although a naive view could easily identify these gods with the objects of their authority and care, there was not the slightest confusion between them. The gods were concealed within them, rather like the motor inside the machine it sets in motion; each area was merely the domain they gave life to, 'created' and organised by them.

Men had been 'invented' and made by the gods, with the precise aim of getting the best out of natural resources. By means of their labour, men produced goods for consumption and use: food, drink, clothing, furniture and buildings, initially for the benefit of their master-gods and, secondarily, for their own. Such an employer–employee relationship had the consequence that, not being anxious to slow down or halt the output of their workers, the gods had not the slightest interest in afflicting them with paralysing ills and troubles without cause.

Of course, men were expected to obey them, in other words, to conform to the endless obligations and sundry prohibitions which governed human existence and which were equally imagined to be decided and promulgated by the masters of the world. As kings on Earth punish trouble-makers and flouters of public order, the gods had to punish those of their subjects who, scorning their divine will, rebelled in this way and 'sinned' against them. To this end the gods resorted to other supernatural entities, of lesser calibre, who had been given to them as executioners and 'police'; on the order of the gods, these 'demons' inflicted on the culprits the illnesses, misfortunes, calamities and upsets of every kind that cast a shadow over life.

A Long Tradition of Divinatory Schools

However, because they were good rulers and by no means sadistic, the gods were deemed to offer mankind (in two principal ways) the remedy at the same time as the ill – however deserved it might be.

On the one hand, in the presence or threat of the 'punishment', they showed themselves capable of being moved; they themselves had prepared procedures of exorcism for use by the unfortunate. These were a combination of prayers and quite expressive gestures, which might well incline the supreme judges to show mercy by ordering their demonic henchmen to suspend the punishment, so as to restore the joys of life to the condemned man, together with full capacity to devote himself entirely to his duties.

But they could also grant their benevolent aid to humans by a quite different route, revealing to them in advance the fate that had been allotted to them, their 'destiny'. If this was bad, people could guard against it by resorting to exorcisms; if favourable, it was a source of comfort and encouragement. The gods unveiled this future through divination.

Like many other people, especially their Semitic close relatives, the Mesopotamians accepted that the future could be revealed to them in direct speech: a 'revelation' of the gods, the latter contacting any individual in a dream, a vision or some other supernatural intervention. This is what we term 'inspired' divination. However, although it was known and accepted in that country, this purely passive method of communication seems to have given way before a very different and highly original method of discovering the future from the gods – 'deductive' divination. This was not based on the model of oral communication, from mouth to ear, but a written message passed on by means of signs that had to be interpreted.

It is essential to recall here a major fact which profoundly stamped the mindset and outlook of the ancient Mesopotamians: around the year 3000 their ancestors had invented and perhaps perfected writing pure and simple, but at all events their own system – the first to appear in a world that was completely ignorant of writing.

In its earliest form, this writing had first worked by 'pictograms', schematic sketches of various objects to each of which a whole semantic cluster was attached. For example, depending on choice and context, the outline of the human 'foot' could designate any behaviour, movement or attitude in which this extremity was involved (standing, local movement, walking, progress, carrying or transporting); and the outline for 'star' could represent everything to be found in the heavens: superior, sublime, dominant, divine. Later improvements to this system always preserved its initial and radical ability in this way to denote real things by things that, although certainly designed and shaped, were no less real in the eyes of those people.

'Deductive' divination was based on the conviction that the gods – again resembling earthly sovereigns – could freely communicate their decisions to interested parties, and were happier to do so in writing. For, just like the designs drawn by scribes on the clay tablets that served as 'paper' at that time, what the gods planned and caused to happen to a person, in their day-to-day government of the world, formed significant pictograms. In the view of the ancient Mesopotamians, the whole of creation was presented as an immense page of divine scripture. When everything was normal and routine, with nothing special to attract the attention, the divine 'writers' therefore had nothing to point out to human beings, their readers. If they had to pass on some particular decision that had been taken, they would arrange to produce some unusual, singular, unexpected or monstrous phenomenon – for example, a six-legged sheep, a heavy downpour outside the rainy season, a redhead or blonde in that country of 'black heads', a horse trying to mount an ox, the particular disposition of a sacrificed animal's entrails and heaven knows what else.

Such an odd occurrence not only immediately caught the attention of onlookers but, by its very happening alone, formed the pictography of the gods' message and had only to be deciphered and interpreted, following the code peculiar to that 'divine writing', analogous with that of the cuneiform signs which had originated the idea. Sometimes the encoding was fairly transparent, and still is, even to our own eyes. Thus, the attempted mounting of an ox by a horse, which in any case would prove fruitless, indicated a reduction in the numbers of livestock; and whoever lost his seal, the legal substitute for his own person, must expect the disappearance of that other replacement of himself – his son. Such clarity, however, was far from commonplace. Thus, understanding all these divine 'writings' in the normal course of events was reserved to a body of specialists, 'diviners' or 'soothsayers', whose long periods of training and study enabled them to decipher all the divinatory phenomena on behalf of the man in the street. They interpreted omens, drawing and deducing from the way these were presented what the future held in store; and *oracles*, which the gods had 'pictographed' in their own fashion.

To facilitate the work of these soothsayers and to teach them its rules casuistically, a long tradition of divinatory 'schools' – in operation as early as the last third of the third millennium at the latest – had patiently assembled all imaginable 'omens': every kind of singular, unexpected, bizarre and abnormal object and event had been classified and each provided with the 'oracle' to be decoded from it. They were all collected in interminable lists, each of which, specified by subject and arranged according to its classified presentations, formed a veritable 'treatise'. These works – thousands of tablets have come down to us – covered all natural orders, because, as it had been shaped and 'written' by the gods, the whole of creation was pregnant with their messages.

After this detour – as necessary as it might appear far removed from the subject – we are back again with the astrology of ancient Mesopotamia.

From the dawn of time, under their almost perpetually clear eastern sky, Mesopotamians had been fascinated by celestial bodies, whose appearances and rhythms they had recorded and studied without respite for many centuries. These included not only the multitude of fixed stars and their constellations, from which they had drawn up a zodiacal sequence in the first millennium BC, but also those great 'lamps' of day and night, the Sun and (above all) the Moon, which ruled their calendar. Lastly, the planets: Venus, whom they called Ishtar, after the patron goddess of Love; Jupiter, 'the white star'; Mercury, 'the mouflon', Mars, 'the inflamed' (?); and Saturn, 'the constant'. whose rising, paths, absences and eclipses they could predict with certainty. It is hardly surprising that they saw in these the most dazzling pictograms, drawn in the sky by the gods to announce their decisions.

Prepared by work covering centuries – of which little has been retrieved so far – astrology thus began to blossom around 1800 BC, but required only a few centuries to flower increasingly. It is known to us, first and foremost, through the remains of a wide-ranging 'treatise', compiled from the mid-second millennium and reworked and enlarged several times with a myriad variations, extracts and explanatory commentaries. At least seventy tablets, dating from the first half of the first millennium, came down to us. They provided thousands of 'omens', each one supplied, according to the rules, with its oracular 'decoding'.

Preceded by a kind of instruction in verse – to emphasise that the stars had been created by the gods not only to define and govern time but also as a means of communication from the heavens – these omens were spread over four 'chapters' of unequal size. First came those shown by the Moon (which was called *Sîn*), the greatest in importance of the astral bodies, and an object of worship: the strange or unexpected phenomena observable at its rising, waxing, waning and disappearance on the last day of the month; the various aspects of its light, its fullness, its crescent; its situation in relation to the other stars; its eclipses. Some twenty tablets were devoted to it.

Next came the section – slightly less well provided for – examining the situations of the Sun, Shamash as it was called. At least to our eyes, the last two parts are rather badly defined and unevenly detailed: some dozen tablets, under the name of Adad, the patron god of rainfall and various meteors, assembling the phenomena concerning them; and the last twenty, in the name of the goddess of the planet Venus, Ishtar, dealing chiefly with the planets, but also the fixed stars, separately or in constellations.

We have as yet retrieved only portions of this impressive work; they are fairly copious but interrupted, and some are mutilated and obscure. A few extracts, culled at random, will give at least some idea of that astrology's presentation and functioning.

> If the Moon, on rising, is partly dimmed, the right point of its crescent broken off, but the other sharp and perfectly discernible – the country's economic activity will stagnate for three years.
>
> If on the first day of the month of Teshrît [September–October] the rising Moon is surrounded by a halo – enemies in the south–east [the Elamites] are going to attack.
>
> If in the month of Nisan [March–April, the first in the Mesopotamian year], there is an eclipse of the Sun – the king will die in that same year.
>
> If, during a storm, thunder sounds eleven times – cattle will be hit by an outbreak of disease.
>
> If, on the 15th of the month of Shabat [January–February], the planet Venus, having disappeared in the east and remained invisible for three days, reappears on the 18th in the west – there will be a heavy flow from springs; abundant rains; much water in the rivers; a king will send a message of reconciliation to another.

All in all, omens are concerned with a kind of astronomy, while the quality of the astrological oracles is of greater interest. For instance, we find forecasts of drought; inadequate or spoilt harvests; famines of greater or lesser cruelty; sickness and disasters among livestock; economic crises, with price rises for goods; an increase in abortions and various calamities; enemy incursions; the capture of towns or territories belonging to the country; military defeats; pillaging or ruining of public buildings; rebellion in the army or uprisings in the population; internecine hatreds and reciprocal massacres in the kingdom; 'loss of civic sense' and general ill-will; dynastic quarrels; illness or death of the sovereign, and a hundred other public misfortunes. Conversely, there are endless stories of luck, successes and happy occasions befalling the populace and its king: abundance of possessions and goods of all kinds; flourishing economy; good relations with and submission to the government; stability of the throne; the promise of many safe births; victories and conquests over enemies, who will be crushed and defeated. The combination of these items of good and bad fortune would seem to compose a realistic, not to say picturesque, view of daily life with its fluctuating highs and lows.

For it will have been noticed that, whether positive or negative, there is never any question in these oracles of other than the 'country', the 'population' and its 'king', the sole leader and one in authority, whose good or bad fortune would of necessity have repercussions on all his subjects. When, occasionally, some discernible personage comes to the fore, it is always someone close to the king – often his wife or eldest son and 'crown prince'; or some highly placed official, an important cog in the political machinery. Unlike the majority of the other sectors of 'deductive' divination, in which messages and warnings concerned the destiny of everybody and anybody, those of astrology in Mesopotamia – probably because of the public display, posted up as they were to the gaze of all on the gigantic screen that served as the world's dome – at first generally concerned only the public good.

The Astrologers of the Last Great Kings of Assyria

Because of this, rather like what we term 'intelligence', astrology was well and truly a means of government. In order to take the best decisions, those in power needed to be informed about the future, to try to discover what lay ahead inside the country or at its gates. That is why, during the first third of the first millennium BC, the last two mighty kings of Assyria – Asarhaddon (680–669 BC) and Assurbanipal (668–627 BC) – took great care to maintain a number of informers or professional astrologers. From their own observatories they each scrutinised the heavens and passed on to the palace – which often questioned them on particular problems – the results of their examinations, often accompanied by their decoding of these 'signs', which in its turn was usually submitted to other professionals for checking. From the 5000 or so items recovered from the correspondence of that period, we can glean countless testimonies to this astrological activity that was centred on the government and the king. We get a real-life view of how those astrologers worked, and at the same time evidence of the curious weight and importance given to their information, examinations and decisions.

> His Majesty having commanded me to observe the movements of the stars and apprise Him of all that is happening, I have taken the utmost care to report to Him, everything that appears to me to be favourable, of good omen and promising well for His Majesty.
>
> Sun and Moon have been clearly visible, except on the 13th of this month; there will therefore be no eclipse. This is my firm opinion, which I convey to His Majesty.
>
> On the 14th of this month an eclipse of the Moon will take place. This is bad news for our neighbours, in the south-east or the north-west, but is a good omen for His Majesty. His Majesty may therefore rest assured. In any case, I had already foreseen and predicted this eclipse as soon as the planet Venus appeared.
>
> His Majesty asked me how to interpret the fact that Mars has retrograded, leaving the constellation of Scorpio, only to return later. I reply that this omen means: Be careful! At the risk of misfortune, His Majesty must not leave the Town by the Great Gate without taking [exorcistic] precautions. This interpretation is not to be found in the *Treatise on Astrology*; it comes from the oral tradition of master

> astrologers. Furthermore, when Mars, retrograding in the same way, has left the constellation of Leo to enter that of Cancer or Gemini, the end of the reign of some western king must be expected. Nor does this appear in the *Treatise*.

Our picture even contains echoes of those arguments between specialists, each charging his opponent with incompetence or stupidity – following a tradition still observed today.

> Regarding the planet Venus, His Majesty has informed me that someone had announced its appearance to Him. To which I reply that only an ignoramus could have said such a thing. No! Venus is not visible at present; tonight it is Mercury that can be clearly seen, and not Venus! Whoever told His Majesty the opposite, I repeat, cannot tell Mercury from Venus!

There is no doubt that such an official role, such governmental and political clout, together with the mainly collective nature of the messages it had to supply, must have conferred unique celebrity and importance on Mesopotamian astrology. Thus it gave astrology the lead over other sectors of 'deductive' divination, some of which had been developed and widely used much earlier – at the beginning of the second millennium BC – especially haruspicy and hepatoscopy, the analysis of the entrails and livers of sacrificed animals. It therefore acquired a reputation and popularity which, once exported outside its native land, must have contributed to its extraordinary credit in the Hellenistic world.

In addition, however, well before its diffusion and in its home country, it had been enriched by an extra advantage that must have considerably enlarged its appeal; the value of the divine messages it purported to transmit was extended from the community to individuals.

Some data peculiar to 'deductive' divination might lead in this direction. First, although by their 'private' quality certain omens seemed intended to disclose only individual destinies (such as those deduced from particular features of a physical nature, of character or dreams), the majority often accompanied their 'public' oracles by predictions of a private kind. Thus, the birth of quadruplets, two boys and two girls, was decoded as 'ravages caused by the enemy and sad times for the country; moreover, the ruin of the house of the party concerned'. This may have encouraged soothsayers to seek an individual interpretation *everywhere*, even in astral presages. In fact, such a beginning is revealed, though still timidly, by the exceptional presence in the *Treatise on Astrology* of some oracles of the type 'this man is doomed to death' or even 'a wet nurse will abandon her infant in the street'.

In another aspect, a divinatory discipline existed whose 'pictograms' were taken from the chance encounter of a turning-point in the life of a man with a specific moment in time – a month, in this instance; and among those decisive moments was that of his birth. If born during the first month of the year (Nisan), he was destined to 'fritter away his paternal home'; in the second month (Ayar), to 'die prematurely'; in the seventh, to 'prosper', and so on. These months, when all was said and done, were well and truly governed by the stars, so there was an angle by which astrology could enter private destinies.

These convergent lines explain how it finally emerged – when, how and by what stages we do not know – as what is known as genethlialogy, the prediction of a personal future based on the astral situation at birth, no longer based merely on the month in which it took place, but the whole celestial picture, the position of the various stars at the moment in which the subject entered this world. The oldest of these 'horoscopes' is dated 410 BC and precedes the first known Hellenistic specimens by more than two centuries. As far as the mediocre condition of the tablet permits, here is a translation:

> In the month of Nisan, the night of the 14th, So-and-So [the name has disappeared where the clay has broken], son of Shuma-usur [?], grandson of Nadin-shumi [?], of the family of Dêkê. The Moon was below one of Scorpio's pincers; Jupiter in the zodiacal sign of Pisces; Venus in that of Taurus, Saturn in that of Cancer and Mars in that of Gemini; Mercury was not yet visible . . . All will go well for you.

Here we have an astral configuration taken at the moment of an individual's birth and which, decoded following the rules of the astrological code, supplied at least a general outline of the newborn's future, in the same way that the 'treatise's' oracles imparted the destiny of the country's sovereign. The existence of a certain number of similar, rather more recent, documents (notably around the year 250) reveals that such a practice was common. Quite early in the second half of the first millennium, therefore, Mesopotamian astrology had become a *complete* divinatory system; capable of foretelling private as well as public futures. At that point it was ready to pass to the Hellenistic world, and Berosus appears to have been astute enough to go there and preach it.

By what steps Hellenism modified it, once it had been accepted, does not concern us here. It is far more important to emphasise in which direction it was transformed – namely, presenting in a completely different way the stars that played a central role in it. As Bouché-Leclerc summed it up earlier: according to our classical astrology, the stars by themselves exert effective action on us; this action is governed by the specific property of each star, recognised as different from the others; and by means of this influence, the future they map out for us the moment we arrive in the world is irrevocable. All we can do is know it. Such exorbitant power could be attributable to them only if *all* – Sun, Moon and planets – had been *deified*, and thus endowed with a capability of absolute decision, with no appeal.

Of course, such a system might keep the general texture of that of Babylon, which had given birth to it; but as regards their profound significance, they were separated by a yawning gulf. To Mesopotamian eyes, the stars, unchanging by nature, were neither more nor less than the instruments of the gods, by their aspect and position composing the pictograms of the gods' writing and merely acting as go-betweens or interpreters of the gods' will. But the decisions they passed on in this way, like those of rulers and judges in our world, represented only the outcome of a *hic et nunc* deliberation, and were therefore never absolute and definitive. Their authors, the gods, after being duly implored according to the *ad hoc* rites of exorcism, could always revoke those decisions, 'changing [as was said] an unfavourable future into a favourable one'. The absolute determinism of classical astrology was diametrically opposed to its original Babylonian model.

When the Greeks transposed into their own view of the world a genuinely and 'logically' divinatory system, rooted in old Mesopotamian culture, they did something ontological – a fundamental alteration. Even if neither presentation stands up to scrutiny, still less when one has witnessed their birth and growth; and even if they are both equally fanciful, nothing will stop my regarding the older one as more humane, imaginative and flexible, more open to the hope and uncertainty that are a necessary part of our lives, more remote from that gloomy and – if one thinks about it – terrifying fatalism that would logically condemn us to remain forever impassive, our hands by our sides.

CHAPTER 12

The Ordeal

Bertrand Lafont

'Strange and poignant, trial by ordeal is an assault upon our reason,' wrote Dominique Barthélemy in an article he devoted to the 'Judgement of God in the Middle Ages'. Illustrating this topic, medieval paintings and miniatures show us the accused holding red-hot irons in their hands, or plunging naked into icy water, bound hand and foot, so that their guilt might be proved or disproved.

Appealing to the supernatural to decide the guilt or innocence of an individual is a feature common to many religions and areas of civilisation; but an ordeal, strictly speaking (from the Old English *ordal*, German *Urteil*, 'judgement'), was not simply a physical test whose victorious outcome allowed the accused to be found innocent. At a deeper level, it provided the irrefutable and irrational proof that such and such a crime had, or had not, been committed by someone.

The origins of the ordeal go back a very long way in history, and research into its oldest traces takes us back some 5000 years to the valley of the Tigris and Euphrates.

What gave its unity to the civilisation that flourished there for 3000 years, up to the last centuries before the Christian era, was the use of cuneiform writing. 'Invented' by the Sumerians around 3000 BC, and taken up a thousand years later for a further 2000 years by the Semites (Akkadians, Babylonians and Assyrians), that writing enabled a wealth of records to be made of many political, religious, economic, cultural and social features peculiar to ancient Mesopotamia. Two of these features in particular catch our attention: first, the importance attributed very early on to law and justice. The proof we have lies first in the 'codes' (like that of king Hammurabi of Babylon, around 1750 BC) which, as early as the Sumerian period, reveal a desire and capacity for legal systemisation; and next in the cuneiform tablets containing contracts, protocols, minutes of trials and so on. All this documentation is evidence of a juridical way of thinking imprinted with empiricism, and a strongly material view of the law and justice. The second characteristic of that civilisation is the very special way it had of expressing its deep religiousness. The ancient Mesopotamians imagined that divine society, organised on the model of their own, governed the course of events, and they invented a number of oracular procedures (and 'magic') to try to understand the decisions of the gods and influence them in men's favour.

It was in this context that an elementary, but fundamental, principle of judicial procedure appeared – no one could be condemned without proof, and even an irrational demonstration of guilt was necessary in order to sentence a criminal.

The most frequent irrational mode of testing to be found in the cuneiform documents is the swearing of an oath. This was indeed a form of ordeal; one swore by the deity that one was telling the truth. The intention of this solemn oath was to avoid lies through fear of perjury and its consequences. This kind of justification, committing one not only before men but before the gods, has persisted throughout the ages. We find it today in American courtrooms, where the accused swears on the Bible to tell 'the whole truth, and nothing but the truth'. This systematised and trivialised oath has, of course, ended by losing much of its impact.

Trial by ordeal, however, was far more solemn and spectacular – it was also more exceptional. In ancient Mesopotamia, the accused person whose guilt or innocence was to be established was subjected to the action of a watercourse, the 'divine river'. In a region truly created by the Tigris, Euphrates and their tributaries, running water possessed a sacred nature and rivers were looked upon as deities.

The cuneiform texts alluding to this type of ordeal are datable to the Sumerian period (c. 2300 BC) for the oldest, and to the last centuries before the Christian era for the more recent. At first, it was a matter of various codes of laws, whether Sumerian (like that of Ur-Nammu, king of Ur around 2050 BC), Babylonian (like that of king Hammurabi, around 1750 BC) or Assyrian (middle-Assyrian at the end of the twelfth century BC). Thus, paragraph 132 of the code of Hammurabi says: 'If a man's wife has been pointed out because of another man, even though she has not been caught with him, for her husband's sake she must plunge into the divine river.' Or again, the second paragraph of the same code:

> If anyone has attributed acts of sorcery to a man, but without being able to prove it, the man accused of these acts will go to the divine river and dive into the river. If the river takes him, his accuser will take possession of his house. But if the river shows the man to be innocent and he emerges safe and sound, his accuser will be killed, and the one who has plunged into the river will take possession of his accuser's house.

Sorcery and Adultery

Those extracts from the code of Hammurabi at once reveal the two types of accusation that are characteristic of trial by ordeal – sorcery and adultery. These offences were similarly typical of the use of ordeal in our own Middle Ages, probably because they are infractions that are particularly difficult to prove, unless discovered *in flagrante*. The collections of Sumerian and Assyrian laws also prescribe trial by ordeal for these types of misdeed. We shall see later that other categories of offences or legal wrangles could lead magistrates to appeal to the judgement of the river-god.

Another feature that immediately becomes noticeable when we read these two paragraphs: contrary to our modern rules whereby the accuser must establish proof of guilt, here it is the accused who must prove his innocence by being subjected to the ordeal. The second paragraph of Hammurabi's code also shows that – following a system of reciprocity common in ancient Near Eastern law – when the river proved the accused's innocence, the accuser suffered the penalty which the accused would have undergone (in this instance, the death penalty).

These codes of laws of ancient Mesopotamia do not allow us to gain a precise idea of the procedure of trial by ordeal. How did the trial take place? Where? In what circumstances? What did it consist of exactly? In order to find out, we have to turn to 'texts relating to practices', provided by administrative reports, public or private letters, items of procedure and so on, which the ancient inhabitants of those regions have bequeathed to us, in tens of thousands and covering 3000 years.

Until quite recently, only some few dozen texts mentioning trial by ordeal were available to us; and those did no more than refer to the decision to resort to the divine river, in this or that case, without once describing in detail the formalities of the trial. One document alone was more explicit; but it was a 'literary' excerpt rather than a legal item, composed in the sixth century BC to the glory of king Nebuchadnezzar II of Babylon (604–562 BC). The text exalts that ruler's acute sense of justice, illustrating it with several examples, one of which retraces the unfolding of an ordeal.

A man has accused another of murder, but without bringing proof of his allegations. The king then commands recourse to trial by ordeal, which takes place on the banks of the Euphrates, upstream from the town of Sippar, not far from Babylon. The procedure begins one evening, in great solemnity, during a ritual vigil. The next morning, at daybreak, the trial proper takes place, during which the culprit plunges into the river. His body vanishes; for half a day it is sought in vain. The disappearance provokes the king's annoyance, and he commands the search to continue.

Thus, the text goes on,

> with hearts full of anxiety . . . the envoys searched the area, but without spotting the man in question; they crossed to the other bank of the river, and walked through the countryside, but as no one had seen him, they could get no response. Supervisors of bridges and sentinels went up and down the river, from one side to the other, examining the banks – in vain! Then at the stroke of noon, his corpse rose from the river. His head was wounded and blood flowed from his mouth, ears and nostrils; moreover his skull was burning, as if it had been exposed to fire, and his body was covered with bruises. When people saw him, they showed their fear, and the whole country was terror-stricken. Enemies, evildoers and rebels then took flight.

The apologetic nature of this text is clear. It was a matter of extolling the infallibility of divine justice and the greatness of the king; the culprit was punished, the people filled with fear and miscreants fled the country. But the text emphasises above all that this took place *after* the ordeal. It is interesting to note the worry with which they searched for the body – the proof of guilt, irrefutably provided when the man went straight down in the water, must not be confused with punishment. Clearly, the outcome of this matter had not been foreseen, and we may note how the author of the text 'recuperates' it to show how punishment was in the end inflicted by the river-god himself, and the effects it produced.

Thanks to the cuneiform archives of the town of Mari, the old capital of the Middle Euphrates region, we are able to follow the process of ordeals more precisely. The archives go back to more than 1000 years before Nebuchadnezzar II's reign. Volume XXVI of the *Archives royales de Mari*) presents several informative texts on the subject – the fifth chapter of the first volume is entirely devoted to this matter. They are accounts of trials by ordeal reported by direct witnesses, and are letters sent to the king of Mari, Zimri-Lim (1775–1760 BC), by several of his 'servitors', governors of provinces and other great officials of the realm. One of their essential tasks was to keep the sovereign informed of every noteworthy event occurring in the area of their jurisdiction.

It is probably not by chance that the author of most of these letters is a man named Meptûm, one of the governors of the province of Hanat, south of Mari. Indeed, in this province, on the banks of the Euphrates, the town of Hît was situated. It seems to have been the very spot where all these ordeals took place. The name of this town is written like that of the river-god (same ideogram). Hît was therefore, *par excellence*, the 'town-of-the-ordeal-river'. And the texts show that people came from far afield so that 'divine justice' could be dispensed, which has encouraged the belief that the custom and ritual of ordeals must have originated in this precise location. At that time, all the Mesopotamian texts that tell us about the people who went to the ordeal bear witness to their travelling as far as the town of Hît.

The texts all underline the liturgical and ceremonial nature of the ordeal procedure. Like the account of Nebuchadnezzar, they mention a ritual of vigil that takes place on the preceding evening. The accused utters ritual formulas and has water poured over his hands. Then, just before the test, there is a solemn statement of the facts, in front of witnesses, consisting of setting forth in detail the reasons for resorting to the ordeal.

After this, the test proper takes place, with two fundamental aspects brought to light by the Mari texts. On the one hand, it is not always the accused himself who is subjected to the ordeal; he or she is often replaced by a third person. In some cases, there is even evidence of veritable 'diving teams', who play the part of 'champions' of the cause to be defended. On the other, we discover that it was not enough to plunge into the river and emerge alive. It was necessary to accomplish a real physical performance into the bargain, as is shown by the example of those servants who, to establish that their masters were in the right, had to 'lift a millstone and get it across the river'.

These two features (substitution and 'sporting' trial) are perfectly illustrated in one of Meptûm's letters to king Zimri-Lim. It concerns a matter of territorial claim, the opponents being two 'vassals' of the king of Mari, Shubram and Hâya-Sûmû – the same Hâya-Sûmû who married two of Zimri-Lim's daughters (Chapter 8).

> To the king, my lord, letter of Meptûm, thy servant. Regarding the people who were to 'dive' for Hâya-Sûmû . . ., to begin with, a woman was thrown in, and she emerged. After her, an old man; he swam a distance of

> 80 cubits 'in the heart of the god', was successful and emerged. After him, a second woman went in, and emerged. After her, a third woman; the river 'married' her. Given that the old man had proved his rights over a distance of only 80 cubits and that the river had 'married' the third woman, Hâya-Sûmû's people refused to let the last three women be subjected to the water. They agreed: 'Town and land are not ours.' And the old man, falling at the feet of Shubram's people, said, 'Do not make the other women dive, for fear that they may die!'

So, in order that Hâya-Sûmû's rights over a city and its territory should be recognised (here it is a matter of civil and not criminal law), it had probably been agreed that a team of six women and an old man must dive into the water and, one after the other without exception, succeed in the special trial of swimming underwater ('in the heart of the god') over a certain distance. Such prior agreements, where the conditions of the ordeal are determined by arrangement between the parties, appear in several documents. In this instance, the team failed; whereas the first two women succeeded, the old man managed to complete only part of the course (about 40 metres), and a third woman drowned ('married' by the god). The ordeal was stopped at the request of the survivors of the team, who acknowledged their failure.

One might well wonder why Hâya-Sûmû's team comprised women and an old man. Contemporaries would have known that the god often 'lent a hand' to the more sporting types. For want of additional information, it is difficult to answer this question, but it could be that Hâya-Sûmû was so sure of his rights that he was able to throw down a challenge of the 'even an old man and some women can defend my cause' kind. Other explanations are possible, however, the more so because we do not know the exact criteria required for the choice of champions.

The end of Meptûm's same letter recounts another ordeal affair, this time concerning one of the women servants of the queen of the land of Zalmaqqum (a region in the north-west of Mesopotamia), the wife of king Yarkab-Addu. Meptûm *tells* why they resorted to the river-god:

> Here are the terms according to which we made her take the plunge: 'Did thy mistress use sorcery against her lord Yarkab-Addu? Did she betray palace secrets? Did another open the thighs of thy mistress? Has thy mistress sinned against her lord?' These are the questions about which she was forced to dive. The river married her; she did not resurface.

In fact, these were the three major accusations that could be levelled at a woman, all very typical of recourse to trial by ordeal: sorcery, political treason and adultery. These attacks on the queen are all concurrent and enable us to guess at an overwhelming inquisition. Probably someone wanted to get rid of this woman and she had been 'charged' with the maximum number of offences. It is difficult to pinpoint the precise content of the accusation of sorcery which heads the list of the three complaints against the queen and therefore seems to be the most serious. Had king Yarkab-Addu fallen sick or lost a war? There is no way of knowing.

Another of Meptûm's letters to the king of Mari gives us a better understanding of what such accusations might mean. This is about a young girl named Mârat-Ishtar, who is accused of having bewitched a boy, Hammî-Epuh, to whose food she must have added something. According to a principle we have already seen, Mârat-Ishtar's mother, substituting herself for her daughter, has to confront the river ordeal. Meptûm relates the oath uttered by the mother to swear her daughter's innocence, and the tragic outcome of the ordeal for both women.

> This is what the woman had to say: 'I swear that my daughter, Mârat-Ishtar, carried out no sorcery against Hammî-Epuh, son of Dâdiya. Neither at the door nor elsewhere did she [Mârat-Ishtar] give Hammî-Epuh, son of Dâdiya, any bewitched wood or make him eat any, in bread, food, beer or anything else.' After she had made this speech, she fell into the depths of the god and died. She did not prove her utterances. The child was freed from the sorcery.

Mârat-Ishtar had been blamed for having cast spells on wood delivered to the young Hammî-Epuh so that he could prepare his food himself. And it was probably in burning this wood that the boy had supposedly unleashed evil spirits, the malign powers having entered what he was eating and making him ill. It will be noted that here divine action was not confined to unmasking the culprit and punishing her; in the end it also liberated the victim from his ill.

Overall in this file of texts on ordeals, one might equally look for something that seems at times to be 'manipulation' of the trial by the judges. For though it is clear that the process was used to safeguard certain legal principles, it is no less true that a wide margin of manoeuvre seems to have existed in the way of assessing the conditions of application and the results. For instance, reading Meptûm's account of the queen of Zalmaqqum, how can we fail to think that she had been condemned in advance, and her servant with her? We could also look at several other recorded cases where the accused refused to subject themselves to the river trial – which boiled down to admitting their guilt and incurring the death penalty. Was it from fear of the god? Or dread of the physical ordeal?

Lastly, we may wonder about the deeper meaning of the ordeal in Mesopotamia. For all matters that were too obscure for them, the ancient inhabitants of those regions, as has been said, always referred to the higher authority of the gods. Appeal to the divine tribunal, in this case the river-god, was a 'cover-up' for the inability of the judges on Earth to decide on rights, innocence or guilt. Ordeal was thus an exceptional procedural instrument in the service of justice.

But it was more than just that, and some studies have shown that a purely juridical view of trial by ordeal is inadequate. As a true historian of mental attitudes, Jean Bottéro for example has tried to replace it in its ideological context. Notably, he has given an 'exorcistic' explanation of the ordeal by river: the running water of the divine river allows the ill to be localised and known before it is acted upon and made to disappear into the depths. Mesopotamian trial by ordeal is also close to divination. Both share the same conviction of the superior power of the gods in the face of human ignorance and impotence. The gods know, and can communicate their knowledge to humans through dreams, omens or other signs that must be asked for and interpreted. To do that, it is enough to put the appropriate words and gestures to work.

So we must be careful not to reduce all the kinds of trial by ordeal down the centuries to one and the same schema. As far as Mesopotamia is concerned, the last word has not yet been said. There are certainly other elements that might enable us to explain more fully why and how the ancients resorted to the river-god. An account from the neo-Assyrian era (seventh century BC), for instance, relates that two people, accused of having broken a taboo, refused to submit to the ordeal. They were accused of having given their son the name of a reigning sovereign or royal prince. Such an accusation, as well as the decision to resort to the divine river, continues to raise a good many questions.

Part III

Myth and Legend

CHAPTER 13

The First Account of the Flood

Jean Bottéro

In those countries that composed the geographical, political and cultural background of the ancient Israelites – the authors of the Bible – for more than 150 years cities, palaces and temples have been unearthed, as well as the remains of early civilisations and an impressive amount of written and decipherable documents. The lion's share comes from the ancient inhabitants of modern Iraq – Sumerians, Babylonians and Assyrians, the inventors of the oldest-known form of writing around 3000 BC – seventeen centuries before Moses; some half million clay tablets on which, with a reed stylus, they inscribed their awkward and strange cuneiform signs. Among these enormous archives are hundreds of historical, literary, 'scientific' and religious works, which have been deciphered and studied by the sparse and almost secret body of Assyriologists.

For those inclined to question, the problem is whether, when faced with the abundant new documentation that historians continue to wrest from their scribbled notes, people can read the Bible 'as in the old days', when it was looked upon as the oldest book in the world and the only one that could throw any light on the earliest ages of mankind.

It is to give 'proof of the pudding' – and to reply to this question not with an aphorism but with a demonstration and what might be called a method exercise – that I have chosen the subject of the Flood, because it is so well known, so much debated and perhaps still so enigmatic.

Assurbanipal

Separate, unexpected, full of precise and vivid detail, included in a book that was deemed to preserve the oldest archives in the history of the world, the biblical record of the Flood (Gen. 6–8) – like so many others from the same background – was for a long time taken to be the account of an event that could hardly be more historical. There is reason to believe that more than one person still thinks so, if we are to judge by the commotion caused some years ago by a 'scientific' expedition which went to carry out research on an Armenian mountain peak on the presumed remains of the famous Ark to which Noah and his menagerie had entrusted themselves.

This account, however, is neither first-hand nor attributable to an eyewitness of any kind. It was only to be expected; we know it now, and Assyriologists began to provide the proof over a century ago. On 2 December 1872, George Smith – one of the first to undertake the deciphering and listing of the thousands of cuneiform tablets from Assurbanipal's[1] library discovered at Nineveh

[1] The Assyrian king Assurbanipal (668–627 BC) had collected the greater part of the ample literary production of his country, carefully recopied on some 5000 'tablets' (we would say 'volumes'), in his palace at Nineveh: everything which, in his time, was considered worthy of being preserved and re-read. In 1852, and then 1872, A. H. Layard and H. Rassam discovered this library, in some 25,000 fragments. Transported to the British Museum in London, it is still the subject of fruitful deciphering. For Assyriologists, it is one of the richest and most irreplaceable sources of our knowledge of the thinking in that ancient land.

– announced that he had found a narrative which was too exactly parallel to the one in the Bible for the coincidence to be attributable to mere chance. This account, in 200 lines, formed the 'XIth Canto' of the famous *Epic of Gilgamesh* (see Chapter 14). Gilgamesh, in search of immortality, having come to the very end of the world to question the hero of the Flood, learns from his lips how the cataclysm had come about in earlier times.

Of course, the edition of the *Epic of Gilgamesh* found in Assurbanipal's library – and dating, like this ruler, to around 650 BC – could not by itself be anterior to what historians have good reason to regard as the oldest narrative stratum of the Bible, known to them as the 'Yahwist document' (8th century) – still more since it is hard to visualise the writers and thinkers of the lofty, dazzling and formidable Babylon going to seek topics among the Israelites.

A century of discoveries amid the inexhaustible treasures of the cuneiform tablets has at least enabled us to obtain a clearer view. We now know that, although the *Epic of Gilgamesh* has a very long literary history, going back far beyond biblical times to around 2000 BC at least, the account of the Flood did not immediately form part of it, but was inserted later, having been plucked from another literary piece where it originally belonged: the *Poem of the Supersage (Atrahasîs)*.

The *Poem of the Supersage* is a work that was little known for a long time (from some scattered fragments), but a series of fortunate finds some years ago has restored two-thirds of it to us; about 800 lines, which are more than adequate for an understanding of its sense and range. Our oldest manuscripts belong to around 1700 BC, and the poem must have been composed shortly before that, in Babylonia. Not only does it contain 'the oldest account of the Flood', which enables us to get a better idea of that event as 'seen' and thought of by those who included it in their writings, it is also quite an admirable composition, in both style and thought, one of those archaic literary works which, because of their quality, breadth of view and inspiration, deserve to become better known.

It begins in the time when man did not yet exist. The gods were the sole occupiers of the universe and, in keeping with the fundamental bipartition in the economy of that time and place, were divided between producers and consumers. In order to provide the 'aristocracy' of the 'Anunnaki' with plenty to live on, an inferior 'class', the 'Igigi' worked the land. 'Their task was considerable,/Heavy their burden and endless their torment!', all the more so, it seems, because there were not enough of them. Finally, exhausted, they launched what we would call the first strike movement, 'Throwing their implements into the fire,/Burning their spades,/Setting light to their paniers', and even going off in the dead of night to 'surround the palace' of their employer and sovereign, Enlil, whom in their rage they propose to dethrone. This throws the 'Anunnaki' into great turmoil and anxiety; what will they do if no one is willing to produce the means of subsistence any more? They gather in full assembly, and Enlil does his best to reduce the rebels to submission; but they declare themselves resolved to hang on to the bitter end. Their drudgery is too unbearable and they are prepared to do anything rather than resume it. Defeated, Enlil then considers abdicating – an even more fearsome upheaval, as that would bring anarchy and breakdown upon the society of the gods.

At this point Ea intervenes; among the major gods, his authority as counsellor and 'vizier' to Enlil is unlike the 'tough rule' of the latter. Ea is the personification of lucidity, intelligence, wiliness, a facility for adaptability and invention and the mastery of techniques. To replace the recalcitrant Igigi, Ea suggests creating a substitute, designed 'To bear the labour imposed by Enlil/And take on the drudgery of the gods': this would be man.

It is not a mere pipe dream. Ea has formed an exact and subtle plan, which he reveals. Man will be made of clay – an omnipresent material in that country – the earth to which he will have to return when he dies. But in order to retain a little part of those whom he is to replace and serve, his clay will be moistened with the blood of a second-rank god, sacrificed for the purpose. The assembly applauds such a wise and advantageous project and, under the direction of Ea, its execution is entrusted to the 'midwife of the gods', 'Mammi-the-Expert'. She perfects the prototype, which is subsequently put into production in fourteen models by a like number of mother-goddesses: seven males and seven females, the first of humankind's 'parents'.

The Three Scourges

Mammi-the-Expert does the job to perfection, and everything goes well, to such an extent that 'the populations having multiplied to such an extreme' and 'the noise they made having become like the lowing of cattle', the peaceful life of the gods is upset until they 'lose sleep because of it'. To put an end to this awful racket, the impetuous Enlil, driven to extreme solutions, takes it upon himself to decimate mankind by means of an epidemic. But Ea, a thoughtful god aware of the risk involved in too great a reduction in the number of men, which would be catastrophic for the gods, warns Atrahasîs, the Supersage – the nickname of a high-ranking person on Earth – whom he trusts and who enjoys great authority over the human population. Ea shows him how they can eliminate the scourge; they need only divert all food offerings to the god Namtar alone (the deity of the killer epidemic), and the gods, reduced to a state of famine, will soon be forced to interrupt the evil; and this, in fact, is what happens. But, with the return of safety, men resume their disturbing and noisy occupations, annoying Enlil once more. This time, he sends drought upon them. A new challenge for Ea, who advises Atrahasîs to have the gods' food reserved for Adad alone (the god in charge of atmospheric precipitation). The gaps in the text allow us to guess that Enlil does not give in at once, but eventually all is restored to order and humankind flourishes again.

From what remains of the tablet, it at least emerges that the king of the gods finally decides to eliminate humans, who are still as noisy as ever, and calls upon an even more radical catastrophe – flood. By now suspicious, he takes every precaution to ensure that his fatal plan cannot be divulged to humans and that no one, therefore, can escape death. But the ever-ingenious Ea manages to warn Atrahasîs indirectly of the imminent disaster and the stratagem he has worked out to save him – but this time him only, together with his family. Atrahasîs will have to 'build a double-decked boat, strongly rigged, duly caulked and robust', for which Ea 'draws the plan on the ground'. He will have to provision it, and at a signal from his god, will 'embark [his] stores, [his] furniture, [his] wealth/[his] wife, [his] nearest and dearest and allies, [his] foremen [to preserve the secrets of acquired techniques], as well as domestic and wild animals'; after which all that remains for him to do is 'go aboard the boat and close the hatches'. What follows (full of gaps in what has been preserved for us of the *Poem*) can easily be supplemented by the account in the *Epic of Gilgamesh*, which is later by several centuries but broadly drew its inspiration from it.

Having found a way of explaining his strange behaviour to those around him, without alarming them, Atrahasîs carries out Ea's orders, 'embarks cargo and family' and 'offers a great banquet'; but during its course he remains anxious. 'He does nothing but come in and go out,/Never sitting down or staying in one place,/His heart broken, sick with anxiety' – he awaits the fatal signal.

This finally arrives: 'The weather changed its aspect And the Storm thundered amid the clouds!' Time to get ready:

When the first rolls of thunder were heard,
Bitumen was brought to him, so that he could seal the hatch.
And once it was closed,
The storm still rumbling in the clouds,
The winds were unleashed.
So he cut the mooring ropes to free the vessel!

The Flood, clearly an enormous inundation caused by torrential rains, then continues:

Six days and seven nights, the tempest raged.
Anzû [the Rapacious, a giant deity] rent the skies with his talons: It was well and truly a Flood
Whose brutality fell upon populations like War!
Nothing remained to be seen
And nothing was identifiable any more in that carnage!
The Flood bellowed like a bull;
The Wind shrieked, like a screeching eagle!
The darkness was impenetrable; there was no more Sun!

When the cataclysm had

demolished the earth, the seventh day having come,
The raging Hurricane of the Flood subsided,
After delivering its blows [at random], like a woman in labour;
The Mass of water calmed; the Storm ceased; the Flood was over!

Then, the hero relates,

I opened the hatch, and the fresh air hit me in the face!
Then I scanned the shore, at the horizon of the Expanse of water;
Some cables' distance away, a spit of land emerged.
The vessel landed there; it finally came to rest on Mount Nicir![2]

Atrahasîs prudently waits a further week before using a stratagem of the first navigators on the high seas.

I took a dove and released it;
The dove flew off but came back:
Having found nowhere to land it returned!
I then took a swallow and released it;
It flew off but came back:
Having found no landing place, it returned!
Lastly I released a crow:
The crow flew off but, finding that the waters had receded,
It pecked, cawed, and did not come back at all!

This is the sign that he can now leave his refuge; so he disembarks the passengers from the boat 'and scatters them to the four winds'; and immediately resuming the essential function of humankind – of which he, together with his family, remains the sole representative to escape – he prepares a banquet for the gods who, having fasted for so long, cluster around him 'like flies'.

[2] According to native sources, Mount Nicir was situated in present-day Kurdistan, in the north-east of the country, some 80 kilometres east of Kirkuk. It was very probably the present Pir Omar Gudrun (almost 3000 metres). It dominates all that sector of the country, and may have been chosen for that reason, or perhaps because its name evoked 'protection' and also 'mystery' in the Akkadian language. The authors of the biblical history of the Flood, who took a more distant view, spoke vaguely of the 'mountains of Ararat' (Gen. 8: 4), in other words, Armenia, north of Mesopotamia, known to be the loftiest in that part of the world. It was only later, by a sort of logical deduction, that one of the highest in the chain was chosen, the Agridagh or Massis (over 5000 metres), obviously the first to be uncovered when the waters receded, to make it the Ark's resting-place.

Then, while the Great Goddess (the one who had had a hand in the creation of men) vainly calls for the condemnation of Enlil, the author of the disaster, he realises that his plan for the total extinction of humankind has been thwarted and flies into a rage. But Ea shows him that he should never have resorted to such an extreme and brutal measure and 'without reflecting, provoked the Flood'. For, if men had totally disappeared, would not the gods have found themselves in precisely the same impasse that had brought about man's creation? A world without producers? And, as if to point out what it would have sufficed to do, the wise Ea suggests the introduction in the new generation, the issue of Atrahasîs, of a kind of 'natural Malthusianism' which, by restricting the births and survival of newborn babies, would moderate the proliferation and tumult. That is why, henceforward, some women will be sterile; others exposed to the implacable extinguishing demon, who will snatch their babies from their breast; others who will embrace a religious status which will prohibit their becoming mothers.

Here, in a last break that conceals the denouement from us, the third and last tablet of the *Poem* ends.

Despite the terseness of the summary just given, it may be seen that this is less a true ancient *history* of mankind – in other words, a sufficiently faithful version of the events that presided over its origins and first avatars – than an explanation of man's nature, place and function in the universe. Rather than a kind of chronology, on the whole it is something akin to an exposition of theology which, despite its lively and descriptive style, intends not to record factual data but well and truly to inculcate definitions, perspectives and an entire system of ideas concerning the universe and mankind. It is what could be called a mythological account.

A Philosophy in Images

In spite of their lively intelligence, universal curiosity, and the enormous intellectual and material advances for which we know they were responsible during the three millennia (at least) while their civilisation and sphere of influence lasted and increased, the ancient Mesopotamians never attained abstract thought. Like many other ancient, and even some modern, peoples – and unlike our own customs – they never disassociated their ideology from their imagination. In the same way that, in their mathematical treatises, they put forward and solved only particular problems – without ever extracting or formulating principles of solution from them – so they presented their general ideas not in their universality but always embodied in some single fact.

Myths, the favourite expression of such speculative thought, were precisely what enabled them to materialise their conceptions, let them flow into images, scenes, series of adventures – certainly created by their imagination, but in answer to some query – to throw light on some problem, to teach some theory – as the writers of fables construct their little tales to inculcate some moral.

The whole of Sumerian and Babylonian literature is filled with this 'philosophy in images' that is mythology, and the *Poem of Atrahasîs* is a very fine example, both by the scale of the picture it embraces and by the intelligence and weight of the questions it airs. All in all, the problem is that of the human condition – and quite naturally, from the viewpoint of its authors. What is the meaning of our life? Why are we committed to exhausting and never-ending toil? Why this division between the multitude, who find themselves exclusively condemned to toil, and an elite who lead a tranquil existence, ensured precisely by the labour of others? If we are aware of immortality, why do we have to die in the end? And why is that death hastened from time to time by more or less monstrous and unexpected scourges? And so many further enigmas, such as the restrictions – in themselves inexplicable – placed on women's fundamental role of bringing children into the world and keeping them alive?

All these difficulties had to be not only formulated but solved in the particular setting in which they were raised – an essentially theocentric system. For those people, the world could not be explained on its own; it had its *raison d'être* in a supernatural society, the gods, whose existence was beyond doubt. In order to gain some idea of those personages whom no one – with good reason – had ever seen, they had merely projected what they saw all around them on to a higher plane: the whole of this world's material, economic, social and political organisation. The gods were conceived as humans, with all the needs of humans; but they were superlative, freed from the fundamental constraints that oppress us, such as illness and death, and endowed with powers far outreaching our own. That being so, how could their persons fail to be modelled on the flower of humankind – the 'aristocracy' of 'the ruling class'?

'Aristocratic' Gods

In such a system, compared with the divine world, and for its benefit, the entire human race could hardly fill any other function than that of subjects in relation to those who govern them; liable to unpaid labour as required, and providers of all the things that were indispensable to a life of opulence, with no worries apart from giving orders. So, of necessity, men owed their existence to the gods, of whom it is self-evident that they could be neither the forerunners nor even independent contemporaries. As on Earth, the divine world simply had to have been self-sufficient, divided as it was into a category of producers and an elite of consumers; and it must have been forced to put an end to that state of affairs because of some internal crisis, similar to those that erupt in our day between employers and employed, when the latter feel they are being over-exploited. Thus man was 'by birth' the servant of the gods; and when they created him, the gods had not failed to provide that he should retain something of them, certainly, their long life, intelligence and power – but all strictly limited, so that he was inferior, weak and transitory. That was the idea that had been evolved of the nature and condition of humankind.

By itself, such an arrangement would have implied the absence of any cloud between gods and men, provided that the latter – as was generally the case – carried out exactly all their duties towards their masters. Leaving aside death, illness and the troubles that attend every individual, because they are implanted in our nature and destiny, how was it possible to explain those enormous convulsions of the great catastrophes that befall humans unexpectedly and apparently without cause, wiping them out *en masse*? What was the reason for those 'cosmic' calamities like epidemics, famines and the sudden devastating assaults of nature? The gods, without whom nothing important could occur, must obviously be the cause. But why? Faced with this problem, the authors of the *Poem* could find no other reason than the capriciousness of the ruling gods. Of course, they could discern a motive – a pretext? – on the part of men; by their prosperity and multiplication alone, and the very gusto and drive of their activities as servants, they might offend their rulers in some way, as the over-numerous and over-busy staff of an irritable sovereign might disturb his repose. But in such a theocentric universe, so far removed from any idea of 'challenge' or rebellion against power, was it not the ultimate in wisdom to feel dependence, submit to one's own condition, accept one's destiny, show resignation and fatalism? When the authors of the *Poem* revealed that, in the dawn of humanity – the 'mythical era' before history when the 'historical world' was being formed – the gods had now and then been moved by the desire to decimate and even annihilate men by visiting collective calamities upon them to this end, they were not only giving their public an adequate reason for the existence of those cyclic scourges, but also stressing their rather 'traditional' nature and therefore their inevitability, before which humans must bow.

But such a lesson in wisdom had its counterpart of hope; 'once upon a time', in those misfortunes men had had a defender and saviour – the god Ea, their 'inventor', the enemy of all futile violence, the same god, moreover (as another series of myths related) who had perfected and propagated every useful piece of knowledge among men. In fact, by one of them he had taught men how to guard against the great universal misfortunes. Now, in 'historical time', they could thus still apply his lessons and in this way fight catastrophes in order to escape them. This is the 'philosophy' that the *Poem of the Supersage* was trying to instill in its users, through the medium of its fables and myths.

The Flood or the Floods?

The account of the Flood had the same value and sense as those of the epidemic and the drought which preceded it. We know very well from our historical documentation that calamities of this kind periodically struck the country, which was as yet so poorly protected medically, and with an economy that was still planned in only a rudimentary manner. By means of a process that was common in literature, especially folklore and poetry, the memories of such experiences, recorded in tradition or lived through, were amalgamated; illnesses that spread like wildfire and raised the death rate, or poor harvests that wore down populations and resulted in epidemic or famine – the Lion or the Ogre, in the storytellers' language – each concentrating the horrors of all and projected, like some terrifying prototype, on the mythical 'once upon a time'. The Flood that follows them would have been imagined and constructed in similar fashion. In that country centred on the Tigris and Euphrates, which immediately reacted to an excess of rain, flooding was not a rarity (we know of several instances) and could be murderous and spectacular to a greater or lesser degree. Archaeologists themselves have found sometimes impressive traces, especially at Ur, Kish and Fâra-Shuruppak, among various strata of the IVth and IIIrd millennia. Based on a certain number of catastrophes that had ravaged one city or another, one region or another, the cataclysm had been composed, submerging the entire country; and a far-reaching legend crystallised around the event, to emerge in the 'history' recounted in *Atrahasîs*, and later enlarged by the authors of Canto XI of *Gilgamesh*.

Of course it is still possible that, in the wealth of details and the importance given to the Flood by Babylonian tradition which – as may be seen in the *Poem* and can be found fairly frequently elsewhere – had turned it into the last act of mythical times and the threshold of the historical era, a rather vague memory of one of those especially fearsome cataclysms may have survived, but it would be very naive to imagine that it happened as described. But resorting to such a disaster is not inevitable; the pivotal role in time played by the Flood may well have been ascribed to it not for its historicity but for the place it occupied in the traditional mythology reflected in the *Poem*: it was the last and most dangerous of the great calamities visited by the gods upon men to make them toe the line and reduce them to the scale that has been theirs since the beginning of history.

Let us now return to the account in the Bible, with which we began and which it will now be easier to see in its true light. Anyone who has really read and reflected on it to any extent will at first admit that it is hard to conceive the idea of such an inundation in a hilly land of streams like Palestine, without the slightest river worthy of the name, or the slightest valley broad and suitable enough for the accumulation of water. *A priori*, the reasonable probability is therefore that the story was borrowed. However, though the more than substantial identity with the Babylonian flood is not in the least doubt, there are too many divergent details between the two for the account in Genesis to be regarded simply as a transcription into Hebrew of the Akkadian text of *Atrahasîs* or *Gilgamesh*.

The Flood, the Bible and Mesopotamia

The Flood is part of a vast harvest of theological, mythological and ideological themes, and more besides, devised by that eminent and prodigious Mesopotamia, which from the earliest times had impregnated the entire Near East with them. One has only to think of the unlikely finds of Ebla in Syria, for half of the third millennium! Like many others – the Creation of the World, the Origins and Ancient History of men, the Problem of Evil and Divine Justice – the theme of the Flood would also have been welcomed by the Israelites who, through their ancestors and themselves, were exposed to the extraordinary cultural sphere of influence of Sumer and Babylon. They even adopted it in its setting: apparently – as in *Atrahasîs* – the primitive 'history' of man, in reality the theological picture of his condition in this world. For it is the purpose of the first eleven chapters of Genesis to inculcate in us, for our guidance, how the universe and men were modelled and remodelled, put in place and 'in working order' before history, properly speaking, began with Abraham. But they did not retain either its native theology or way of looking at things; as they did with everything that they took from the ancient Babylonians, they profoundly reworked it, imbuing it with their original religious ideology. Their system, too, was theocentric; but, as the 'inventors' of monotheism, their divine world was concentrated on the one and transcendent God, who had not the least anthropomorphic feature, or the slightest need for 'servants' to ensure His way of life. That is why, in the Flood as they 'rethought' it, they replaced the multitude of deities with the one God, and the capriciousness and futility of the masters of the universe with moral demands: if God sends this cataclysm upon men, it is because of their 'corruption' (Gen. 6: 5ff.), in order to propagate a new human race which will be capable – at least through the best of its representatives (the people descended from Abraham) – of leading a life from now on fully in accord with an elevated ethical and religious ideal.

It is this Flood, the one in the Bible, that lingers in our memory, imbued as we are – like it or not – with the scenes and teaching of that ancient book. But the aim of history is to seek to understand by 'going back', by 'what was there before', children by their fathers and rivers by their sources. That is why, in addition to what they recover *en masse* from our oldest forefathers in direct lineage, from those incomparable Sumerian and Babylonian civilisers and their heritage that has come down to us, filtered, reworked, enriched, sometimes impoverished, by the millennia, Assyriologists can also throw light on the Bible for us. They do so by reintroducing its content into its 'historical continuum', which illuminates it so particularly. Peaceable and unobtrusive, these people's calling is not exactly easy; spending one's life deciphering, analysing, penetrating the secrets of thousands of clay 'notebooks', hatched with spiky and daunting cuneiform characters! One may wonder, however, whether this arduous immobility is not more fruitful than all the mighty to-ings and fro-ings to bring back a few worm-eaten planks, which with touching naivety are assumed to be a relic of the shipwreck of an 'Ark' as fabulous as the Giant's seven-league boots.

CHAPTER 14

The Epic of Gilgamesh

Jean Bottéro

In the rich literary heritage of ancient Mesopotamia, together with the code of Hammurabi, *Ishtar in the Underworld* and the famous *Poem of the Creation*, the *Epic of Gilgamesh* is undoubtedly one of the rare pieces which nonprofessionals may have heard about at some time or another. But their acquaintance will be scanty and poor, at that; they will not know its worth, or with what vigour of thought and imagination it brings us face to face with the fundamental problem that is forever nagging us, although we may not consciously recognise it. When all is said and done, we shall in our turn enter endless night, and willy-nilly our existence is therefore nothing more than an insignificant interlude.

The *Epic of Gilgamesh* does not impart such a feeling of our impermanence and the inevitability of our end as that other great book in the Bible, Ecclesiastes, showing point by point how everything is negligible and frail. It instils it more subtly and perhaps more effectively, through the prowess and disappointments of a man like ourselves, sublime and heroic enough to impress us, but close enough to us to move us and enable us to understand that his destiny is ours, too. Only great minds and great writers can create such unforgettable, universal types in whom we each entirely recognise ourselves, even if their remoteness in place, time and culture confers a kind of unreality upon them.

An explanation of the impressive and fascinating work of which Gilgamesh is the hero is worth while for more than one reason, but first of all perhaps because after lengthy studies we are now in a better position to know it more fully and discern its story, composition and meaning more precisely and with clearer hindsight. Great discoverers of secrets buried for millennia in subterranean tombs, Assyriologists are never in a hurry to divulge them, but let us at least extract from them what they know at present about this ancient masterpiece.

The Sumerian Legends of Gilgamesh

Not the slightest identifiable trace remains of the person, but we know from a reliable source that, around 2600 BC, Gilgamesh (whose name, Sumerian and archaic, tells us nothing for certain) had been one of the sovereigns of the venerable city of Uruk and had built its first defensive walls, which were rediscovered in 1932 by German archaeologists. We also know of two or three mighty ancestors in his country, whose exploits and glory had, in the view of their compatriots, elevated them to supernatural rank fairly swiftly after their death. The Greeks would have made 'heroes' of them, but being unaware of that category, the Mesopotamians had regarded them as more or less 'divine'. We are ignorant of the merit that had earned Gilgamesh such advancement, but the fact is that he rapidly passed into legend, and generally speaking legends manifestly include many genuine features; but we are scarcely in a position to distinguish them from their aura of fantasy.

Of this somewhat fabulous archaic vision of Gilgamesh,

there remain – rather knocked about by the damage of time in their framework of clay – at least five legends, lofty in style and in the Sumerian language, composed at the latest around the end of the third millennium (in other words, about 4000 years ago), but the manuscripts discovered are slightly more recent. One legend merely recalls Gilgamesh's military glory and his magnanimity, telling how, after defeating a king of the neighbouring town of Kish, he treated him with clemency. The second legend depicts the arrival of his 'phantom', after his death, in the immense and shadowy subterranean cavern of the 'Land-of-no-return', and in this Kingdom of the Dead confers upon him an important supernatural role, which he was to keep throughout later tradition. The three other tales seem to refer to special episodes in his life, most probably 'historical'. In them he is usually accompanied by a character called Enkidu (whose Sumerian name seems to mean that he was a 'creation of the god Enki/Ea') and who is always portrayed as Gilgamesh's servitor' or right-hand man.

In the first of these tales, both set off on a campaign for the 'Pine Forest', situated somewhere in the mountains of the east, access to which is blocked by a formidable supernatural monster named Huwawa, a fierce and vigilant guardian. The two companions take him by surprise and kill him, and from then on are free to exploit the riches of his forests. This is a clear transposition of ages-old and continual sorties, peaceable or warlike, to which people in Mesopotamia had always been compelled, being in search of raw materials that were almost totally lacking, especially wood for building. The second story must have evoked a famous catastrophe that had hit Uruk, disguising it under the veils of fable and folklore, in the form of atrocious ravages by a gigantic Celestial Bull, dispatched against the town at the request of the goddess Inanna/Ishtar in a rage; it is eventually killed by the two heroes.

The fifth and last of these legends would seem to celebrate the death of Enkidu in its own fashion. It is presented as an initially voluntary descent into Hell to retrieve precious talismans that Gilgamesh had let fall there; but the bold traveller finds himself held among the dead, with permission – just once – to return to his master to explain to him the mysterious existence of the deceased in their doleful habitation.

We know that, from the last part of the third millennium, a profound change took place in Mesopotamia, the indirect consequence of the final elimination of the Sumerian section of the population, which was absorbed and swallowed by the Semitic component. The Sumerians' cultural predominance was succeeded by the rise to prominence of the Semites, Akkadians as we would say. From then on the sole possessors of their ancient patrimony, they were at that time reinforced by a fresh wave of their brethren – immigrants in their turn – whose most famous son, Hammurabi (c. 1750 BC), created a large, enduring and prosperous kingdom centred on the city of Babylon. From this Semitisation and advancement was born a broad movement of development and rethinking of traditional values, together with a notable cultural progress which produced, among other things, several literary masterpieces, remarkable for the widening of their horizons and their concern for synthesis. The most celebrated is the mythological picture of the first history of human beings, from their creation until their entry, through the Flood, into a properly historical era: the *Poem of Atrahasîs (the Supersage)* (see Chapter 13).

From that period we have found some ten scattered fragments, in Akkadian, relating to Gilgamesh, and in texture, tone and range they are very different from the Sumerian legends quoted above. Two are whole tablets, one following the other and each of 250 lines; and there is every reason to suppose that there was at least another tablet, before and after – which would bring the total to a minimum of one thousand lines. Far removed from the meagre accounts in Sumerian, limited, short-winded and with no breadth of horizon, here we have the impression that we are in the presence of the remains of a coherent, extended and complex work, and each fragment – even those whose pitiful state of preservation seems to have reduced them to one episode – says enough for us to assume preceding ones and anticipate others, like the toothed cog of some complicated machinery.

It is therefore likely that some unknown author of the period, some 3600 years ago, wanted to assemble an entire rich fresco based on Gilgamesh in a single and far-ranging account. It was esteemed and famous enough to be exported to distant parts; remains have been discovered in Palestine, and fragments of a translation into the Hurrite language, spoken in the north and north-west of Mesopotamia; and even the well-known and distant Hittites of Anatolia abridged it for their own use, as evidenced by various scraps that have been found among them, and in their language. We do not possess the first true *Epic of Gilgamesh* in its complete state, but only in bits and pieces, and are therefore unable to form a sure idea of its various episodes, their sequence and the overall impression it might have given.

However, bearing in mind the obstinate traditionalism that seems to be one of the peculiarities of the ancient Mesopotamian civilisation, and the similar case of a fair number of comparable works, there is every likelihood that this first version of the *Epic of Gilgamesh* is to be rediscovered, altered and enlarged with time, adapted to changes in outlook and taste, but substantially identical, in a more recent and much better-known presentation, the earliest evidence of which is datable to the cusp of the second and first millennium. In some ten manuscripts and quite a few fragments, we have as yet recovered only two-thirds, but quite sufficient to gain an often distinct, and at least panoramic and coherent, view of it. For it *is* impressive – certainly much more so than the ancient and fragmentary version composed, as we have seen, six or seven centuries earlier and mentioned above. Originally, it comprised eleven tablets, each of 200–300 lines, to which a twelfth was later added as a kind of supplement, much shorter, obviously appended and extrinsic. This re-edition of the *Epic of Gilgamesh*, touched up and enlarged, was probably completed shortly before the end of the second millennium. Its 'author' was said to be a certain Sîn-leqe' unnennî, who is otherwise unknown. It is sometimes called the 'Ninevite' version of the *Epic*, because the first and most important manuscripts were found among the remains of Assurbanipal's library in the ruins of his palace at Nineveh (see Chapter 13, n. 1).

It is through this Ninevite version that we become best acquainted with the prowess and setbacks, the mighty deeds and ultimate failure of Gilgamesh, as the fragments of the earlier version allow only a fairly small number of episodes to emerge. This is the one we must read in order to get the measure of such a masterly and profound work, which is penetrating, moving and so far-reaching.

Of the historical Gilgamesh, ancient tradition must have retained the fact that he was haunted by death in one way or another. One of the legends in Sumerian in which he is the hero has him anxiously questioning Enkidu, who had been released for a short while from the Land-of-no-return, in order to learn from him the mysterious condition of the shades. Another accompanies his phantom, after his death, to their torpid and dismal place of sojourn. It is precisely on this trait in his character – fondness for life and denial of death – that the author of the Akkadian story (by a real synthesis of the folkloristic material available to him, especially the Sumerian legends of the cycle of Gilgamesh) has centred his broad and powerful composition, which is perfectly structured and developed, *crescendo*, like a tragedy in several acts. The drama of an accomplished, most favoured man, both the happiest to live life to the full and the worthiest to live forever, whose gigantic effort to evade death will end in lamentable failure – he is the paragon for all of us who cannot manage to accept truly and light-heartedly, or to overcome, that remorseless prospect of seeing the thread of our existence finally severed once and for all.

In the first half of the *Epic* – the first six tablets of the Ninevite version – Gilgamesh initially appears in all his imposing presence, perfection and success. 'An exceptional monarch, famous, prestigious', 'Returned from his wanderings, wearied but at peace', after 'seeing everything,/Knowing and committing the entire world to memory', he is supposed to have 'carved all his mighty deeds on a stele'. The account of his roving destiny – of which the *Epic* will thus provide the main theme – is to inculcate in us the lesson of his terrible failure: resignation to our fatal destiny. He is the king of Uruk, living a life of luxury, adulated and prosperous. He is a kind of superman, and such are his vigour and exuberance that he cannot help tyrannising his people; with the result that, alerted by the laments of his subjects, and in order to calm him down a little, the gods resort to a kind of psychological subterfuge that they are glad to use. They create a rival for him, of his own size and appearance, to rid him of his feeling of absolute superiority and channel his excess of forcefulness and belligerence.

This is how the Enkidu of the legends is introduced in Sumerian; but to place him in better contrast with his future adversary, here the author has made him a kind of symmetrical opposite of Gilgamesh. Where the latter is civilised, refined, a man of the city, Enkidu is wild and primitive, born isolated in the steppe, with wild animals and their herds for his only companions, which he closely resembles in his way of life and habits. The archaic comparison between a nomadic and crude population, gradually subjugated, if not swallowed, by highly cultivated citizens, probably shows through in this contrast. What memories did it evoke?

Informed that such a creature exists, Gilgamesh sends a courtesan to tame and attract him; she is known as 'The Joyous One' (*Shamhat* in Akkadian), a woman, like many in Mesopotamia, devoted to the practice of 'free love' – held to be one of the prerogatives of early civilised life. Indeed, she seduces him, and Enkidu makes love to her for 'six days and seven nights on end'. Then, feeling that he is no longer 'one of them', the animals flee him, while he becomes attached to his mentor and learns from her how 'to become a man', a real man, civilised and urbanised. She takes him to the town – Uruk. Thus by 'free love' with a true woman, not just a mere female, this wild creature is introduced to great culture, which completely brings him out of his former brutishness.

Meanwhile, in Uruk, Gilgamesh has had warning dreams of the advent of a rival, as powerful as he, with whom he will be fighting, before making him his best friend. This is indeed what occurs; the first contact of the two supermen when they meet is a rough fist fight. But afterwards, they 'embrace and become friends'. This is another considerably far-reaching innovation; the one who, in the Sumerian legends, was never anything more than the 'servitor' of Gilgamesh, has become his 'inseparable friend', his alter ego, and we shall soon see what use the author makes of such a metamorphosis.

I should mention in passing that here, in the Ninevite edition, begins the series of lacunae – shattered or fragmentary manuscripts – that render it mute or barely intelligible in places. Luckily, the two successive tablets of the ancient version opportunely fill part of the present void. Here we have Gilgamesh prey to a nostalgia for great adventures, unheard-of dangers, and glory – a way of ensuring at least the immortality of fame: 'If I succumb, at least I shall have made a name for myself/Eternal renown.' In this way the author has tried to make him approach the central theme of the work, as if his young, fiery hero was not yet clinging sufficiently to life to beware of risking it, and had not yet a clear enough notion of death to flee it at all costs. 'Since we have to die,' the luminous Pindarus would say in another time and place, 'why sit in the shadows, dragging out a useless old age without glory?'

To ready his hero for a confrontation with one of these dreams of exploits, dangers and fame, here the author of the *Epic* has incorporated the Sumerian legend of the 'Pine Forest', revised and adapted in his own fashion. In the mean time, however, the theatrical setting has changed; the old eastern reserves of essences being no doubt exhausted, he turns to the north-west, and the 'Mountain' and 'Forest of Cedars' from now on are Lebanon and Amanus (see Map). The dreaded guardian Huwawa (the spelling slightly altered to Humbaba) has been transferred there by the author who, besides, has immediately turned him from a fearsome obstacle into an enemy to be wiped out. The tale of the hero's long journey, in six stages, crossed as if by giant steps and in each case preceded by a dream to give some sort of presentiment of both the perils and the happy outcome of the undertaking, is badly preserved in our manuscripts. We can get a fair glimpse of it, however, enough to see how in the end, after neutralising the terrifying keeper of the forest, they decide to kill him – seemingly on Enkidu's suggestion – cut down trees to their heart's content and carry off the trunks on board their ship, which goes down the Euphrates and brings them back to Uruk where they are given a triumphal welcome.

At this point, our author inserts his own version of the legend of the Celestial Bull. Ishtar – the patron goddess of 'free love' – seeing Gilgamesh parading like a peacock in all his might and glory, immediately falls in love with him and tells him so in fairly coarse terms. But he, being aware of her frivolous nature and the scant consideration she shows her lovers once she is tired of them, scornfully rejects her, throwing in her face his poor opinion of her, together with a list of her failed love affairs. That is why, in a fury, she goes to her 'father', Anu, to demand that he send against the city of the man who has insulted her a giant Bull, which wreaks carnage there. But the two heroes overpower and kill it. Enkidu even contemptuously hurls one of the animal's hooves at Ishtar, who is impotently watching the ruin of her plan for vengeance, and goes as far as to threaten to festoon the goddess with its guts. Gilgamesh's triumph is complete; he senses it, demonstrates it and, proclaiming himself 'the finest/the most glorious of men', holds a great feast in his palace.

The author of the *Epic* has homed in on the cruel inevitability of our life which turns our most striking successes into the foretaste and beginning of our downfall. From the outset of the heroes' wanderings, he has cleverly prepared the grounds for this downfall by scattering here and there excesses that they indulge in which cannot meet with the gods' approval: the pointless murder of the supernatural Huwawa/Humbaba; the insults to Ishtar, which are equally unnecessary; and perhaps the dizzying and 'over the top' feelings that are almost always a parasite on our greatest achievements. At the beginning of tablet VII, luck has turned. In a dream, Enkidu sees the gods condemning him to death. He does in fact fall ill, goes downhill, curses the courtesan who by promoting him to a higher plane of life in reality set him on the road to misfortune, and finally dies in the arms of his despairing friend, who is at first unwilling to believe it and holds his corpse 'until the moment when worms fall from his nostrils'. Then he intones a heart-rending threnody to his alter ego whom death has snatched from him. Although the whole passage, which is in a fairly bad state, barely enables us to follow the account step by step, it immediately becomes clear that the author had a deep reason for changing the status of Enkidu. He had to be no longer a simple servant, inferior and a stranger, but the closest person possible to Gilgamesh's heart, so that his demise overwhelms not only the latter's spirit but his entire life. For the first time, here he is in the presence of *actual death*; the cruel fate of his friend has presented him with a pitiless and hideous image of his own death, as well as a kind of advance notice and presentiment: 'I, too, shall have to die like Enkidu!/My heart is drowned in despair.'

Nevertheless, in the end he resolves to fight – it is part of his nature – against such a fate. At the far end of our world, on the fringe of that of the gods, he knows of the existence of a man like himself who yet leads an endless life. This is the hero and sole survivor of the Flood, here called Utanapishtî. 'I have found my life!' He will go and visit this man and ask him his secret, so that he can profit from it. So he sets off on an interminable, exhausting and wondrous journey to the ends of the Earth. It is a great pity that most of the tale is lost or damaged.

Before crossing the last perilous sea – and this is a new twist brought in by our author – he receives a warning from the mysterious nymph Siduri:

> Where are you rushing off to now, Gilgamesh?
> The endless life that you seek you will never find!
> When the gods created men,
> They also allotted them death,
> Keeping immortality for themselves alone!
> Far better that you should fill your belly,
> Have fun day and night . . .
> Wear fine clothing,

Wash and bathe your body!
Look fondly on your little boy who holds your hand
And make your wife happy, clasped to you!
That is the only prospect for men!

But, lost in his hopes and dreams, he refuses to heed her, crosses the sea with its thousand perils, and at last reaches Uta-napishtî-the-faraway whom he bluntly questions. 'You are just like me,/Yet the gods have granted you life without end!/What did you do to obtain it?'

In reply, his interlocutor undertakes the long account of the Flood, which the *Epic*'s author, again using an entire pre-existing folklore, has borrowed and adapted from the famous *Poem of the Supersage*. It emerges that, favoured by the superintelligent Enki/Ea who, according to the myth, had invented men so that by their toil the gods could live in happy idleness, Uta-napishtî had been chosen to ensure men's return after the brutal, stupid and thoughtless cataclysm inflicted by Enlil, sovereign of the gods and the world, 'because their noisiness had prevented him from sleeping'. Because Uta-napishtî had fulfilled this duty, which was to their advantage, the gods had transferred him to this 'suburb' of their domain, as far removed as possible from less happy mortals, thus granting him life without end, a unique and exceptional situation that could not be repeated for Gilgamesh, whose unprecedented efforts have consequently been in vain.

As if to show him more clearly that he is not fitted for immortality, Uta-napishtî puts him to the test, challenging him to remain only 'six days and seven nights without yielding to sleep', the image of death. He accepts the wager – but almost immediately falls into a deep sleep, and is therefore forced to admit, in consternation, that living forever is not to be his lot. Anguish and confusion are revealed in the conclusion he draws: 'And now, what can I do? Where can I go?/Now the Reaper will seize me!/Death is already close to me!/Wherever I flee, it awaits me!'

However, filled with pity to see him so unhappy and cast down after so many incredible dangers and trials which he has confronted with such courage, Uta-napishtî's wife persuades her husband not to let Gilgamesh depart completely empty-handed. He therefore tells him of the existence and hiding-place of a mysterious plant, which certainly does not ensure true immortality but at least allows an old man to rediscover his youth, thus postponing the fateful day of reckoning. It must be sought at the bottom of the sea in a secret cranny, where it is protected by terrible thorns. With great difficulty Gilgamesh reaches the spot, dives and seizes the Plant of Youth. He will therefore not have wasted his time and trouble completely.

Alas! On his homeward journey, wanting to refresh his tired limbs, he leaves the marvellous Plant for a moment on the bank – just the time it takes for a bath – and a serpent steals it from him! So his last hope crumbles, and the very gain – however derisory in comparison with his ambitions – that his wearisome journeys have earned him disappears: 'What was the good of wearing myself out?/ What was the good of punishing my heart to such an extent?/I have gained nothing for myself:/All I have done is profit the Serpent!' – for it was believed that when the snake sloughed off its skin it regained its vitality.

It would appear that this is when Gilgamesh becomes resigned: the adventure over, the poet is concise. Without more ado, he brings home his hero 'exhausted but at peace with himself', to make no more of him than the great man 'Who has seen everything,/Known the entire world and committed all to memory', ready to leave to others, to all men who will come after him, the cruel and profound lesson of his experience. For here the author manages to bring us back full circle to the very beginning of his work, letting us understand that the person he originally presented, before the account of his adventures, was in fact the one *after* the events, who at the end of the tale has become a man like other men and resigned to his fatal destiny. He has realised that so much expenditure of energy, so many efforts, have in no way served to prolong his life or postpone death, and considers it more worth while to live without giving it thought, contenting himself at best with the immortality of renown and glory which he had originally aimed for and obtained. As the wise Siduri advised him, he will now gather in full measure all the joys of existence without paying too much heed to their ultimate fatal interruption.

What would be the point of making the slightest addition to this long tale of a grandiose illusion lost, an immense hope collapsed, so many futile efforts? Yet, although we do not know at what point in the manuscript tradition, someone added a twelfth tablet – at all events before the time of Assurbanipal, in whose library it was found. This, too, revolves around death, and is purely and simply the translation into Akkadian of one of the Sumerian legends of the cycle of Gilgamesh; the one in which Enkidu has descended to Hell and been held there. From the evidence, it is in no way part of the *Epic*; merely a kind of supplement slipped into the file, an addendum, which is moreover in complete contrast to the whole work itself. In the VIIth tablet we learned of Enkidu's illness and subsequent death, yet here he is presented in perfect health and offering to descend to the Land-of-no-return, where his courageous venture will come to nought because he will be kept there, dead like all the other inhabitants of this sinister place. In the logical and dramatic sequence of the *Epic*, as conceived and developed by its author, such a snippet does not merit the least place; it is merely the piously preserved echo of quite another folkloric tradition.

Even if one decides to take the words at face value, the *Epic of Gilgamesh* is not an explanatory account, a myth, although it happens to have been treated or qualified as such. Here and there a few true myths have been incorporated, for instance the amours of the fickle Ishtar or the Flood, but these are dealt with more explicitly elsewhere in literary tradition. Its hero is not one of those prototypes whose fate, by mythological rules, explains the nature and destiny of his descendants. He is a superior personality, the greatest of men, but not the first, the archetype of our entire race. In recounting his travels the author has not at all sought to explain why we are all condemned from the very outset to die. The ancient readers of his work knew the explanation only too well, and in any case the sensible Siduri clearly referred to it in her harangue quoted earlier.

The Gods Invent Mankind

Several myths, the most famous and exemplary of which is that of the *Supersage*, give details of how and why 'the gods, when they created humans,/assigned Death to them,/ Keeping for themselves eternal life . . .'. Men had not been 'invented' and created until the archaic time when the gods, seeing that work was indispensable for survival, had refused to exhaust themselves any more, thus running the risk of dearth and famine. The wisest of them all, Enki/Ea – the author of this 'invention' and constructor of its 'working drawing', the human prototype – had carefully worked out a dosage of enough energy and intelligence to keep the first 'workers' fit to accomplish the tasks assigned to them; but he gave them a constitution radically different enough for it never to be possible for their descendants to claim an identical nature with the gods and demand the same destiny – the right not to work. He had therefore incorporated into his 'raw material' the blood of a sacrificed god; but for that raw material he had chosen clay, the soil of the country, into which eventually the body which returned to dust would inevitably be absorbed. In this way, he had written death into our nature, thus essentially separating us from the gods. That is the mythological explanation, not set out but only suggested, in the *Epic of Gilgamesh*.

It is therefore not a myth, but a heroic legend, in a sustained and serious style – a long and solemn epic which offers us not a demonstration but a model, to be admired, undoubtedly, but also to be imitated. Through the shining example of the most celebrated and greatest of men, one who would have been the most worthy and capable of achieving his grandiose *personal* design and whose wonderful adventures dazzle us, it seeks to remind us that, like him, no one escapes death. His fame, in men's rapturous memory, is merely a derisory palliative, and no one, any more than he, can abrogate laws and bring down barriers set up by those who are stronger than we; no one can do anything to counter this state of affairs, which was instituted outside our control. We enter it, at birth, not of our own choice, only to leave it, even rebelliously, at our death, so we should only 'think about living . . .'.

In an almost forgotten past, when much less was known about things, but when understanding was perhaps all the more penetrating and profound because the world was not as crammed with knowledge and ideas as it is today, and presented itself to the mind in a less cluttered and more easily explorable state, were not those ancient Semites very wise when they emphasised our limitations so forcefully? It might perhaps be salutary to lend them an ear, listen to them again, through their ancient books, across a distance of 2000 or 3000 years, and hear an echo of their great voices nowadays, when our prodigious technical progress tends to go to our heads and let us believe that we are verging on the ultimate power – that we are at last going to master the universe and our own lives?

CHAPTER 15

How Sin Was Born

Jean Bottéro

I remember an autumn stroll around Cap d'Antibes in the company of an old friend, long since departed, a godly man and renowned Hellenist. Beside the 'sea of a thousand sounds' we were chatting, each bringing up his own familiar world; he boasted about his Greeks and I about my Semites. At first that name made him frown, drawing together his bushy, menacing eyebrows. 'Those unbearable Semites,' he exclaimed, 'without whom we would not have acquired the sense of sin which poisons our lives!' He was right. Totally unknown to our Greek and Roman ancestors, who were aware only of infractions of social order and ritual, and failure to observe conventions, our sin was a Semitic invention.

The name 'Semites' was applied to an entire group of people, still flourishing after five millennia, defined by the fact that they all spoke related languages which for the most part are still living – Hebrew, Aramaic, Arabic, Ethiopian; others, especially the Akkadian of ancient Mesopotamia, were swallowed up in ancient shipwrecks. Like our Romance languages (French, Provencal, Italian, Spanish, Portuguese and Romanian), those languages were sufficiently different for those who commonly used them not to understand each other. But they had enough common features so that, in linguists' eyes, there is not the shadow of a doubt that they all represent transformations of a unique and same 'mother tongue', which became diversified both by the dispersal of those who spoke it and the prolonged specialised development, over generations, of the differences in pronunciation and usage encouraged by the separation of the groups. By assembling these variations, classifying them into constants and discovering their laws of transformation, linguists are able to trace their way back to the original language and, at least partly, restore it. In the case of our Romance forms of speech, the original is perfectly well known – it was Latin. For the much older Semitic languages, verging on prehistory – which ended at the earliest around 3000 BC with the invention of writing in Mesopotamia – nowhere is there any evidence of it; but its existence is no less certain, just like that of Latin, and for want of a better term it is known as 'protosemitic'.

The essential instrument of communication within a society, implicit in every language is the existence of a group who speak it. But language is also the product and record of the original culture that gives life to the group, and is passed on from generation to generation. This culture is composed of characteristic social habits which are preserved and modified with time to a greater or lesser degree in the separate communities that emerge from the original collective group. By virtue of this linguistic dialectic, we are able to posit – even before history begins, around the sixth millennium BC at the latest, probably in the environs of Arabia – a 'protosemitic' community with an original language and culture, later to be disassociated and developed concomitantly, but separately, into various groups which had emerged from those archaic Protosemites.

The most ancient, who are fairly well known to us

through plentiful and intelligible documents, were first of all the old inhabitants of Mesopotamia, whose Semitic element quickly 'absorbed' the native Sumerians. They are familiar through the ample literature they have left us, from the first half of the third millennium until shortly before the Christian era. Much later, in Palestine, we have the Israelites, whose history and thinking for over a thousand years, beginning in the thirteenth century BC, are preserved in the Bible. Concerning sin, I must mention both of them.

Among the cultural constants – which are as likely as linguistic ones to have formed many original and distinctive features of archaic Semitic 'mentality', and to have been preserved, with various developments, both in Mesopotamia and, later, in Israel – the first thing that catches our attention is a profound religious feeling. It repercusses all the way down to us because, Buddhism aside, the three great 'universal' religions of our time – Judaism, Christianity and Islam – are Semitic in origin.

Because of that potent religiousness, the Semites always attributed responsibility for all the happenings that affect us and cause us problems in this world to supernatural beings – gods. Not only were these gods the originators of the universe and mankind, but they remained their supreme masters and guided their existence and evolution from day to day. For that reason, they were regarded as the promoters and guarantors of all the infinite obligations – positive or negative – that govern human life. All stemmed from the explicit decision of the gods, and whoever infringed so much as one of them was thus resisting their will, scorning their commands or neglecting them, rebelling against the gods' authority – shades of meaning which, in the Semitic languages, synonymously contributed to a definition of that disobedience towards the gods that was the fundamental essence of sin, through which one might at any moment enter into conflict with the supernatural world, since no area or moment of life eluded their authority.

How was such a 'doctrine' lived and adapted by the most ancient and enduring autonomous community of Semites in Mesopotamia?

The Catalogue of Sins

In that country, dedicated since the dawn of time to monarchical government, the world 'On-high' – master of the universe and its inhabitants – was conceived on the model of secular government and organised in the same way. But whereas civil powers could control only the rules that governed social life, the sovereignty of the gods ranged far more widely and commanded the entire life of all and sundry, thus multiplying to infinity the likelihood of sinning. To get some idea of the number and variety of those occasions, we have a long catalogue of such 'offences'. It figures in the great exorcistic liturgy called *Shurpu*. Here are some excerpts.

It goes without saying that ritual transgressions are to be found:

> Failure to respect a god, by word or deed; diverting sacrificial material promised to a deity; assuming an arrogant attitude for saying one's prayers, or neglecting to wash one's hands; during a sacrifice, failing to mention the name of the god one is addressing; disturbing the arrangement of an altar prepared for worship; having sexual relations with a woman consecrated to some deity . . .

Similarly, we see violations of public order, for which responsibility also fell on the civil authorities. Some were serious, in that they caused disorder or a grave hindrance in social life:

> Use of counterfeit money or false measures; unjustified moving of boundaries or barriers demarcating property; falsely acquiring an inheritance; theft, adultery; bearing false witness or making groundless accusations; murder and assassination; calumny or scandal-mongering; rebellion against a representative of public authority; lack of respect for parents.

Others, by all the evidence milder, were concerned rather with simple courtesy or *savoir-vivre*, even a feeling of personal dignity or what is called moral order:

> Lying or using unseemly language; gossiping or speaking maliciously; speaking boastfully or improperly; committing some unsuitable act; refusing to help a man who has nothing; helping to send someone to prison; not freeing a prisoner [when one has the power to do so]; not keeping one's promise; stopping up a channel; eating stolen meat.

A good number remain that apparently have nothing to do with religious, social or personal duties; they seem to be customs derived from fairly irrational representations, probably dating from time immemorial and no clearer to the ancient Mesopotamians than to us when, for example, we bless someone who has just sneezed. For instance,

> Walking on the site of a massacre; pointing at a lamp; lighting a fire in the presence of a third person; drinking from a cup made of unfired clay; putting one's finger on the wound of a sheep that has had its throat cut; refusing or asking for something in bad weather; plucking blades of grass on the steppe or reeds in the marsh, or even pulling a reed from one's boot; tearing a clod of soil from a field, or breaking it up or throwing it into water; urinating or vomiting in a stream or river.

Although some prohibitions may be explained by beliefs held at the time (the last mentioned above, for example, is in keeping with the supernatural nature attributed in ancient times to rivers and streams), the least that can be said about any of these transgressions is that it was hardly likely to provoke the slightest disorder in religious, social or individual life, and that, judged on this level, the sins thus committed appear to have been the most venial and excusable.

The most astounding feature of the *Shurpu* catalogue is that the sins it enumerates (totalling over 250, but distributed with the categories intermingled, not as I have done in classifying them) clearly all had the same supernatural scope; they are all explicitly deemed to provide a justification for the ill or misfortune endured by the individual concerned, who would turn to exorcism only to rid himself of them.

Those people were therefore logical in representing the gods as the source and guarantee of all men's rules of conduct; viewed from this aspect, these rules were all equally important, because it was not a matter of the gravity of their repercussions on social life, but their intrinsic dignity and their nature as expressions of divine will. Those who, by violating them, rebelled against the gods, resisted or neglected them and, in short, scorned them, deserved to be punished by those same gods, as the civil powers suppressed those who contravened the rules of community life. The ills and misfortunes that occurred all of a sudden, without obvious reason, in everyone's life were thus regarded as chastisements sent by the gods to punish the sins committed against them. But, just as the sovereign on Earth was compassionate and, being duly implored, could always repeal a sentence, so the gods were looked upon as capable of wiping the slate clean, pardoning the offence and removing the consequent punishment it had incurred. As in civil courts, the prior condition needed to implore this absolution/deliverance was admission of one's own responsibility by confessing the sin committed. And it is against the background of such a confession that the ritual of exorcism in question included the list from which I have just quoted a few details.

But why such a long list, when one avowal alone would have sufficed to overcome the ill or misfortune to be combated? From all the evidence, because by reciting it – for it had to be recited in its entirety, not selectively – the sufferer had all the more chances of lighting upon a real misdeed that had been committed and confessing. For in order to cover everything that might have been omitted, the catalogue ended with the generalising rubric 'or any other sin, whatever it may be'. Sinners were not necessarily conscious of the sin they must have committed, which had unleashed the trouble upon them. The proof lies in the fact that in the enumeration of situations, some also crop up which – of necessity – are incompatible with the least imaginable personal responsibility. For instance: 'A blemish inherited from one's parents, or passed on by those around' the sinner; and even the simple (accidental) 'contact with a third person already afflicted by some supernatural curse'. These 'blemishes' and 'curses', being obviously unnoticeable on the countenance of their bearer, who in any case was presumed to be an unknown person, were therefore supposed.

Here the key word is revealed: supposition or deduction played a major role in such a form of reasoning. In this representation of sin and its punishment, the point of departure was not *a priori* the sin itself – discovered first and leaving its punishment to be awaited – but *a posteriori* from the instant ill and misfortune (interpreted as punishment sent from the gods) deducing that they must have had good reason to inflict them: namely, that the person involved must have perpetrated a sin. That is why sinners need not have retained a clear memory of their sin; it was enough that they should have committed it, or even had contact with another sinner or object of divine wrath; and the gods were aware of this!

Such ignorance of the offence for which one suffered the punishing result is a known theme in religious literature. Many arguments have been devoted to it, including a long monologue in which a man, conscious of the uprightness of his life, complains that he has been plunged into the worst of misfortunes and wonders why – a topic that will be found again in the Bible, treated in its own way. Here are some of the exclamations that – in one form or another – recur more than once in prayers and exorcistic addresses: 'O gods Ea, Shamash and Marduk, what sins have I committed/For such a curse, such misfortune to have befallen me?'; 'My god, your punishment is a heavy burden,/ And yet I know not the reason!'; 'What must I have done, O god, and what must I have committed/To find myself like river water, flowing I know not where/Like a boat not knowing where it will land?'. This uncertainty even affects name-giving. In Mesopotamia, as among other ancient Semites, anthroponyms were frequently kinds of pious exclamations that one imagines must have been uttered by the father and immediately conferred as 'proper name' on the newly born infant. There is no lack of examples of individuals who have been given the name 'What-sin-have-I-committed?' or 'What-have-I-done-against-my-god?' – as if the one asking the question had been a prey to some ordeal at the time when his child was born.

All in all, in the view of ancient Mesopotamians, sin was a rebellion against the gods, an infringement – deliberate or not, conscious or not – of any one of the countless rules and regulations with which they had peppered human existence. In the unfathomable wisdom of their plans, the offended parties might well fail to be outraged and might leave these escapades unpunished – as happens with the authorities on Earth. But they might also punish them by illnesses, irritations, misfortunes directed upon the sinners. Sin did not impinge upon the consciousness until the vengeance was happening. Only then did people start to worry about it, certainly not moved by woe, anguish or contrition for having offended the masters of the world, but simply in order to take the necessary measures to rid themselves of such punishment. So they implored the mercy of the gods, in accordance with the exorcistic rituals provided, and started by confessing their offence, so as to put them in a more kindly frame of mind. It was therefore not in Mesopotamia that a feeling of sin could, by itself, really 'poison existence', as my devout Hellenist maintained.

Thou shalt not Commit Adultery! Thou shalt not Steal!

Things would change in Israel. For a better understanding of the situation, we must not forget that, unlike Mesopotamian religion and nearly all similar 'primitive' religions (ancient or contemporary), Israel's religious system – whose doctrine and development are recorded in the Bible – was of the 'historic' type, like Christianity, Islam and Buddhism. It was not a simple expression of a community's traditional and immemorial attitude regarding the supernatural, deeply rooted in its culture; in the fullness of history, in the thirteenth century BC, it had been thought out, elaborated and propagated by one man alone, Moses, who had imposed it on his fellow men. In such systems, not only do adherents keep an ever-present memory of the founder, but they also make constant reference to what they think must have been his ideas and wishes – present among them in the form of 'holy books' and set out in writing with the embellishments and improvements of later tradition. That ensures a soundness, clarity and unity of 'doctrine' and behaviour, and also a profound adherence of heart and mind, a 'personal commitment' that one would look for in vain among 'primitive' systems.

Moses had founded his religion on two or three fundamental inspirations. First, whether or not other deities existed, one alone must count in the eyes of the Israelites: Yahweh. He had revealed Himself to them shortly before their 'liberation' from Egypt – a god with a new name, in isolation, mysterious and with no pantheon surrounding Him; truly unfathomable, unlike all the rest. They were deemed to have been linked first with this god by one of the solemn pacts of 'alliance' practised freely by the ancient Semites. They had become Yahweh's own special people and, as the gods of other nations did for them, He would take the Israelites' side, defend them and make them triumph in all their plans, in particular the one they cherished at that time – to carve out a territory that would really belong to them and would gather them all together. In return, they would pledge themselves never to regard or serve any other god than Yahweh, and scrupulously to render the worship He demanded; not in offerings and pompous ceremonies, but above all by strict observance of a fundamentally ethical and religious code, condensed into what was called the 'Decalogue'. This concentrated all prescribed religious conduct in some ten rules, positive or negative, that from then on would govern the social life of these wandering semi-nomads which the Israelites still were.

> I, Yahweh, am your God: I led you out of Egypt: You will have no other gods but Me! You will make no idols; you will not prostrate yourselves before them or worship them, for I, Yahweh, am a jealous god! Never take the name of the Lord your God in vain! Do not forget to keep holy the day

of rest: six days shall you labour, but the seventh shall be a holy day reserved for Yahweh your God! Honour your father and mother! Kill no one! Do not commit adultery! Do not steal! Do not bear false witness against one of your fellow men! Do not covet your neighbour's house, his wife, his servant or anything that is his! (Exod. 20: 2–17)

The Sole and Universal God, Master of All

In this founding pact we see the same essential representations that we came across, although quite differently materialised, in Mesopotamia. The god is still the originator and one responsible for the duties and prohibitions that guide men's lives; at that time, every infringement of the divine will, with regard to the supernatural power, would constitute resistance, negligence, scorn – in one word, a sin.

Israel's entire religious history lies in the development of those propositions, depending on period and circumstance.

First, the Israelites would radically alter their way of life by a gradual conquest of Palestine from its occupants, also Semites, who were divided into small urban kingdoms and known under the collective title of Canaanites, in order to settle there themselves. From a confederation of semi-nomadic tribes, without hearth or home, and with a basically collective existence, they would change into peasants and townsfolk, initially neighbours and imitators of the Canaanites, from whom they learned everything they could before 'absorbing' and replacing them.

Like all the other Semites, those people also had their own gods, who played an active and daily role in the settled agricultural life, since they were the 'masters' of the benefits of the climate, the richness of the soil and general prosperity. The followers of Yahweh, despite the 'jealousy' of their

God, were therefore exposed to the living and constant temptation to resort to these other deities and serve them almost as much as their national Yahweh. Furthermore, they would ultimately adapt the pomp and ritual of the Canaanite deities for Yahweh, thus running the risk of being satisfied by such ostentatious ceremonial, instead of rendering homage to Him mainly by their own conduct, as He had commanded. Lastly, the new regime of independent working of the land and private property ownership would make it far more difficult to practise that law of fraternity and sharing between 'neighbours', traditional among nomads, on which the 'Decalogue' had been based. On all sides, therefore, occasions increased for failing to live up to their ancient promises – for sinning against their God.

After a century which steadily led to triumph and power, crowned around 1000 BC by the establishment, under David, of a glorious, respected and wealthy kingdom, political decline rapidly set in. Fifty years after David, the country was split in two: a more powerful state in the north, the other round Jerusalem. From then on they would be rivals, even enemies on occasion, although they retained the feeling of a deep 'national' unity centred on Yahweh. Soon, the formidable campaigns of the Assyrians, then the Babylonians, who had come to Mesopotamia to open up an outlet for themselves on the 'Upper Sea', at the same time appropriating the wealth of the little Syrio-Palestinian kingdoms, would plunge the country into a series of disasters. The kingdom of the north was the first to go and, a century later, that of the south, whose elites were deported for many years to Babylonia.

It was precisely those unhappy events which would broaden and deepen Israel's religion to the limits. An elite of great religious minds, including the most famous of those preachers we call the Prophets, in the name of unconditional allegiance to the first Alliance, and their total faith in an omnipotent, just and retributory Yahweh, brought together in a single strand the dual threads of political decadence and religious and moral decline. The one explained the other, bearing in mind the need for Yahweh to punish the sins of His disloyal people. Such an inference went a long way!

Its first result was an extraordinary development of the potency and grandeur of Yahweh. He had been capable of bringing the most powerful people and army in the world at that time from their distant Mesopotamia to carry out His mighty works. He had therefore commanded them, and was obviously far superior to their famous deities. But after all, He was the God not only of the people of Israel but of the entire universe, the Only God, the Omnipotent. That was how the conviction of Yahweh's absolute monotheism developed.

It was impossible not to ascribe absolute justice to this unique and universal God, placed above everything and master of all on Earth, who pulled all the strings in the history of man, and Israel's misfortunes provided a striking demonstration. Things were not as in Mesopotamia, where once the tribulation had occurred and been interpreted people then began to think about the sin that must have deserved it, deducing it *a posteriori* since no one had been aware of it beforehand. Where Yahweh was concerned, immediately the offence was committed the punishment was to be expected, ineluctably, for He was too absolutely just to let the slightest offence againt Him pass without reacting. The Prophets endlessly predicted fresh catastrophes – and the course of events proved them right, thus confirming the truth of their analysis – unleashed by the Israelites' inability to return to a pure and simple observance of the Alliance.

From the latter, meanwhile, by dint of an age-long work of reflection and, in short, casuistry, a wealth of rules and duties had been drawn up and put in writing, setting out the potentialities of the primitive and all-enveloping 'Decalogue', detailing with increasing minuteness the conduct to adopt in order to comply with Yahweh's will. It is instructive to read Deuteronomy and certain chapters of Leviticus about this process. In the thinking of 'theologians' of the period, these details only explained the profound and collected thoughts of Moses, presented as they had been revealed by Yahweh, and so they began to be assembled under the name Torah: both the 'teaching' of God for a righteous life and the 'manifestation' of His will over His people – in short, the proper total content of the Alliance. In the Torah there was no question, as there would have been in Mesopotamia, of seeking out the minutiae at all costs, resorting to superstitious trivia, unworthy of the name of Yahweh. He had put forward only the major orientations of human life, certainly detailed in all imaginable potentialities but, when all was said and done, covering only the field of relations with God and other human beings.

Another advance that occurred in the meantime, and one of incalculable scope, besides, was the evolution of a personal religion. The people of Israel had been the first partners in the Alliance and, after receiving the blessings of Yahweh, had been the first to find themselves responsible for and punished for their sins; and the Prophets promised them new misfortunes if they did not return to their sworn loyalty. Shortly before the fall of Jerusalem, following a long process of maturing religious faith, the conviction came to be held that such a universal and sublime God must have before Him, under His rule, not only the entirety of His own people – a vague and anonymous mass – but each and every person.

On those principles the religion of Yahweh was re-established when, in 538 BC, Cyrus, king of the Persians and conqueror of Babylon, freed the Israelites from their distant exile. During the half-century of bitter reflection on their past misfortunes, their responsibilities and those of their fathers, the exiles had had time to admit to all that their spiritual leaders had been vainly preaching to them for so long, and prepare for a fresh start, forging a religious attitude for themselves that was in keeping with their new convictions.

For this renewal, some took the wider view: they suggested interpreting the fundamental privilege of 'Yahweh's people' as a mission to be undertaken henceforward by Israel to make the one true God known to all men; He was their own God and had chosen them for this purpose. But the exiles preferred to look upon this prerogative with a quite different eye. Heedless of the rest of the universe, they regarded themselves and behaved as a community apart, set aside and pledged first and foremost to genuine worship of the true God, who had chosen their people precisely so that there should be at least one group of men in the world who were entirely devoted to Him. And this worship would resume its original meaning and content – sworn at the time of the Alliance but for centuries unfortunately forgotten or refuted – of strict obedience to God's will as presented and explained in the Torah, the corpus of 'holy writ' that had gradually been compiled since Moses and, so it was thought, in his own spirit, complemented and detailed to the nth degree, in the dual field of relations with God and with other men. This religious community, which naturally included only the descendants of Israel, by birth, was the final form taken by the ancient Israelite religion after the Exile to Babylon from the fifth century BC. It was called Judaism, and has hardly budged since.

As a fundamental rule of life, Judaism therefore imposes obedience to a superior Will, laid down in written detail and governing the daily relations with God and other people: a code of supernatural regulations – a Law. Everything that complies with it is good and virtuous; everything that strays from it is bad and a sin. A similar ideal is reflected everywhere in the biblical books composed after the Exile: for example, in a number of those spiritual canticles known as Psalms, or the wise pieces of advice entitled Proverbs. Here is an eloquent example, taken from a Psalm (119: 10–15), made up of interminable variations on this theme:

> With my whole heart have I sought Thee:
> O let me not wander from Thy commandments.
> Thy word have I hid in my heart
> That I might never sin against Thee!
> With my lips have I continually declared
> All the Commands from Thy mouth!
> I have found more joy in following Thy Commandments
> Than in any riches!
> I wish nothing else than to meditate on Thy Instructions
> And contemplate Thy Rules-of-conduct!

And so on, in 176 'verses' divided into 21 'strophes'.

This passage emphasises the deep feeling that can be generated by ascribing such importance to the Law-to-be-observed – to be precise, the happiness that can be derived from such obedience. 'I have found more joy in following Thy Commandments/Than in any riches!' And it is true that such spirituality in itself could bring its reward and surface as true mysticism, taking its delight in the very submission to the Will of a God who is not only sublime, incomprehensible and overwhelming in Himself, but who would henceforward be someone to talk to, a confidant, a close companion and, in short, a Friend. Here and there we may find this somewhat enraptured attitude; once or twice it seems to have triumphed even over the terrible ordeal of death, which at that time was conceived as a definitive slumber for all, without exception, in the vast, subterranean cavern of She'ol, of the Grave. 'I bless Yahweh who counsels me' says the author of Psalm 16: 7–11:

> And who even in the night teaches me docility!
> I have set Yahweh always before me:
> Because He is near me, I shall not be moved!
> Therefore my heart is glad, and my soul rejoices:
> My body also rests in safety! No, Thou wilt not leave my soul in She'ol!
> Thou wilt not let Thy devoted servant endure the Abyss!
> But Thou wilt show me the path of Life
> The richness and joy of Thy Presence,
> And the sweetness of dwelling with Thee forever!

These are exceptional attitudes, however, reserved for religious minds of great loftiness of view and depth of feeling, as are to be found – rarely – in all religions. Is it possible that the greater number, far removed from those summits, did not ask themselves questions in the light of what their own faith imposed upon them? Of course, it was an inestimable privilege and honour to belong to the people chosen and preferred by the God of the universe, and such an advantage was well worth the obligation to conform to His Law. But in reality, could there not be other benefits to be found, in keeping with the ancient promises?

For a time, people nurtured dreams of a new accession by Israel to power and glory, and a whole literature – grandiloquent, rather prophetic and abstruse (it is called 'apocalyptic') – exploited the theme of a thunder-and-lightning intervention by God, who would restore David's kingdom, change the face of the world and bring back prosperity, peace, happiness and a prime position to His chosen people forever. But although such themes inspired writers for a while, they seem hardly to have aroused the enthusiasm and adherence of the multitude; even less were they enough to assuage the need for reward that was necessarily created by religious obligations.

After all, religion had become a personal matter. So if children no longer had to pay for the sins of their fathers, as before, should they not also receive a reward for lives spent in conformity with the Law; while sinners, who defied it, should obligatorily be punished, by virtue of the ancient doctrine of Yahweh's absolute justice? After the Exile, this controversy greatly exercised minds, and gave birth to an incomparable masterpiece of poetry, and also of thought – the Book of Job. In it, the author poses the problem of why a righteous and absolutely irreproachable man, like Job, recognised as such by God in person, could nevertheless be plunged into the deepest misfortune. The wretched man's three friends, using the ancient and hackneyed *a posteriori* reasoning, stubbornly maintain that he must have sinned; but he, knowing his own innocence, asks God for an explanation.

God Himself gives the answer to this formidable problem of the sufferings of the Righteous Man and, all in all, of suffering pure and simple, the universal evil. In sublime and magnificent words, it is enough for Him to recall His own incomparable role of creator and ruler of all, His fundamentally superior position over everything on Earth, for Job to realise that all he can do is 'put his hand over his mouth'; hold his tongue, not only in submission to, but also wonder at, decisions which come from so high above that, by definition, no one is capable of understanding them. This solution to the inextricable difficulties of evil, the only one possible in a system that posits a unique and transcendent God, was definitive. But who could accept it, be satisfied with it, find serenity and joy in it despite misfortune, unless they were, again, very high-flying religious minds, an exceptional elite?

For the masses, then, there remained a hope that God

would carry out His promises, henceforward transposed on to the personal plane. Let me quote another Psalm (1: 1–4) which sums up this ideal very well:

> Blessed is he who hath not mingled with the ungodly
> Or stopped on the way of sinners . . .,
> But delighteth in the Law of Yahweh And reciteth that Law night and day!
> He is like a tree planted by a stream,
> That bringeth forth fruit in his season
> And his leaves never wither:
> Whatsoever he doeth, he shall prosper!
> For the ungodly it shall not be thus:
> They will be as chaff before the wind!

Shunned or committed, as we see, sin was at the centre of the religious life and preoccupations of the religious man. All the more so because, unlike the ancient Mesopotamians, to get rid of it he did not have at his disposal the almost automatic rituals of exorcism. The sinner, therefore, could only utter his repentance and implore forgiveness by directly addressing God, who had no need of rather incantatory formulas or manipulations to give His own reply and cancel out the sin and its consequences; for He was believed to be compassionate, and He was too essentially good not to react to the misery of the one who had offended Him.

> Of Thy goodness, have mercy upon me, my God:
> Wipe out my sins, by Thy great compassion!
> Cleanse me thoroughly of my iniquities
> And purify me from my sins!
> I acknowledge my transgressions:
> My sin is ever before me!
> Against Thee, and Thee only, have I sinned
> And done what is evil in Thy sight!

Turn Thine eyes from my sins,
Purge me of all my iniquities!
Grant me the joy of Thy deliverance!
(Psalm 51: 3–6, 11, 14)

It is obvious that, in the religion of Yahweh – Judaism – disobedience to divine will (or sin) occupied a greater place than it had in Mesopotamia in religious life, or in life pure and simple since the latter was part and parcel of one's entire existence. Whether it led to legalism and solely the literal execution of the 'commandments', or tended to go further and higher, giving pride of place to respect for the 'spirit' of the commandments, sin and the haunting fear of sin pervaded the whole field of religious consciousness. This could even become obsessive, to the point where the entire existence of the believer was nothing more than the scrupulous and meticulous observance of a certain number of directives, in return for which he thought he could count, in this world or the next, on the reward of a satisfied God – as if true religion had anything to do with this mean and derisory settling of accounts!

It is a fact, and we have learnt it the hard way, that sin and its attendants weighed heavily in the heritage received from Israel by Christianity which, although imbuing it with its own spirit, really passed on the whole 'bag' to us. To be sure, it does not necessarily 'poison' everyone's 'existence', as my Hellenistic friend lamented. Nevertheless, it played a major role – which it would be instructive to study – in the formation of our conscience; notably, it has accustomed us to the constant feeling that we are 'responsible before Another' for our conduct (rather than dependent solely on our own judgement) and, where we fail, guilty towards Him rather than dishonoured in our own eyes – as is the case, and always has been, for instance, with Far-Easterners, whose 'moral' life is consequently quite differently organised. Perhaps, after all, we still tell ourselves that we could have managed quite well without it, and been content to clash with laws and conventions, quelled if caught by civil authorities or the fleeting disapproval of our own *amour propre* or of our nearest and dearest, without our heart and innermost depths being disturbed in the slightest.

Chronology

	Mesopotamia	Israel
Prehistory		
From the 6th millennium	Slow emergence of the Mesopotamian territory from the north to the south. It is peopled by unknown ethnic groups, from the foothills of the north and east; probably Semites also, from the northern fringes of the great Syrio-Arabian desert. A little later, perhaps, the Sumerians arrive (from the south-east?).	
In the 4th millennium	Between all these races and their cultures, the osmotic process of copenetration and exchange is established or continued, composing early Mesopotamian civilisation, which rapidly becomes an urban system through the merging of originally autonomous primitive villages around a larger agglomeration. Through large-scale cereal farming and intensive breeding of small livestock, the country soon grows wealthy and begins to seek farther afield, by trading and war, the materials it lacks: wood for building and also furniture, stone and minerals.	

	Mesopotamia	Israel
Historical Era		
Proto-dynastic	**c. 3200.** First invention of writing. **2900–2330.** Independent city-states. The Sumerian language in general use. The Uruk dynasty and its king, Gilgamesh. The First Dynasty of Ur and its Royal Cemetery.	The Canaanites in Palestine.
Palaeo-Akkadian epoch	**2330–2100.** First Semitic Empire founded by Sargon the Great: Dynasty of Akkad. The Akkadian language begins to supplant Sumerian. **2100–2000.** Kingdom of Ur: Third Dynasty of Ur, which still prefers Sumerian and develops a brilliant literature in this language. First arrivals of Amurrite Semites.	
Palaeo-Babylonian and Palaeo-Assyrian epochs	**2000–1600.** Rival kingdoms. Dynasties of Isin Larsa, Esnunna and Mari (the last notably between 1800 and 1750). First sovereigns of Assyria. First Dynasty of Babylon, from 1894. Hammurabi (1792–1750) unites the entire country around this town in a single kingdom which his successors will maintain. Blossoming in all areas, notably literature, of the Akkadian language, Sumerian remaining only in scholarly and mannered use.	
Middle-Babylonian and	**1600–1100.** Invasion and seizure by the Cassites, who plunge the country into political torpor, favouring a vigorous cultural development.	The ancestors of Israel lead a nomadic life, from east to west along the Fertile Crescent, then pass into Palestine.
Middle-Assyrian epochs	**From about 1300.** Assyria, around Assur as its capital, gains its independence and asserts its importance. **1100–1000.** First infiltrations of Aramaic Semites. Then struggles for hegemony between Assyria and Babylonia. Even when the latter is dominated by the former, it will keep its cultural supremacy.	**Early 13th century.** Moses, then the conquest of Palestine and settlement.

	Mesopotamia	Israel
Neo-Assyrian epoch	**1000–609.** Predominance of Assyria centred on first Kalah, then Nineveh as capitals. The first great invasions in the east and the Sargonids (Asarhaddon, Assurbanipal).	**End of 11th century.** The kingdom of Israel and its first three sovereigns (Saul, David, Solomon). **Second half of the 10th century.** The Schism and there are two separate kingdoms: of the north (Israel) and the south (Judah). The first great prophets, then the great writer-prophets. **End of the 8th century.** The kingdom of the north disappears
Neo-Babylonian epoch	**605–539.** Babylon masters Assyria and resumes control of the country. Nebuchadnezzar and the Chaldaean dynasty. Aramaisation continues.	**Beginning of the 6th century.** Downfall of the kingdom of the south, then the Great Exile to Mesopotamia.
Persian epoch	**539–330.** In 539, Babylon is vanquished by the Achemenid Cyrus, and Mesopotamia incorporated into the Persian Empire.	The return of the exiles and organisation of Judaism.
Seleucid epoch	**330–130.** In 330, Alexander conquers and supplants the Persians, bringing all the Near East into the Hellenistic cultural orbit. His successors, the Seleucids, keep control of Mesopotamia.	**First half of the 4th century.** Completion of the Bible by the collection and arrangement of the principal biblical writings, to which others will be added until the **end of the 1st century AD.**
Arsacid epoch	**130– .** Mesopotamia passes into Parthian hands in 129. The country has lost not only all autonomy but also any actual significance, either political or cultural. Its writing, language and written works fall into oblivion.	

Further Reading

Trevor Watkins

Primary texts

Burstein, S. M. 1978. *The Babyloniaca of Berossus*. Malibu, CA: Undena. This is a critical edition of what remains to us of Berossus' work.

Dalley, S. M. 1989. *Myths from Mesopotamia: Creation, the Flood, Gilgamesh, and Others*. Oxford: Oxford University Press. Affordably published in Oxford World's Classics.

Foster, B. R. 1995. *From Distant Days: Myths, Tales and Poetry of Ancient Mesopotamia*. Bethesda, MD: CDL Press.

George, A. 1999. *The Epic of Gilgamesh*. Andrew. London: Penguin.

Jacobsen, T. 1987. *The Harps that Once . . . : Sumerian Poetry in Translation*. New Haven and London: Yale University Press.

Kramer, S. N. 1979. *From the Poetry of Sumer: Creation, Glorification, Adoration*. Berkeley: University of California Press.

Secondary works

General

Black, J. and Green, A. 1992. *Gods, Demons and Symbols of Ancient Mesopotamia: An Illustrated Dictionary*. London: British Museum Publications. This useful reference work provides a key to most of the names encountered in the texts in section 1 of this guide.

Bottéro, J. 1992. *Mesopotamia: Writing, Reasoning, and the Gods*. Chicago: University of Chicago Press.

Bottéro, J., Cassin, E. and Vercoutter, J. 1967. *The Near East: The Early Civilizations*. London: Weidenfeld & Nicholson.

Dalley, S. M. 1984. *Mari and Karana: Two Old Babylonian Cities*. London: Longman.
Hallo, W. W. and Simpson, W. K. 1971. *The Ancient Near East: A History*. New York: Harcourt.
Jacobsen, T. 1970. *Towards the Image of Tammuz, and Other Essays on Mesopotamian History and Culture* edited by W. L. Moran. Cambridge, MA: Harvard University Press.
Jacobsen, T. 1976. *The Treasures of Darkness: A History of Mesopotamian Religion*. New Haven and London: Yale University Press.
Kramer, S. N. 1944. *Sumerian Mythology: A Study of Spiritual and Literary Achievement in the Third Millennium BC*. Philadelphia: American Philosophical Society.
Kramer, S. N. 1958. *History Begins at Sumer: Thirty-Nine Firsts in Recorded History*. London: Thames & Hudson.
Kramer, S. N. 1963. *The Sumerians*. Chicago: University of Chicago Press.
Kuhrt, T. A. 1995. *The Ancient Near East*. Two volumes. London: Routledge.
Matthiae, P. 1980. *Ebla: An Empire Rediscovered*. London: Hodder & Stoughton.
Nissen, H. J. 1988. *The Early History of the Ancient Near East, 9000–2000 BC*. Chicago: University of Chicago Press.
Oppenheim, A. L. 1964. *Ancient Mesopotamia: Portrait of a Dead Civilization*. Chicago: University of Chicago Press. An excellent account. Oppenheim and Jacobsen (above) provide contrasting interpretations of Mesopotamian religion.
Pollock, S. 1999. *Ancient Mesopotamia: The Eden that Never Was*. Cambridge: Cambridge University Press.
Postgate, J. N. 1977. *The First Empires*. Oxford: Phaidon.
Postgate, J. N. 1992. *Early Mesopotamia: Society and Economy at the Dawn of History*. London: Routledge.
Roaf, M. 1990. *Cultural Atlas of Mesopotamia and the Ancient Near East*. New York and Oxford: Facts on File.
Roux, G. 1990. *Ancient Iraq*. London: 3rd revised edition, Penguin.
Saggs, H. W. F. 1962. *The Greatness that was Babylon*. London: Sidgwick & Jackson.
Saggs, H. W. F. 1986. *The Might that was Assyria*. London: Sidgwick & Jackson.
Van de Mieroop, M. 1999. *The Ancient Mesopotamian City*. Oxford: Oxford University Press.
Van de Mieroop, M. 1999. *Cuneiform Texts and the Writing of History*. London: Routledge.

Origins of the Sumerians

Jones, T., editor, 1969. *The Sumerian Problem*. New York: Wiley.

Archaeology and the Excavations at Dilmun

Bibby, G. 1970. *Looking for Dilmun*. London: Collins and Penguin. This archaeological autobiography is a vivid description of the beginning of excavations in the Arabo-Persian Gulf, notably in Bahrain.

Crawford, H. 1998. *Dilmun and its Neighbours*. Cambridge: Cambridge University Press.

Potts, D. T. 1990. *The Arabian Gulf in Antiquity*. Oxford: Oxford University Press. Potts and Crawford provide general views of the results of recent excavations, and Crawford in particular offers a simple outline of developments in the Gulf and relations between Dilmun, Mesopotamia and further flung neighbours such as the Indus valley civilisation.

Languages and the Cuneiform Script

Walker, C. B. F. 1990. Cuneiform. Chapter 3 in Hooker, J. T. (ed.). *Reading the Past: Ancient Writing from Cuneiform to Alphabet*. London: British Museum Publications.

Ur and the Royal Cemetery

Moorey, P. R. S. 1997. 'What do we know about the people buried in the Royal Cemetery.' *Expedition* 20, pp. 24–40. An invaluable guide. (*Expedition* is the magazine of the University of Pennsylvania Museum.)

Woolley, Sir L. revised edition by P. R. S. Moorey, 1982. *Ur 'of the Chaldees'*. London: Herbert Press. A good popular account that subtly updates Woolley's own, now outdated, interpretations.

See also Chapter 15, pp. 268–36, of Bottéro 1992 above.

Love and sex

See 'Free love and its disadvantages', pp. 185–98, in Bottéro 1992 above.

Women

Batto, B. F. 1974. *Studies on Women at Mari*. Baltimore: Johns Hopkins University Press.

See also Dalley 1984 above. Stephanie Dalley takes a particular interest in the female members of the two Mesopotamian palaces.

Index

Geographical names are in italics. Names of gods and goddesses are followed by an asterisk.